BIRTHRATE
POLITICS IN ZION

Perspectives on Israel Studies

S. Ilan Troen, Natan Aridan, David Ellenson, and Arieh Saposnik, *editors*

Perspectives on Israel Studies is sponsored by the Ben-Gurion Research Institute for the Study of Israel and Zionism of the Ben-Gurion University of the Negev and the Schusterman Center for Israel Studies of Brandeis University

BIRTHRATE POLITICS IN ZION

Judaism, Nationalism, and Modernity
under the British Mandate

LILACH ROSENBERG-FRIEDMAN

Translated by HAIM WATZMAN

INDIANA UNIVERSITY PRESS

This book is a publication of

Indiana University Press
Office of Scholarly Publishing
Herman B Wells Library 350
1320 East 10th Street
Bloomington, Indiana 47405 USA

iupress.indiana.edu

The paper used in this publication meets the minimum requirements of the
American National Standard for Information Sciences—Permanence of Paper
for Printed Library Materials, ANSI Z39.48-1992.

Manufactured in the United States of America

Cataloging information is available from the Library of Congress.

ISBN 978-0-253-02889-1 (cloth)
ISBN 978-0-253-02898-3 (paperback)
ISBN 978-0-253-02911-9 (ebook)

1 2 3 4 5 22 21 20 19 18 17

On the cover: WIZO Nursery (babies home) in Jerusalem (the babies were
evacuated from Kibbutz Kfar Etzion accompanied by their nannies, during
Israel's war of Independence); February 1948.

Source: Central Zionist Archives in Jerusalem, Photograph Collections–
PHWI/1245347.

*In memory of
my beloved father, Shmuel Friedman*

CONTENTS

ACKNOWLEDGMENTS

THIS BOOK COULD NOT HAVE BEEN written without the support of many wonderful people, all of whom deserve my gratitude.

First in line is my teacher and mentor Margalit Shilo, who opened up the world of women's and gender history for me, and who steered me through the serpentine paths of historical research. I could not have produced this work without all the values and skills I learned from her, as a historian and as a human being. Her keen scrutiny of my work and her wise comments have been instrumental in turning my research into a book.

I am also grateful to my colleagues, friends, and all those who took an interest in this study, followed my progress, and offered good advice and valuable information. Special gratitude is due to Deborah Bernstein, whose scholarship provided an important foundation for my research and whose recommendations made a great contribution to this book. Heartfelt thanks also go to Zvi Zameret, who believed in me from my first steps as a scholar, and to Tami Razi, who has been attentive, supportive, and offered useful suggestions, as well as to Muki Tzur, who enriched my knowledge. The Taub Center for Israel Studies in New York University, in which I stayed for a short time as a visiting scholar, was a scientific framework that allowed the development of the ideas regarding the book. The center's director, Ron Zweig, was a valuable source of support and encouraging. My dear friend, Joel Rapel, shared some of his knowledge with me and offered good advice, and so did Tamar Schechter, Esther Carmel-Hakim, and Smadar Sinai. I greatly appreciate their friendship.

I would like to thank my dear colleagues in the Martin (Szusz) Department of Land of Israel Studies and Archaeology at Bar-Ilan University, and especially to Eyal Regev for his extraordinary support. Special warmly thanks go to Tamar Magen, Talia Shlosberg and Sima Kurzberg, who have helped me steadily in various ways over the years, and always with a smile, as well as to my students over the years, who have been fascinating interlocutors on the subjects of my research, and from whom I never cease to learn.

My many hours of searching for every scrap of information passed pleasantly, due to the professional and efficient assistance of the staffs of the archives and libraries I used. I thank them all and regret that there is no space to name each and every one. The English translation was produced by Haim Watzman, who is far more than a translator. His keen eye, comments, questions, and precision with words improved my manuscript, and I am grateful to him.

Special thanks also go to Ilan Troen, who had faith in my research. The book is the product of that faith. It has been a real pleasure to work with the editorial staff at Indiana University Press, especially, Dee Mortensen, Paige Rasmussen, Rachel Rosolina, Charlie Clark, and Katherine Faydash, who resourcefully and amiably provided supportive professional support in all stages and levels during the complex process of publishing my book. I could not have chosen a better publishing house.

I am in debt to thank warmly a number of bodies that provided the generous support that enabled the publication of this book. First and foremost, I want to thank the Hadassah-Brandeis Institute (HBI) at Brandeis University for its support of my research as a whole and for this project in particular. The HBI has for years been a source of major material and spiritual support for my work. I am so grateful to Shulamit Reinharz and Sylvia Barack Fishman for their confidence in my abilities and for their invaluable support over the years, which spurred me to continue my studies of gender history as a whole and of Jewish women in particular.

I received important support from the Israel Institute and the Memorial Foundation for Jewish Culture and I thank them all. I am also grateful to Judy Baumel-Schwartz and the Fanya Gottesfeld Heller Center for the Study of Women in Judaism at Bar-Ilan University for supporting my research over the years, and to Bar-Ilan's chamber of the vice president for research, for granting me fellowship. Further generosity came from Zeev Safrai, head of Moskowitz Cathedra and the Koschitzky fund of the Martin (Szusz) Department of Land of Israel Studies and Archaeology at Bar-Ilan University.

The support all these people and organizations provided were important encouragements for me to carry out this study and bring it to conclusion, in part because of the material assistance they provided, but no less so because of their recognition of the importance of my work. I offer them my most wholehearted thanks.

My research would not have been possible without the support of my family, nuclear and extended. They are the anchor of my life. I especially want to thank my dear parents, my late father Shmuel and my mother Mira, who together with my wonderful brothers Aviv and Ohad were the most loving and caring platform for my personal development; my soul mate, husband, and friend, Asaf, a great believer in my abilities from the beginning of our joint way and my constant companion who made it all possible; and my dearest children, Ofri, Iftach, Tuval, and Achinoam, whose love and sustenance are always with me. I love and value them all beyond measure.

A NOTE ON THE TRANSLATION

TO MAKE IT EASIER TO IDENTIFY and locate the sources used in this book, I have preferred to transliterate the titles of books and articles rather than translate them. The aim of the transliteration is to enable a Hebrew speaker to reconstruct the title in Hebrew script quickly and easily, so that it can be located in libraries, on the internet, or in the relevant archives. I have thus departed at times from strict "scientific" modes of transliteration in the name of clarity and user-friendliness. I represent both the letters ח and ה as *h*; ע is represented as ʻ, א as ʼ where it is vocalized, and צ as *tz*. When, however, a note refers to an archival document by describing it rather than providing its title, that description appears in English. As tastes in and methods of transliteration abound, I apologize in advance to those who find my system unwieldy or annoying.

PROLOGUE

MY LATE FATHER WAS BORN IN Tel Aviv in the early 1940s and grew up in a working-class neighborhood on the edge of the city. When I was a girl he frequently told me stories about his own childhood and adolescence, which coincided with the period of the struggle for Israel's independence and the new young country's early years. I listened avidly. One of the things that came up in his stories from time to time remains etched in my memory. It had to do with his elementary school class. There were two notable things about it, he told me. One was that the great majority of the children had no grandparents—this was one impact of the Holocaust on Israel's young immigrant society, he explained. The second was the fact that most of his classmates grew up in small families in which they had at most one sibling. He found that strange—why was that and what could it mean?, he asked. How did it come to be?

Years later, as a student and scholar, when I chose the field of women's, gender, and family studies, I began to study the Yishuv—the Jewish community in Palestine before the establishment of Israel—among other things, from the perspective of its birthrate. My father was no longer with me, but his astonishment remained.

BIRTHRATE POLITICS IN ZION

INTRODUCTION

"IN THE DAYS OF THE TEMPLE, the High Priest concluded the Yom Kippur service with a prayer for his people. In the prayer, he beseeched God that no woman lose the fruit of her womb in the coming year," wrote Dr. Ze'ev Binyamin (Wolfgang) von Weisl, a Jewish physician and journalist in Mandatory Palestine, in 1947. "For us, this is the gravest problem of all, a threat to our very existence. Not just the high priest, but every one of us—every Jewish man and woman—must pray that the scourge of non-natural abortions . . . is lifted from us."[1] Von Weisl, writing just before the establishment of the state of Israel, was protesting elective abortions, which were a key reason for the low Jewish birthrate in Palestine under British rule, from 1920 to 1948.

Natality in prestate Israel and in Israeli society today represent opposite ends of a spectrum. Israel has one of the highest fertility and birthrates in the Western world. In 2009, an average of 2.9 children were born to each Israeli woman, above the average for developed countries. Most Israeli women want even more children—the desired birthrate ranges from three to four.[2] This yearning for motherhood was shared by the Jewish women of the Yishuv— the Jewish community in Palestine before the establishment of the state. "Women in the Land of Israel want children," wrote Lilia Bassewitz, a leader of the Women Workers' Movement and member of a kibbutz, in 1933.[3] Ostensibly a personal choice, the desire for children intensified in response to national needs. Building up a Jewish majority in Palestine in anticipation of statehood was a top Zionist priority.[4] This primary goal has been studied from the perspective of immigration but not from the perspective of the birthrate. The birthrate was a critical public issue at the period under discussion. Yet, despite the common wisdom that having many children was a national imperative, fertility and birthrates in the Yishuv steadily declined (the birthrate is defined as the number of births relative to the size of the population). The trend was all the more worrying in view of the high rate of

1

natural increase (births less deaths) among the local Arabs.[5] Contraceptive practices were blamed for the decline, and even more so abortions, which women sought out on a large scale during this period. This became a matter of great public concern, with public figures and medical professionals declaring that the practice had to be fought.

As the infrastructure for a Jewish state took shape under British auspices, the Yishuv found itself grappling with conflicting value systems and goals. On the one hand, it aspired to establish a Jewish majority, which meant encouraging large families; on the other hand, it envisaged a modern Jewish society modeled after those of the West—where small families were increasingly the norm. A further challenge faced by the Yishuv was the absorption of immigrants, who arrived with different customs and mind-sets. This juggling of national objectives and individual needs sparked conflict in an already complex and difficult situation. The Yishuv was caught up in a contradiction between nationalism and modernity, between incompatible religious, social, and cultural ideas, between West and East. Childbirth was encouraged as an act of patriotism but discouraged in the name of modernity, and women flocked to abortionists despite national campaigns to deter them.

This book is divided into six chapters. Chapter 1 offers an account of the Yishuv's low natality, and especially the practice of abortion. Chapters 2 and 3 consider the multiple causes of the shrinking birthrate, with special attention to Western influences and their impact on local culture. These chapters look specifically at abortions, the chief method of family planning used by Yishuv families. Despite the pervasive practice of pregnancy termination, it was widely condemned on a variety of economic, social, hygienic, and nationalist grounds. Chapter 4 presents the concrete manifestations of birth control, especially the practice of abortion. Chapter 5 focuses on the discourse about what the birthrate ought to be, with an emphasis on its nationalist overtones. Chapter 6 recounts the practical attempts to craft and implement policies to counter the low birthrate and high abortion rate.

A number of significant and even crucial themes emerging from my analysis of the sources appear throughout these chapters, among them the effect of the outbreak of World War II, the gap between a mobilized society in which people were expected to subordinate their individual needs and desires to ideological goals, and the actual choices that people made. Other such themes are the difficultly, to the point of inability, faced by public figures, policy makers, and the Zionist establishment in their attempts to have a significant impact on the birthrate. The book as a whole illuminates the complexity of the Yishuv and the generation of pioneers who carved the social and ideological underpinnings of Jewish society in the State of Israel and the events as well as the ideas and thoughts that accompanied its formulation.

A mother's decision to conduct abortion is today perceived as an intimate matter, not to be spoken of in public. When taken up by the media, it is branded as sensationalism and yellow journalism. In the Yishuv, however, abortion and pregnancy prevention were not anecdotal. They were not a footnote to the historical narrative but rather a highly sensitive issue that pierced deep into the nation's soul. In 1941, doctors who performed abortions were accused of "naked commerce in the nation's most precious resource in the name of pure and innovative science."[6]

For generations, abortions had been a private act, known only to the woman, her immediate family, and those assisting her. But abortions are more than "women's history." Their impact extends beyond the woman, her body, and her personal health. They have attracted public attention since the nineteenth century, becoming the object of legislation and of discourse by doctors and public figures, both symptomatic of social and gender change and a trigger for change. Societies differ in their attitudes toward and practice of abortions and contraception. Sex, age, social class, profession, education, geography, and epoch all come into play, as do economics and industrial and technological developments. Not just a matter of biology, their prevalence and acceptance are a reflection of society at particular point in time. As such, historical scrutiny of shrinking birthrates and, in particular, the incidence of abortion, are an indivisible part of social history and a means of chronicling history from below, with an emphasis on everyday life analyzed in sociogender terms.[7] Such scrutiny provides a platform for discussing social issues of utmost importance.

The book uses a wide array of sources, weaving a tapestry of the story as completely as possible. Among these are official documents of Zionist agencies and the British Mandate, records of local medical institutions, and correspondence of societies and organizations that were directly or indirectly involved, as well as private letters and diaries. Contemporary newspapers are a particularly valuable resource, reflecting as they do the tenor of public discourse. Nevertheless, I faced formidable methodological problems. The most serious of these was the difficulty of assessing the scope of the phenomenon and finding accurate figures.

During the period in question, the Yishuv was a young, evolving society in the process of establishing its public institutions. These institutions began to collect and tabulate data, the efforts becoming more professional over time and encompassing a larger range of subjects. With respect to birthrate and abortions, however, documentation is very sparse, especially in the early years. In 1928, Dr. Reuven Katzenelson, deputy director of Hadassah Hospital in Tel Aviv,[8] admitted to Dr. Yossef (Gustav) Aschermann, founder of the hospital's gynecology and obstetrics department, that he was unable to provide information on the number of births in Tel Aviv in 1924–1926 "because we do not keep records of births."[9] Needless to say, the same was true for abortions, which were illegal at the time, as they were in most Western countries. Few reliable figures are thus available on how many were performed in these countries,[10] all the more so because many were done privately, either by gynecologists or by primitive means, leaving behind no paper trail at all.[11]

Oral testimony can fill in the gaps in the documentary record but presents its own problems: in particular the vagaries of memory exacerbated by the passage of time.[12] There is, for example, a story about Teddy Kollek, later the well-known mayor of Jerusalem. In 1937, Kollek helped found Ein Gev, a kibbutz on the banks of Lake Kinneret. According to people who lived at the kibbutz in those years, Kollek hung a sign on the kibbutz notice board saying that no babies were to be brought into the world until further notice.

When Kollek was later asked about this legend, he said that he had, at a general meeting of the kibbutz membership, suggested that a number of requests be turned down given the difficult living conditions at the kibbutz—among them, permission to have children.[13] But no written record from kibbutz assemblies confirms either this or the sign that the kibbutz members spoke of. Still, those in the know say that the "babies who were not supposed to have been born" congratulated Teddy Kollek on his eightieth birthday.[14]

As always when writing women's history, tracking down the voice of women themselves proved difficult. Women are so involved with their duties within the home and family that they are often left out of the documentary loop. The documentation from that time rarely addresses the everyday and offers little on the personal lives of women, let alone a topic as intimate as abortion, which was also illegal. It was a time when family planning and sex life were not openly discussed.[15] Moreover, in contrast to Western countries like Germany, France, England, and the United States, where women rallied and demonstrated on abortion-related issues, there was no such activism in the Yishuv. Women rarely broached the topic in public. Their position was articulated through their deeds—by having abortions.

Another problem is that Hebrew does not differentiate between *miscarriage* and *abortion*. The use of a single term, *hapalah*, makes statistical analysis difficult. Records from Hadassah Hospital in Tel Aviv in the 1930s contain figures for both births and abortions.[16] However, as no linguistic distinction is made between spontaneous and induced abortions, these records are of limited use for my study. Even at the time, this problem was acknowledged. In 1936, the Hebrew medical journal *Harefu'ah* criticized the practice of lumping different types of abortions together.[17] Nothing, however, was done to rectify the confusion.

With these problems in mind, I have sought out for every shred of information on the subject, attempted to fill in the blanks, and adopted a cautious and critical approach to the diverse source material at my disposal. Examining local trends in their broader historical context has helped me in this task.

Birth and Birth Control in the West

Zionist historiography long treated the history of the Yishuv as a self-standing historical unit featuring unique phenomena and requiring its own special terminology. The period has been examined within the Zionist supernarrative, which has rarely looked at the international influences that helped shape it. That has begun to change in recent years, with the appearance of a number of studies that shed new light on the Yishuv by placing the local narrative in a wider context.[18] An in-depth study of births in the Yishuv, a society composed largely of immigrants from Europe, shows that life in Mandatory Palestine cannot be comprehended in isolation from the broad canvas of Western history.

Mortality rates dropped significantly in Europe beginning in the eighteenth century. With more children surviving, the economic burden on families increased in both cities and rural areas. One response was emigration, with people leaving Europe to seek better economic opportunities in the territories opened up by colonization. Another response was to have fewer children, a phenomenon that became pronounced in the second half of the nineteenth century. The decline in the birthrate intensified in the twentieth century, especially in the period between the two world wars.[19] Initially, the drop in births resulted primarily from the postponement of marriage; later, contraception and abortion came into play.[20]

In 1869, the Catholic Church declared abortion to be murder, on the grounds that life begins at the moment of conception. It banned the practice.[21] In addition to the strict Catholic proscription, regardless of the wishes of the woman or her husband, and regardless of the circumstances of the pregnancy,[22] many Western countries passed stringent legislation, especially in the first half of the twentieth century, motivated by demographic concerns.

However, before abortion was criminalized, it was the first resort of pregnant women who did not want to have a child. Abortions were firmly anchored in local custom and common wisdom, outside the purview of the state and church. Sometimes they were performed by midwives and sometimes by women themselves, using primitive methods that often put their lives at risk. Yet neither the religious ban nor draconian civil laws stopped women from terminating their pregnancies on various pretexts.[23] Although birth control and pregnancy termination have been practiced in all societies throughout the ages, induced abortions were not widespread before the nineteenth century because there was no incentive to limit family size, and because the infant mortality rate was so high.[24]

This changed in the nineteenth century in most European countries.[25] Sociological and demographic studies show two distinct waves of low fertility: from 1870, continuing until the 1930s, and again from the 1960s onward. These waves and the resulting demographic swings are attributable to a number of factors, from social, economic, cultural, and anthropological processes to urbanization, industrialization, modern technology and medicine, secularization, education, changing attitudes toward children, and feminism.[26]

The wars and revolutions that raged on the European continent in the nineteenth century and the first half of the twentieth century, most notably the two world wars in which many millions died, drastically depleted the population of Europe. This came on top of the already-low birthrates of the turn of the century. During World War I births plummeted drastically at the same time that abortions reached a high in Britain and Germany.[27] The paucity of births triggered nationwide anxiety in some countries, which saw the birthrate as a national asset, not a private affair.[28] The first to express such concerns was France, which had, until the French Revolution and Napoleon, been one of Europe's most populous countries, but began to experience demographic decline after the revolution and especially in the early nineteenth century.[29] Other European countries were also plagued by sagging birthrates.[30]

A principal factor in the decline of birthrates in the Western world was the introduction of contraceptive devices such as the diaphragm.[31] These were distributed at family-planning clinics founded by women activists seeking to alleviate the suffering of women who endured numerous pregnancies and the financial burden imposed by large families on breadwinners and society as a whole. Among the outstanding pioneers in the campaign to provide women with information and contraceptives were Margaret Sanger, a campaigner for women's rights who began her long career in the United States in 1916; Aletta Jacobs, a Jewish feminist and the first woman physician in Netherlands, who was active in the 1880s; and Marie Stopes, beginning in 1920 in England.[32] Their efforts were met by furor and controversy, but the women carried on in the face of opposition and under threat of criminal proceedings.[33] Between World Wars I and II, the use of contraceptives began to gain acceptability in the West. Attitudes toward abortion, however, did not change; the procedure remained illegal throughout most of Europe, in part because many countries regarded fertility as a strategy for national survival.[34]

Pro-natal policies were already implemented in Europe in the seventeenth century.[35] In the nineteenth century, with the rise of nationalism and concern that populations were shrinking, boosting fertility assumed even greater importance.[36] In democracies and dictatorships alike, the reproductive rights of the individual were tethered to the demographic needs of the nation.[37] In many countries, birthrate regulation became a hot-button political issue and legislation was passed to stop abortions and encourage childbirth.[38] This was especially true of Nazi Germany, Fascist Italy, and Spain under Franco.[39]

Nevertheless, unwanted pregnancies proliferated in the West. Contraceptives were not always available, and when they were, they were unreliable and expensive. This made avoidance of pregnancy especially difficult for poor women. Thus, despite the legal and religious sanctions, the intensive propaganda against abortions, and the personal risk involved, illegal induced abortions were widespread in Europe and the United States from the late nineteenth century and through the first half of the twentieth century.[40] In the 1930s, during the Great Depression, the fertility rate in some Western countries dropped below the replacement level.[41]

After World War I, the Yishuv was ruled by Britain, where the number of births had been shrinking since the late nineteenth century.[42] However, British influence in this context was mainly legislative—the Mandate promulgated a law forbidding abortion. In actual fact, fertility rates and abortion in Palestine were more influenced by practices in Germany and the Soviet Union. Many members of the Yishuv came from these countries, so that local patterns were very much shaped by the way of life they brought with them. The culture of abortion in Germany and the Soviet Union is thus essential background for understanding it in the Yishuv.

From 1871 to 1945, Germany experienced three kinds of government. It was an absolutist monarchy until 1918, a republic between that year and 1933, and then a dictatorship until 1945. The birthrate fell under all three regimes.[43] In 1871, a law was issued making abortion a criminal act and imposing heavy penalties on offenders. Contraception and family planning were mainly the prerogative of the elite and educated middle class. Birthrates were especially low among the assimilated Jewish bourgeoisie. At the turn of the century, few well-off Jewish families had more than two children. By the early twentieth century, however, small families became the norm among the German middle and working classes.[44]

In the early decades of the twentieth century, abortions in Germany soared to unprecedented heights.[45] Under the relatively liberal climate of the Weimar Republic (1918–1933), abortions became a political issue and cultural phenomenon. Two children was the societal norm, and German women turned to abortion as a first resort to keep their families small. For every thousand pregnancies culminating in a live birth, 650–1,000 fetuses were aborted.[46] On the average, every German woman underwent at least two abortions in her lifetime. But the belief that fertility was a guarantee of national stability was deeply rooted. Weimar Germany thus became a battleground—while the government launched a campaign against abortion, a populist struggle arose to fight for its legalization.[47] Medical professionals fought against self-induced abortions and the practice was censured for moral reasons, while the left, feminists, and women from all walks of life railed against the country's abortion law. Legislative reforms in 1926–1927 eased the prohibition somewhat, making Germany's abortion law one of the most liberal in the world. Yet the fight to overturn the law continued. In 1931, during the Great Depression, over one million abortions were performed in Germany and demonstrations called for the procedure to be legalized. By 1933, Germany had the lowest birthrate in all of Europe.[48]

This relatively permissive approach to abortion was abolished by the Third Reich, which declared terminating pregnancy a crime not only against life but against the German people. The Nazi regime tightened surveillance and meted out stiffer sentences for abortionists, although abortions were sanctioned for the sake of racial purity in 1935. During World War II, the authorities dealt harshly with women who sought abortions and called for the death penalty for anyone assisting them. After the war, the two Germanys, seeking to purge Nazi laws from the books, canceled the death penalty for abortionists and compulsory abortions on racial grounds. The law was also amended to allow for abortions after rape and a clause permitting abortions for health reasons was reinstated.[49]

In czarist Russia, fertility rates began to drop at the end of the nineteenth century, and the trend accelerated during World War I and after the Bolshevik Revolution in 1917. This downward slide continued until the 1970s (apart from an occasional growth spurt), intensifying during outbreaks of civil war and the two world wars.[50] Soviet birthrate policy, however, changed over the years. The most salient adjustment occurred during the period between the Bolshevik Revolution and the end of the 1930s. After the end of World War I and the Civil War, the Soviet Union found itself with millions of homeless children and broken families, in part a product of the upending of the model of the traditional family. The Soviet Union of the 1920s conveyed conflicting messages to women and about the birthrate. Despite regime's declared commitment gender equality, women were expected to bring children into the world for the sake of the proletariat and to revive a society ravaged by war and revolution. In contrast, in 1920 the Soviet Union became the first country in the world to legalize abortion. The move did not mean that the state applauded abortion; it resulted, rather, from concern for the health of women and their right to have the procedure done in a safe, professional environment. Abortions were extremely widespread among city-dwelling women in the Soviet Union in the late 1920s and the first half of the 1930s. The authorities were alarmed by the trend—they viewed population growth as a source of labor for modern industry and warfare.[51] To strengthen the family, a law was passed in 1936 prohibiting abortions unless the pregnancy endangered the woman's life. The birthrate rose slightly in 1935–1937 but dropped again after the outbreak of World War II, largely as a result of illegal abortions. Women paid a physical and emotional price, but they took control of their own fertility and balked at the state's expectations that they bear children when the state didn't offer support for feeding, clothing, and educating them.[52]

In the 1940s, demographic trends began to shift in the Western world. The downward slide in births turned into a baby boom. Among the contributing factors were the end of World War II, the rise in living standards, and better employment opportunities. Some argue that the social security benefits that some countries paid out to large families were an incentive to have more children.[53] But despite these general throughout the West, each society has its own natality history deriving from local conditions.[54] The Yishuv, for example, was at this time in the throes of its national struggle for the establishment of a state, a struggle that escalated into a full-scale bloody war in 1947–1948. It was also, overwhelmingly, a society of immigrants from a multitude of places. Before looking at how these factors affected the Yishuv's birthrate, however, it is important to look at birthrate patterns in the Jewish Diaspora societies from which the Yishuv sprang.

Birthrate Patterns in the Jewish Diaspora

"It was mainly fertility and natural increase that saved the dispersed Jewish people from extinction,"[55] wrote economist Yitzhak Kanievsky (later Kanev), one of the founders of the Histadrut, the Yishuv labor organization, and Kupat Holim, the Histadrut's health services organization.[56] Although abortion and contraception were practiced in the ancient world, he maintained, "Jews completely rejected this practice." As he saw it, the nineteenth century was a golden age of Jewish demographic proliferation.[57]

The Jews of Europe, who would become a majority in the Yishuv, were characterized by a high birthrate. In the nineteenth century, better economic conditions and sanitation led to a drop in infant mortality. Hygiene, which then meant not just cleanliness but also the rational management of all aspects of life, from sleep and eating habits to the home and work environments, was viewed by some as a key factor in the growth of the Jewish population. For example, the Zionist demographer Prof. Roberto Bachi, who came to Palestine from Italy in 1938, argued that European Jews were pioneers in implementing advances in the field of hygiene.[58] Furthermore, Jewish law considered reproduction an obligation. Bachi maintained that good hygiene and religious tradition together contributed to robust population growth.[59] The numbers show that a high rate of natural increase and rapid population expansion were indeed hallmarks of European Jewish society in the nineteenth century. From a global population of 2.5 million Jews in 1800, the number rose to 7.75 million in 1880, 10.5 million in 1900, and more than 13 million in 1914. By 1939, on the eve of World War II, the world was home to close to 17 million Jews.[60]

The growth rate was especially high among Russian Jews, despite the fact that millions emigrated to the United States and Western Europe in the late nineteenth century.[61] In 1800, there were 800,000 Jews in Russia. By the end of the century, there were more than 5 million, and by 1914, nearly 6 million.[62] Records from czarist Russia for 1897 show an exceptionally high birthrate among the Jews, with an average of six children per woman.[63]

But the trend reversed itself in the twentieth century, with a significant drop in Jewish births. In 1934, Arthur Ruppin, a sociologist and demographer who arrived in Palestine from Germany in 1908 to head the Zionist movement's office in the country, noted that the very conspicuous decline in the Jewish birthrate was a disruption of the Jews' long-standing tradition of high fertility.[64] The figures in Table 1 for Jewish births in Europe in the twentieth century indicate a steady downward spiral.[65]

In the 1930s, births continued to plummet. From thirty-three births per thousand persons at the beginning of the twentieth century, the number dropped to between seventeen and eighteen in 1934–1937.[66] Due to a decline in mortality, the smaller volume of births did not immediately affect natural increase, but as the numbers continued to drop, the impact became unmistakable.

Table 1. Natural Increase among European Jews

Years	Births per 1,000 people	Deaths per 1,000 people	Natural increase
1750–1650	45	40	5
1800–1750	40	30	10
1850–1800	40	25	15
1900–1850	35	20	15
1905–1901	33	15	18
1910–1906	32	15	17
1914–1911	30	14	16
1924–1921	23	13	10
1929–1925	21	12	9

According to Ruppin, a tradition of smaller families first developed among the Jews of Central and Western Europe and was evident as early as 1860–1870. In the 1930s, he saw the use of contraceptives taking root among the educated classes in Europe and believed that, within a generation or two, it would reach the proletariat and small towns. "Since the Jews are mainly city-dwellers and belong to the progressive elite," he wrote, they would be the pioneers, and set an example for their Christian neighbors.[67] This perception of the Jews of Central and Western Europe as the forerunners of birth control in Europe was confirmed by other sources. One argument was that assimilated Jews were indifferent to the decline in births because in their hearts they were glad the Jewish population was shrinking: fewer Jews would solve the painful "Jewish question."[68]

In the 1920s and 1930s, birth control methods that had been used for generations in the Jewish communities of Western and Central Europe began to seep into Eastern Europe, and a growing number of East European Jews began to practice birth control.[69] According to a census in 1926, there was no ethnic group in all of Russia that had a birthrate as low as the Jews.[70] Births among the Jews of Russia barely exceeded deaths.

A significant decline in fertility was also evident in the Jewish communities of the United States and Canada from the end of the nineteenth century through the end of the 1930s.[71] Bachi, a demographer at the Hadassah Medical Organization in the early 1940s, viewed the Jews in these countries as birth regulation pioneers.[72] "No population group in the United States stands out more than the Jews in mass utilization of artificial abortions and contraception," he wrote.[73] He found that the decline in births among American Jews began earlier and proceeded at a faster pace than among Christians, and he attributed that to immigration and secularization.[74]

In contrast with Western Jews, natural increase among the Jews in Asia and North Africa soared in the first half of the twentieth century as mortality rates dropped and the number of births remained relatively high.[75] The high birthrate among the Jews in Islamic countries was a product of early marriage, a long childbearing period, and short intervals between pregnancies. Jewish religious laws on reproduction and family purity were contributing factors. In Islamic countries, a married woman was subject to social and family pressure to bring children into the world. As in Muslim society, the status of a Jewish woman was determined by how many children she had. Having a large family brought honor and respect to her husband and the family as a whole. Barrenness was seen as a severe defect.[76] The use of modern contraceptives was not widespread during this period.[77] Nevertheless, reports from the 1940s show that the trend toward smaller families was becoming more entrenched in some Arab countries, particularly Egypt.[78]

The shrinking Jewish birthrate in Europe, which began to seep into Jewish communities in Arab lands, coupled with assimilation and mixed marriage in Western and Central Europe, culminated in dire demographic predictions for the Jewish people even before the Holocaust.[79] After the Holocaust, the annihilation of millions of European Jews, the gender imbalance among the survivors and the mad dash to leave Europe intensified the demographic fears.

In 1944, as World War II was raging and the scope of the tragedy in Europe became known, Bachi alerted the Yishuv and Zionist leadership to the sad state of Jewish population growth in the United States: "Today, the last large bloc in the Diaspora where life is still more or less normal uses abortion and family planning more than any population group in the United States."[80] Over the following few years, fertility in North America, and among the Jews in particular, recovered.[81] In the Yishuv, however, the picture was more complex, with the birthrate affected by a particular combination of origins and local conditions.

A Profile of the Yishuv

The term *Yishuv* designates the Jewish population of Palestine under the British Mandate, and more specifically that section of the Jewish population, sometimes also called the New Yishuv, that aspired to establish a Jewish state there.[82] The Jews were a minority of Palestine's population during this period. At the end of World War I, about 56,000 resided in Palestine, along with about 600,000 Arabs. On the eve of World War II, the Jewish population had increased to about 450,000, constituting about 30 percent of the country's inhabitants. The Arab and Jewish populations were distinguished by religious and culture and rival national aspirations that often resulted in violent clashes. The Jews who aspired to establish a Jewish state in Palestine established separate urban and farming settlements, developed their own local and countrywide political institutions, conducted internal democratic elections, and chose their own leadership, whose authority they voluntarily accepted. They partook of a new culture centered on the Hebrew language. All this was designed to promote the Yishuv autonomy as it strove for political independence and sovereignty. As Aviva Halamish has written, "The Yishuv viewed itself as a separate entity and acted to assert this view in practice."[83] Halamish adds that the aspiration for autonomy in all areas of life was encouraged by the British Mandate administration and its policies.

The Yishuv wished to conduct its affairs on its own to the greatest possible extent during the period before the establishment of an independent state, but it was nevertheless subordinate to the Mandate. British rule began at the end of 1917, when that country's forces began to seize Palestine from Turkey at the end of World War I. During the initial period a military government was in charge and sought to preserve the status quo. British civilian rule began in the summer of 1920, and since 1922 was under the terms of the mandate granted to Britain by the League of Nations, an international organization founded in 1920 to prevent war and promote world peace. Such mandates granted European states the authority to govern territories in a custodial capacity, for the purpose of readying them for independence. The Mandate for Palestine, approved in 1922, also charged Britain with assisting the Yishuv in the establishment of a national home for the Jewish people in Palestine, in the spirit of the Balfour Declaration of 1917. The Mandate administration governed Palestine until May 1948. The entire period of British rule is thus called the Mandate period. During the initial part of this time, in the 1920s, the country's borders were established. The Mandate administration governed in accordance with the accepted principles of British colonial rule. Most of its officials had gained experience in other British colonial governments and, according to Anita Shapira, applied their experience in those places to Palestine.[84] The high commissioners appointed by the British government to serve as Palestine's chief executives worked to advance the region in a variety of areas. They modernized the country, improving its health services, water supply, agriculture, industry, and transport, and they carried out other infrastructure projects that improved life for the entire population, Jewish and Arab.

The British set the policies and laws for all the country's inhabitants. In practice, Palestine's society was triangular, its three sides being the British rulers, the Arab majority, and the Jewish minority. Relations between the three sides were complex and sometimes vicious, with waves of violence creating ever more alienation and enmity between any two parts of the population.

Relations between the Yishuv and the Mandate administration were also not simple. In the larger picture, the 1920s and 1930s were a period of cooperation between these two sides, during which the Yishuv grew stronger. It benefited from greater security, better transport, and improved sanitation. Most of the Mandate administration's welfare, education, and health efforts were for the Arab majority, while the Yishuv established its own institutions in these areas that offered a high level of service, especially in the health field.

Under British auspices, the Yishuv established autonomous self-governing bodies and fostered its cultural identity. Yet there was a disparity between the facts on the ground and the Yishuv's expectations. It was a source of constant friction. British policy did not always accord with Yishuv aspirations.

In 1937, following the outbreak of the Arab Revolt, the British sent a royal committee, the Peel Commission, to study the situation in Palestine. The commission's report asserted that Palestine was a dual country in which two nations and cultures lived side by side. It proposed to partition the territory into two states, Arab and Jewish, in the view that this was the necessary outcome of the development of the two nations. The commission also found that the Yishuv was ready for independence.[85] But the plan was not implemented. In the 1940s, especially after the end of World War II, the Yishuv's relations with the British worsened precipitously. In 1939 the British instituted a policy of getting tough with the Yishuv. In particular, they severely restricted Jewish immigration to Palestine. In response, the Yishuv began to oppose British rule and seek its end and the establishment of an independent state. In the end the British pulled out in May 1948, in the wake of the United Nations decision of November 1947 to partition Palestine into separate Jewish and Arab states.

The Mandate's thirty years enabled the Yishuv to establish its own society and economy in Palestine. Without the British, declares Anita Shapira in her history of Israel, the Yishuv could not have developed past the point of no return in terms of its size and power.[86] One of the most important manifestations of this was Jewish immigration, which continued to grow despite the obstacles.

The basis of the Yishuv was the immigration of Jews from Europe in ever-increasing numbers, beginning at the end of the nineteenth century. As a society of immigrants, the Yishuv retained strong ties to the Jewish Diaspora, where members of their families, movements, and political parties remained, as well as business and financial connections. The Zionist Organization was an international organization dedicated to the establishment of a Jewish state, but most of its members lived outside Palestine. On this organization's basis, the Jewish Agency was established. It was also international in nature and a more inclusive body that aimed to include non-Zionists and that served as the Zionist's autonomous self-governing authority and its representative before the Mandate administration. Its executive arm was the Jewish Agency Executive (previously the Zionist Executive). The Yishuv also had its own leadership institutions, among them an elected Assembly of Representatives, which had its own executive board, the National Council. These were responsible for the Yishuv's internal affairs, such as immigrant absorption, education, and health. In practice, it and the Jewish Agency, which represented the Yishuv to the British and oversaw immigration and settlement, complemented each other, and together they made up the leadership of the Yishuv.

The Mandate was a period of extremes marked by dramatic events unfolding within a short span of time: great waves of immigration, civil disturbances, economic hardship, world war, and above all the death of millions of Jews in the Holocaust, followed just two years later by the decision to establish a Jewish state. This combination of circumstances, within a brief but intensive period, became a breeding ground for complicated social issues, some universal and some localized. Childbearing and birth control were part of the picture.

Two main factors played a role in Yishuv demography: immigration and natural increase. Immigration was affected by British Mandate policy, which until the end of the 1930s was based on considerations of the country's economic absorption capacity. In keeping with this approach, the British classified immigrants into a number of categories, the most important of which were "capitalists," for whom there were no restrictions if they arrived with a specified amount of money; "dependents," who were supported financially by existing inhabitants of the Yishuv and were not meant to join the labor force; and "labor immigrants," who intended to earn their own livelihood. The numbers of the latter allowed in were determined by estimates of the country's ability to provide jobs for them. The Zionist Executive was responsible for providing "certificates," as immigration permits were called, to labor immigrants.[87] Under this immigration policy, in force in the 1920s and 1930s, the Yishuv population grew rapidly.

Until the late 1930s, immigration was the key component in Jewish population growth. "It enriched the country with young forces who built the homeland with their own hands and replenished the population through natural increase,"[88] wrote Kanievsky, emphasizing not only the numbers but also the fact that the newcomers were young and hardy, with the potential to substantially boost the population. In practice, the influx of immigration camouflaged the birth slowdown that characterized the Yishuv in the 1930s.[89] From 1937 onward, immigration decreased sharply and World War II halted it altogether.[90] By the time it resumed, the makeup of the group had changed in terms of age and physical and mental state. Natural increase was even more crucial.

The Yishuv was a society of immigrants consisting of families and young people. Most hailed from Eastern Europe, but after the rise of the Nazis in the 1930s, they also came from Central and Western Europe. Men slightly outnumbered women, a product of immigration policies. The Yishuv was young: in 1931, the average age was 26, rising to 29.2 in 1941.[91] When the State of Israel was declared on May 14, 1948, there were 649,633 Jews in the country, accounting for more than 30 percent of the population. Most were European in origin—78 percent at the end of the 1940s, compared to 22 percent from Islamic countries (Mizrahi Jews).[92] Most of the Jewish population (75 percent) was clustered in cities, the most populous of which were Jerusalem, Tel Aviv, and Haifa. About a quarter of the Jewish population lived in the countryside, in over 250 rural settlements.[93] Most of the Jews lived in a family setting. The centrality of the family, which was rooted in Jewish tradition, became even more important in the Yishuv, where it was assigned social and national roles.[94] "Healthy, hardy, happy families are the foundation for a strong, healthy nation," stated a manual on infant nutrition published by Hadassah in 1939.[95]

Families in the Yishuv, apart from the minority living in kibbutzim, followed the traditional patriarchal model revolving around gender-based division of tasks, dependency of women and children on the head of the family as breadwinner, and the perception of the woman as a wife and mother whose calling is to bear children and care for her family.[96] However, social and economic conditions during the Mandate period reshaped the Jewish family as a whole, and female identity in particular.[97] There were women in the Yishuv who sought to free themselves from the traditional gender stereotypes of Jewish patriarchal society and become "new Hebrew women," whose duties went beyond motherhood.[98] But traditional gender stereotypes became even more entrenched in the Yishuv because of the accentuation of the national mission of Hebrew women as mothers, a familiar phenomenon in nationalist societies.[99] The Zionist leadership, consisting of the Zionist Executive (the Jewish Agency Executive after 1930, chaired by David Ben-Gurion), and the Jewish National Council (Va'ad Le'umi), the executive body of the semi-autonomous Yishuv government under the Mandate, saw the birthrate as a tool for achieving national demographic objectives. It thus embraced a pro-natalist policy.[100] Consequently, there was tension in the Yishuv between the desires of the individual and national goals, and between the aspirations of women to take part in the national struggle in a variety of ways and traditional gender roles that confined them to the private domain and motherhood.[101] The battle over the birthrate was both ideological and practical. It is these conflicts and tensions, and the way they tell the story of the Yishuv, that constitute the essence of this book.

NOTES

1. Zeev (Wolfgang) von Weisl, "Me'et Ha'elef She'avdu Lanu Lanetzah," *Hamashkif*, Oct. 10, 1947, 3.
2. Sicron 2004, 72–73, 90.
3. Lilia [Bassewitz], "Isha, Em Vayeled," *Mibefnim*, April 1933, 14.
4. On the Zionist aspiration to create a Jewish majority in Palestine, see Halamish 2006, 13.
5. Melamed 2004, 69–96; Yuval–Davis 1987, 37–59.
6. Zvi, "Min Ha'et veLifanim," *Hatzofeh*, Jan. 26, 1941, 2.
7. Usborne 2007, 11; Gordon 1976, xiii; Tone 1997, 229–230; Hoffer and Hull 2010.
8. Hadassah, the Women's Zionist Organization of America, was founded in New York in 1912 and was very active in Palestine, especially on health issues. In 1918, the organization founded a hospital in Tel Aviv. See Katzburg-Yungman 2008.

9. Letter from Dr. Reuven Katzenelson to Dr. Yossef Aschermann, Aug. 27, 1928, CZA J113/401.

10. For example, on Germany see Usborne 2007, 9; Kaplan 1998, 82.

11. The social worker Sidi Wronsky headed the Center for Children's arrangement of the National Council, in a meeting of the Committee on Birthrate Problems, June 22, 1943, CZA J1/3717/1.

12. Usborne 2007, 15.

13. Zameret 1987.

14. Interview with Muki Tzur, Aug. 7, 2013.

15. Schechter 2011, 252; Margalit-Stern 2013, 114.

16. Patient diagnosis lists, Hadassah Hospital, Maternity and Gynecological Department, 1932–1936, TAA 4-4645, 4644.

17. "Sifrut Refu'it," *Do'ar Hayom*, June 12, 1926, 7.

18. Engel 2012, 315; Shapira 2009, 307–309.

19. Kanievsky 1944, 15

20. H. Myuzam, "Sekirah 'al haMegamot haDemografiyot haNokhehiyot ba'Olam, be'Am Yisra'el, uveYisra'el, 1964," CZA A516/276.

21. Triger 2014, 84.

22. The Catholic Church has been the most stringent Christian denomination with regard to abortions. Protestant, Anglican, and other churches have opposed abortion for religious and moral reasons but allow them under certain circumstances. See Noonan 1970; Lustig 1993, 96–100, 163–170, 218–219, 249–252; Baird and Rosenbaum 2001.

23. Hoffer and Hull 2010, 11–12, 49–50.

24. Coale 1986, 2; Andorka 1978.

25. Coale and Treadway 1986, 79

26. For example, see Van de Kaa 1999, 1–49; Therborn 2004, 235–239; Lesthaeghe 2010, 211–251; Coale and Watkins 1986.

27. Kanievsky 1944, 18, 44.

28. Usborne 2011, 140–161.

29. Reggiani 1996, 725–755; Abrams 2002, 110; Grushka 1958, 193.

30. Van de Kaa 1999, 18–19; Abrams 2002, 306; Taylor Allen 2008, 17; Alpern Engel 2004, 161; Bridenthal, Grossmann, and Kaplan 1984, 1–28; Kanievsky 1944, 39.

31. Contraception had been practiced from time immemorial. It did not require devices but could be accomplished through the cooperation of the partners, via coitus interruptus or the rhythm method. Physical and chemical devices, of questionable and varying effectiveness, came into use in the sixteenth century. Remennick 1996, 8–16.

32. Sanger 1931; Jacobs 1996; Rose 1992.

33. Pass Freidenreich 1996, 185.

34. Drezgic 2010, 955–970; Anson and Meir 1996, 43–63.

35. Maynes and Waltner 2012, 95–96.

36. Abrams 2002, 123.

37. Hoffmann 2000, 35–55.

38. Maloy and Jones Patterson 1992; Zahra 2009, 45–86.

39. Saraceno 1991, 196–212; Nash 1991, 160–177.

40. Coale and Treadway 1986, 37–38; Cotts Watkins 1991; Cotts Watkins and Danzi 1995, 479. Theodore Grushka estimated the abortion rate in the United States in the mid-1940s to be at 140–175 per thousand births. Grushka 1958, 193.

41. H. Myuzam, "Sekirah 'al haMegamot haDemografiyot haNokhehiyot ba'Olam, be'Am Yisra'el, uveYisra'el, 1964," CZA A516/276.

42. Abrams 2002, 106.

43. Grossmann 1995, 3.

44. Frevert 1997, 111, 186.

45. Kozma 2010, 96–124; Woycke 1988.

46. Grushka 1958, 193.

47. Frevert 1997, 186; Grossmann 1995, 8; Usborne 2007, ix.

48. Grossmann 1995, 4; Mouton 2007, 108.

49. Usborne 2007, 3–5, 19; Kaplan 1998, 82.

50. Coale, Anderson, and Harm 1979, 15–17.

51. Alpern Engel 2004, 161–162, 177.

52. Ibid, 178–180.

53. H. Myuzam, "Sekirah 'al haMegamot haDemografiyot haNokhehiyot ba'Olam, be'Am Yisra'el, uveYisra'el, 1964," CZA A516/276.

54. Van der Tak 1975.

55. Kanievsky 1944, 50.

56. Kupat Holim was founded in 1911 by several dozen Jewish workers as a mutual-aid society. In 1921, shortly after the establishment of the Histadrut, several such entities united under the auspices of the Histadrut. See Shvarts 2002, 2008.

57. Kanievsky 1944, 19, 50.

58. For detailed portraits of the central figures who appear in this book, see Chapter 5. On Bachi specifically, see Leibler 2008.

59. Bachi, radio talk, 1943, CZA J1/3717/1.

60. Ruppin 1934, 142–143; "The Jewish people in numbers, 1961," YTA, Oticker, 15-3/8/5; *Encyclopedia Judaica*, 2nd ed., s.v. "Demography" (Keter, Jerusalem & Macmillan Reference).

61. H. Myuzam, "Sekirah 'al haMegamot haDemografiyot haNokhehiyot ba'Olam, be'Am Yisra'el, uveYisra'el, 1964," CZA A516/276.

62. "The Jewish People in Numbers, 1961," YTA, Oticker, 15-3/8/5.

63. Bachi 1977, 196.

64. Ruppin 1934, 144.

65. Ibid.

66. Kanievsky 1944, 19.

67. Ruppin 1934, 155.

68. Bachi, radio talk, 1943, CZA J1/3717/1.

69. Dr. Tova Berman, lecture on the politics of births, June 17, probably early1940s, CZA A516/165; Bachi 1977, 199.

70. Committee on Birthrate Problems, political program to encourage motherhood, 1945, CZA A516/210.

71. H. Myuzam, "Sekirah 'al haMegamot haDemografiyot haNokhehiyot ba'Olam, be'Am Yisra'el, uveYisra'el, 1964," CZA A516/276.

72. Roberto Bachi, "Maskanot Politiyot metokh Hakirotay 'al haHitpathut haDemografit shel haYehudim veha'Aravim beE"Y," Oct. 1944, CZA J1/3717/2, 1.

73. Roberto Bachi, Draft of the Political Conclusions from my Investigations on the Demographic Development of Jews and Arabs in Palestine, 1944, CZA S25/8223.

74. Bachi 1943a, 8.

75. H. Myuzam, "Sekirah 'al haMegamot haDemografiyot haNokhehiyot ba'Olam, be'Am Yisra'el, uveYisra'el, 1964," CZA A516/276.

76. Sabar 2006, 16–17.

77. Bachi and Matras 1962, 215.

78. Bachi, "HaYeludah be Yisra'el uvaYishuv vehaDerakhim le'Idudah," apparently 1944, CZA J1/3717/3.

79. Roberto Bachi, "Be'ayat haYeludah BeYisra'el veHatza'ot leMediniyut haUkhlusiyah," undated, ISA 5588/2c; Bachi, radio talk, 1943, CZA J1/3717/1.

80. Roberto Bachi, "HaYeludah be Yisra'el uvaYishuv vehaDerakhim le'Idudah," apparently 1944, CZA J1/3717/3.

81. H. Myuzam, "Sekirah 'al haMegamot haDemografiyot haNokhehiyot ba'Olam, be'Am Yisra'el, uveYisra'el, 1964," CZA A516/276.

82. Not all of the Jews under the Mandate shared this nationalist goal, nor were they party to the new cultural milieu that took form as a result of Zionist immigration. A minority, the Old Yishuv, did not take part in the Yishuv's political and cultural life. Yet in many scholarly works the term *Yishuv* is used to designate the entire Jewish population under the Mandate. I follow that practice here.

83. Halamish 2004, 20.

84. Shapira 2014, 96. For more on British rule in Palestine, see Shapira 2012.

85. Some argue that the partition plan was a product of the Mandate's policy of preferring Jewish interests by fostering the economic and cultural separation of the two nations. For more on this, see Shapira 2014, 96–97.

86. Shapira 2014, 98.

87. Halamish 2004, 271–272.

88. Kanievsky 1944, 61.

89. Dr. Tova Berman, lecture on the politics of births, June 17, probably early 1940s, CZA A516/165.

90. Alroey 2004.

91. Dr. A. [Avraham] Katzenelson, "Vital Statistics in Palestine," lecture delivered at the International Congress of Tropical Medicine and Hygiene, Cairo, Dec. 1928, CZA J1/33,045; Bachi, Israeli Birthrate Problem, ISA 5588/2c; Bachi, Demographic Material for Mr. Kanievsky, Jan. 1944, CZA A516/201; Jewish Agency, Department of Statistics, "The Yishuv at the End of 1945," CZA S90/2217/5.

92. Ben-Gurion Diaries, vol. 2, Feb. 11, 1952, BGA K218888, 11; Jewish Agency, Department of Statistics, "The Yishuv at the End of 1945," CZA S90/2217/5; Bachi 1977, 199.

93. Jewish Agency, Department of Statistics, "The Yishuv at the End of 1935" and "The Yishuv at the End of 1945," CZA S90/2217/5.

94. On the family in Jewish society in the early twentieth century, see Weinberg 1988, 3–40. On the family in the Yishuv, see Razi 2010.

95. Sara Bromberg, Infant Feeding, 1939, CZA A520/15, 3.

96. Fogiel-Bijaoui 1999, 109, 128; Triger 2014, 13–23.

97. Razi 2010; Alroey 2010, 97–101.

98. Shilo 1998; Shilo, Kark, and Hazan-Rokem 2001.

99. Bernstein 1998, 287–311; Margalit-Stern 2011, 170–197. On the phenomenon in nationalist societies, see Yuval-Davis 1997, 626.

100. Stopler 2008, 473–516; Winckler 2007, 197–237; Portugese 1998.

101. Bernstein 1993, 83–103.

CHAPTER ONE

"COLLECTIVE SELF-SUICIDE"

The Decline in the Yishuv's Birthrate

Overview

"THE STATISTICS SPEAK A CRUEL LANGUAGE," wrote a Yishuv newspaper, *Hamashkif*, in 1941. The Jewish birthrate in British-ruled Palestine had reached a nadir, while the local Arab population was producing children at an exceptionally high rate.[1] The figures were from the previous year, which had set a record for both a nadir of births and an acme of abortions until 1941 came and broke it. Yet the Yishuv had been keeping its birthrate low for years.

A census was conducted by the British Mandate administration in 1922, but it was a limited operation. From that year onward there are partial figures regarding the number of births in Palestine.[2] The first comprehensive census was conducted in 1931; presumably, another such census would have been done in 1941, in keeping with the ten-year census cycle that was common practice throughout the British Empire,[3] had World War II not intervened. The Statistical Department of the Zionist Executive was founded in 1924, in recognition of the crucial importance of quantitative statistical data collection and analysis for the realization of the Zionist idea and the Yishuv's development. The Statistical Department conducted its own surveys, designed to provide precise snapshots of the Yishuv over several dimensions, among them population, immigration, birthrate, death rate, agriculture, and manufacturing. Its first statistical compendium on the Yishuv, which set the template for those that followed, was published in 1929 by David Gurevich, who had headed the department from its inception.[4] But its data collection project provided the Yishuv's governing bodies with only some of the figures they needed. There were difficulties, most centrally the relative scantiness of raw statistical material about births, and all the more so about abortions carried out outside the law. Two other problems required special attention. The first was that the Yishuv was a young population. The percentage of young people of childbearing age was unusually high, much more so than in European countries.[5] As a result, there were, relatively, a large number of births, more than in societies with a more balanced age distribution. The statistician had to take this into account in seeking out "the *true* intensity of births and deaths,"[6] as the Yishuv's senior statistician and demographer, Roberto Bachi, put it. The second problem was the multifarious nature of the Jewish population. True, the Yishuv was small and young, but it also was extremely varied in its origins and included a large number of subcultures and communities. That being the case, an authentic portrayal of the Yishuv's birthrate and birth prevention could not be drawn simply by examining the data regarding the Yishuv as a whole. It was necessary to analyze the demographic information in depth and see how it broke down in relation to the social divisions that were salient characteristics of the Jewish population.

On the eve of World War I, a typical Jewish family in Palestine brought an average of five children into the world.[7] The marriage rate was high and the marriage age relatively young.[8] Very few marriages were childless.[9] On the face of it, this situation might have been expected to continue following the war and the establishment of the British Mandate in Palestine. But over the course of the Mandate, from 1920 to 1948, the birthrate steadily declined. The story of the Yishuv's birthrate is presented in this chapter as a story of decline. That decline's varied causes are analyzed in the chapter that follows.

The figures in table 2 show the birthrate declining from the 1920s onward. This decline is especially pronounced given the significant nominal growth in the Yishuv's population from successive waves of Jewish immigration (411,000 immigrants during the years 1920–1946).[10] The absolute number of births also needs to be considered in light of the notable increase in the population. For example, while in the years 1936–1942 the number of births remains almost the same, the fact that the size of the Yishuv increased significantly means the birthrate was actually declining, as the figures in the second column show.[11] Furthermore, the numbers provided by the Mandate administration, on which the Yishuv's statisticians based their calculations, showed the Jewish birthrate declining year by year.[12] But the rate was computed on the basis of the number of Jews who immigrated legally and were thus registered with the Mandate administration. They did not take into account the number of illegal immigrants, which rose steadily during the 1930s.[13] If these were included, the Yishuv birthrate was even lower than table 2 shows. Such considerations provide the basis for the full picture presented in this chapter.

For most of the 1920s, the percentage of births in the Yishuv was relatively high, twice that in Western countries and three times as high as that

Table 2. The Yishuv Birthrate

Year	Birthrate per 1,000	Absolute number of births	Jewish population of Palestine
1917			56,000
1922	32.6	2,370	83,790[a]
1923	36.4	3,269	89,660
1924	38.2	3,623	94,945
1925	32.6	3,974	121,725
1926	35.5	5,309	149,500
1927	34.6	5,263	149,789
1928	35.0	5,289	151,656
1929	33.6	5,263	156,481
1930	33.0	5,434	164,796
1931	32.2	5,540	174,606
1932	29.2	5,282	192,137
1933	29.2	6,113	234,967
1934	30.2	7,671	255, 500
1935	30.8	9,867	355,157
1936	29.7	11,009	384,078
1937	26.7	10,297	395,836
1938	26.3	10,563	411,222
1939	23.0	9,888	445,457
1940	23.7	10,817	460,100
1941	20.7	9,714	475,000
1942	23.2	10,884	483,600
1943[b]	29.0	14,317	498,700
1944	30.2	N/A	522,600
1945	30.3	N/A	553,400
1946	N/A	N/A	579,100
1947	29.0	N/A	609,000
1948[c]	23.0	N/A	650,000
			(May 1948)

Sources: These figures are compiled from several sources that differ only slightly in their figures. See, for example, Memorandum from Hadassah's Statistics Department with regard to Dr. Rivlin's letter, 1939 (precise date not given), CZA J113/2312; Kanievsky 1944, 64; Roberto Bachi, "Sekirah Ketzarah 'al haYeludah vehaTemotah beE"Y beTekufat 1939–1941," CZA J1/1957/2; Roberto Bachi, "Be'ayat haYeludah BeYisra'el veHatza'ot leMediniyut haUkhlusiyah, undated, ISA 5588/2c; Ben-Gurion Diaries 2, Feb. 11, 1952, BGA K218888, p. 11; Report by Bachi, 1944, CZA J1/3717/3; Bachi's data are also from his report, Feb. 1945, CZA J1/31393. The figures on the Jewish population are based on British Mandate government figures and are taken also from Halamish 2002, 375; Halevy 2008, 585. I was able to find only partial figures for some years and was unable to find figures on births from any source for 1946.
[a]The Arabic population in Mandate Palestine: Most of the Arab population was Muslim. In 1922, there were 589,177 Muslims and 71,464 Christians (660,641 in total); in 1931, there were 750,000 Muslims and 100,000 Christians (850,000 in total); in 1945, there were 1,196,820 Arabs; in 1948, there were 1,300,000 Arabs.
[b]Figures for births in the period 1943–1945 are from Ba'al Heshbon, "Hidat Tenu'at haUkhlusin ha-Eretzyisraelit," Hamashkif, September 8, 1946, 2.
[c]The figures for 1948 relate to the beginning of the year. In his diary, Ben-Gurion cited a figure of 26 per 1,000 for 1948, Ben-Gurion Diaries 1, Feb. 11, 1952, BGA K218888, p. 8. The disparity between his number and that of the other sources is probably due to his number relating to the entire year, that is it includes the months after May 1948, when Israel gained its independence and large numbers of immigrants began to arrive.

of the Jews in those countries.[14] The year 1924 marked the beginning of a large wave of immigration and a period of economic optimism and relative calm in Jewish-Arab relations. In that year, the Yishuv recorded the highest birthrate of the 1920s. The maternity ward of Hadassah hospital in Tel Aviv, in danger of not being able to serve enough people with a deluge of births, desperately asked for more beds, equipment, and midwives.[15] Two years later, the hospital's director, Dr. Mechulam Levontin, warned the Hadassah executive in Jerusalem that the situation in the maternity ward was no less than a catastrophe. No more women could be admitted; there simply was not enough space.[16] The ward's medical staff complained daily about overcrowding when, at the end of 1927, between twenty-three and twenty-five women were admitted each day. The doctors and nurses warned that the crush was a health hazard. "We are sorry, but also happy, to note that during the month of December our maternity ward has suffered from a huge bout of women in labor," the hospital cautioned in a report, even as it rejoiced in the high birthrate.[17]

The relatively high fertility of the 1920s could be attributed not only to the Torah's command to "be fruitful and multiply," which Dr. Avraham Katzenelson, a member of the Zionist leadership, claimed "is the Hebrew nation's oldest instinct," but also to the young profile of the Jewish immigrants to Palestine, the high marriage rate, and in particular the relatively high proportion of ultra-Orthodox Jews (today called Haredim, but then referred to as the Old Yishuv) and of Jews from the Islamic world (Sephardim or Oriental Jews, today usually referred to as Mizrahim). Both these populations were noted for their high birthrates.[18]

In 1929 the trend began to reverse and the first signs of a declining birthrate became evident. It is known that Europeans of a certain strata seek to reduce their number of births, Katzenelson remarked at the time. The trend continued in the years that followed, when, with the growth in the Jewish population, the birthrate declined. It was especially notable in Tel Aviv, the first Hebrew city, founded in 1909, which attracted tens of thousands of immigrants and grew rapidly as a result. (In 1914, Tel Aviv had 3,600 inhabitants; by 1925 there were 34,000, and in 1936 the city's population reached 120,000.) Yet the number of births actually declined, from 1,500 in 1929 to 1,200 in 1931.[19] The number continued to shrink in the years that followed, and the ebb in births grew more pronounced by the year, as the figures in table 3 show.

Some 280,000 Jews settled in Palestine in the 1930s, but this did not quell Bachi's demographic fears. The Yishuv, including a large swathe of both the new immigrants and the veteran population, was, in his words, "committing collective suicide."[20] All those cognizant of the problem were aware in 1939

Table 3. Average Number of Births by Jewish Women
in Palestine throughout Their Fertile Years

Year	Average number of children
1926–1927	3.7
1931	2.84
1937	2.35
1938–1941	2.1

Source: Bachi 1944, pp. 171, 243. Elsewhere he offered the
figure 3.86, Bachi 1977, 199. See also Katzenelson 1929, 7; Roberto Bachi, "HaYeludah be Yisra'el uvaYishuv vehaDerakhim
le'Idudah," apparently 1944, CZA J1/3717/3.

that the birthrate was insufficient to keep the population at its current level.[21]
Yet the trend continued and grew even worse. The lowest point seems to have
come in 1941, when less than 10,000 babies were born in a Yishuv that num-
bered 475,000 inhabitants.[22] The number of births was virtually identical to
that in 1935, when only 320,000 Jews were living in Palestine.[23]

In 1941 the Hebrew press reported that the birthrate in the Yishuv's
"modern" settlements was as low as in the European countries with the most
meager fertility figures. "Among the Jews, a fourth child is an exception. Even
a third and second child are rare," one newspaper item related.[24] Dr. Tova
Berman-Yeshurun, a public health professional and advocate for larger families,[25] reported that, among a sample of 2,180, a full 10 percent were childless,
45 percent had one child, 30 percent had two, and only 15 percent had more
than two children.[26] Her figures are consistent with Bachi's more comprehensive findings of 1943, according to which half of all families were childless
or had one child only, a quarter had two children, and only a quarter had
more than two children.[27]

Bachi was pessimistic about the Yishuv's future. According his statistical model, the Yishuv's rate of natural increase in 1927 was 40 percent per
generation (13 percent per year), while in 1941 the rate of natural increase was
negative—he predicted an 11 percent decline in population over a generation
(14 percent a year). Bachi termed this a threat to the Yishuv's development.[28]
Demographers were not the only ones concerned. "Even a person unfamil-
iar with the numbers," wrote Yocheved Bat-Rachel, a kibbutz member and a
leadership figure in the Yishuv and the Women Workers' Movement, "can see
the peril in this situation."[29]

The number of births rose somewhat in 1943.[30] On average, that year
families in the Yishuv had 2.96 children. In this year, natural increase (births
minus deaths) rose to 21 per 1,000. The previous year it had been 14. The

birthrate per 1,000 Jews rose from 23 in 1942 to 29 in 1943.[31] But the demographic alarm did not diminish; it continued through 1944. Given the growth in the Arab population, the feeling was that it was not sufficient for the Yishuv to maintain its population. It had to expand. The general consensus was that, to guarantee the Yishuv's future, each of its families had to have at least three children.[32] Immigration had dwindled considerably and could no longer be depended on to make up the difference. In the face of the Holocaust, Bachi argued, the Yishuv could not "live on the precipice of the frighteningly swift demographic attenuation of what remains of the Diaspora." In other words, the Jewish population in Palestine could no longer look to immigration to increase its numbers. It could accomplish that only itself, by having more children.[33]

The birthrate recovery continued in 1945. More than 14,000 babies were born, and the average number of children per woman rose to 3.3.[34] That was not enough, however, to cause optimism among those fearful of the Yishuv's demographic future. In 1946, the Committee on Birthrate Problems established by the Yishuv leadership in 1943, argued that the rise was not a long-range phenomenon. There was reason for concern that any economic downturn or political problem would again send the birthrate careening down a slippery slope.[35] Articles in the Hebrew press argued that the upswing in the birthrate was anomalous, a product of specific circumstances rather than a fundamental change. Some writers argued that the increased birthrate did not, in fact, signal any improvement in the demographic situation. After all, the rate had merely equaled that of ten years previously,[36] meaning that it was far from guaranteeing a significant increase in the Jewish population.[37]

They were right; the recovery was short lived.[38] *Hatzofeh*, the newspaper of the religious Zionist movement, reported in June 1945 that the birthrate was declining again.[39] In the first half of 1946 it was lower than it had been in the comparable part of 1945.[40] The decline continued in 1947 and 1948, years in which thousands of young people died in Israel's long War of Independence.[41] Concern about the Yishuv's future only grew more acute.

The Ethnic and Communal Breakdown

The picture offered so far is a general one. But the birthrate varied widely within the subgroups that made up the Yishuv. The economist Yitzhak Kanievsky offered a detailed breakdown of this sort in 1944. It showed that, with the exception of mothers of Russian origin, all Yishuv mothers of European (Ashkenazi) origin had less than two children.[42] Small families were largely an Ashkenazi phenomenon. In 1941, Ashkenazi mothers had, on average, fewer children than any other sector—only 1.7. Yet even within the

Ashkenazi community there were differences. Families of Austrian extraction held the record for the fewest children, 1.38 on the average. These were followed by Germans, who had an average of 1.47 children, while families from Czechoslovakia had an average of 1.49 children.[43]

These low numbers stood in stark contrast to those of Mizrahi families, who in the same period had an average of four to five children. Again, there were differences of degree between countries of origin (see table 4).[44] Hedwig Gellner, a well-known social worker in Austria who settled in Palestine and headed the Tel Aviv municipal Department of Social Welfare, reported at the beginning of the 1940s that many Mizrahi families caring for large numbers of children required assistance.[45] Yemenite families were more than once singled out as having record large families.[46] One newspaper claimed that they were the only community that strictly observed the commandment to be fruitful and multiply.[47] Of the five women who were awarded a procreation prize in 1945, three were Mizrahim who had given birth to more than ten children. The other two were Ashkenazi women of the Old Yishuv.[48]

In contrast to religious Zionists, who practiced birth control, the Haredim of the Old Yishuv were characterized by high birthrate.[49] The Haredim lived primarily in the four "holy cities" of Jerusalem, Safed, Hebron, and Tiberias. In addition to strict observance of Jewish law, the men of these families devoted themselves to Torah study. This sector, in general, opposed the Zionist political project of establishing a Jewish state.

When general figures were discussed, the high birthrate among Mizrahim and Haredim, which in 1943 meant that each woman in these groups had an average of five children,[50] often ameliorated the extremely low birthrate of the Zionist community, or New Yishuv. Yet these two groups still did not have enough children to keep the total Yishuv birthrate up. In other words, the birthrate deficit in the New Yishuv, where most of the women of childbearing age were of European extraction, was huge.[51] Furthermore, at the beginning of the 1940s it became evident that Mizrahim who assimilated into the New Yishuv adopted Ashkenazi birthrate profiles. "There are clear signs that these strata are beginning to imitate the New Yishuv and restrict their childbearing," Bachi argued in 1944.[52] Indeed, the fertility of Mizrahi women displayed a gentle downward trend during the Mandate period. On the whole, however, this trend was milder than it was among Ashkenazi women.[53]

Further insights can be gained from the figures for the Yishuv's birthrate per family figures in the years 1939–1941, the high point of birth control, when they are broken up according to the mother's origin, the father's profession, and place of residence.[54]

Table 4 shows huge ethnic, geographic, and class disparities in the birthrate. Jews from North Africa and Asia have the most children, while those of

Table 4. Yishuv Birthrate per Family, 1939–1941

Mother's place of origin	Birthrate	Father's profession	Birthrate	Place of residence	Birthrate
Germany-Austria	1.5	White-collar professions, arts	1.7	Haifa	1.8
Czechoslovakia and Hungary	1.6	Agriculture	1.8	Moshavot (farming villages)	1.9
England and Northern Europe	1.7	Private and public office workers	1.8	Tel Aviv	2
America (apparently North America)	1.8	Manufacturing and crafts	2.4	Petah Tikva	2.4
Soviet Union	2.7	Trade and transport	2.4	Jaffa	3.5
Balkans and Italy	3.0	Housekeeping services	3.0	Jerusalem	3.5
Palestine	3.7	Religious professions	4.7	Tiberias	4.2
Egypt, Syria, Turkey	4.0	Porters and peddlers	5.2	Safed	4.8
Jordan, Iraq, Afghanistan	6.7				
Yemen	7.8				
Morocco	8.0				

European background are the most successful practitioners of birth control. But even within these groups there are shadings—Eastern Europeans have more children than Western Europeans, and there are pronounced differences among the Mizrahim as well.

The numbers also show that white-collar professionals restricted the number of children, a phenomenon well known from other Western countries as well, while porters and peddlers, most of whom were Mizrahim, had many. Unsurprisingly, so did Jews engaging in religious professions, who were presumably strictly observant of the obligation to propagate. Other data, beyond those in the table, indicate that among the Mizrahim there were large differences between the socioeconomically well-off and the poor. Mizrahim on the lower social rungs had an average of 5.7 children, while those higher up the ladder had a birthrate approaching those of the Ashkenazim,

2.8 children per family.[55] But such class disparities were not apparent among the Ashkenazim, who had small numbers of children no matter what their socioeconomic level. This included farmers, who in many other countries served as the most important demographic reserve for the maintenance and growth of the population.[56]

These ethnic and professional differences can be seen also in the breakdown by geographical location. Cities that were home to Jews of the Old Yishuv and Mizrahim, like Safed, Tiberias, Jerusalem, and Jaffa, showed relatively high fertility.[57] Farming settlements and cities populated largely by members of the New Yishuv, such as Tel Aviv and Haifa, displayed the lowest birthrates.[58] A census conducted in Haifa in 1938 shows that the average number of children per Jewish family was 1.41.[59] In the years 1939–1941 Haifa had the lowest birthrate in the country.[60] Bachi pulled no punches in describing Tel Aviv, the world's first totally Jewish city and home to a healthy proportion of Palestine's Jewish population, "of which we are so proud": its birthrate was so low, he said, that it survived "only thanks to unremitting immigration."[61]

But the leadership was most disappointed with the Yishuv's farmers. The expectation was that this sector would produce a large number of children, as it did in other countries, and thus serve as a symbol and example for the Yishuv as a whole. But the Yishuv's farmers were not like their counterparts elsewhere. On the contrary, the Jewish agricultural communities of Palestine under the Mandate stood out for their dearth of children. That is, the very settlements whose inhabitants embodied the Zionist revolution in practice, who were intent on creating a new Hebrew society, were not reproducing themselves.[62] In the early 1940s, the average number of children per family in Yishuv farming communities ranged from 1.32 to 1.59, reaching 1.9 in 1943. "And so," Bachi grieved, "in our agricultural centers, built to be a foundation for the rebirth of the nation and an example for the entire Zionist movement, there is a severe demographic deficit."[63] He was particularly concerned about the situation in the kibbutzim, cooperatives where the aspirations of the individual were entirely subordinated to the needs of the collective and the highlight of the Zionist endeavor, in which the second generation might be much smaller than the current one. In the 1920s, one child for every two couples was the average in the kibbutzim. In 1937 the average kibbutz woman had 1.67 children.[64] In 1940, the average number of children per family in the kibbutzim was 1.35, despite the fact that the vast majority of inhabitants of these communities were of prime childbearing age.[65] A newspaper reported in 1945 that at many kibbutzim most couples had only one child, if that. Families with two children were rare.[66] In fact, until the establishment of the state in 1948, the number of children born on kibbutzim was less than two per family.[67]

In Bachi's view, the danger presented by these figures was not only that the survival of Yishuv agriculture, including the kibbutzim, was at risk, but also that the rest of the Yishuv viewed the farming settlements as a model to be imitated.[68]

The reluctance of kibbutz members to bring children into the world was characteristic of these communes from the time of their first appearance, on the eve of World War I. The famous Yiddish novelist and playwright Shalom Asch visited one of them at the time. At a meeting with the members, he banged on a table and cried: "Why are you creating a madhouse in this land? I have not heard the voice of a child in any of the places I have visited. Is this possible?"[69] The educator David Idelson, who devoted himself to the care of abandoned children in Tel Aviv, wrote in the 1920s that the establishment of children's houses at the kibbutzim, where the ideal of communal education could be implemented, was not feasible because there were so few children. For the time being, he suggested, the kibbutzim should think of bringing in orphans from elsewhere.[70] In the 1930s the kibbutzim held open discussions about restricting the birthrate, a policy most of the settlements favored.[71] By the 1940s, when kibbutzim were home to many families, the birthrate continued to be low.[72] It is hardly surprising, then, that Yitzhak Tabenkin, one of the founders of the kibbutz movement, declared in November 1944 that the kibbutzim needed four things, the first of which was a high birthrate.[73]

Most farming communities, including the kibbutzim, were part of the secular New Yishuv, with its characteristically low birthrate. Farming communities inhabited by Mizrahim had higher birthrates,[74] as did agricultural communities of a religious cast. The first religious kibbutz, Tirat Zvi, was founded in 1937 by a group of single men and women and twelve married couples and families. By 1941 there were 35 families with 33 children. Most of the families had had at least one child by then, and some had two. "As far as the birthrate goes," said Meir Orlian, one of the founders of Tirat Zvi, "the situation can be seen as satisfactory. The issue of the birthrate does not today constitute a special problem and is of a dimension appropriate to a religious kibbutz."[75] But the Religious Kibbutz Movement was nevertheless part of the Yishuv and thus influenced by its larger trends. In 1941, when the Yishuv birthrate reached a record low, even the religious kibbutzim were concerned. "It could be," Orlian wrote, "that we, too, will face this [demographic] problem if this [security and economic] situation continues."[76] In 1947, when Tirat Zvi's hundredth child was born, its members wondered, "Is it not a dream? After all, not much time has passed since we held disputations over whether it was permissible to bring children to Tirat Zvi!"[77] In other words, despite Orlian's pride in the number of children his commune was producing, the issue of whether that was the right thing to do was certainly on the table.

Birth Control in the Yishuv versus the High Arab Birthrate

To properly understand the significance of the Yishuv's declining birthrate, it has to be placed in a broader context. "The bitter truth is," Bachi wrote in 1943, "that we are a nation with an increasing dearth of children, surrounded by nations with a wealth of children, multiplying by the year."[78] Despite the lack of reliable quantitative data about the Arab population in Mandate Palestine, and about Arab women specifically,[79] the available information clearly shows that the Arab birthrate was much higher than that of any other society in the world, including other Muslim societies.[80] The practice of birth control by the Jews was all the more evident given that the Arabs were a majority of the population in Mandate Palestine.[81] When the Jewish birthrate was at its nadir, in 1939–1941, the average number of children per Jewish woman was 2.1. The average number of children per Muslim woman at this time was 7.51, and this figure grew in subsequent years, reaching 9.42 in 1943–1945.[82] The disparity between the fertility of Jewish and Arab women was huge, with few parallels in international statistics.[83]

Not only was the Muslim birthrate higher; it was also growing as the Jewish birthrate decreased, as table 5 shows.[84] It was already clear by the beginning of the 1930s that the natural increase among Muslims was much higher than that of the Jews. This was the case despite the fact that the Muslim age distribution was wider and that most of the Yishuv consisted of young people of fertile age and the fact that Yishuv mortality "had reached a minimum that the most enlightened countries would be proud of," as Berman put it.[85] Among Muslims mortality declined rapidly as the economy and medical care improved.[86] Together with their high birthrate, the result was a huge rate of natural increase.[87] In 1946 the trend pointed to a doubling of the Muslim population within twenty-five years.[88]

The grounds of the birthrate gap lay in the difference between marriage and birth practices. Muslim women began to have children earlier and continued having children much later in life than Jewish women did.[89] The fertility of Palestine's Muslim women, Bachi noted in 1943, "is the highest today registered by statisticians in all the world's countries. Such high fertility could be found fifty years ago in southern Russia, at a time and in a place where the movement toward birth control had not entirely begun."[90] Unlike the Jews, the Muslims of Palestine showed no inclination to learn about and use artificial means to restrict their number of children.[91]

Table 5. Jewish and Muslim Births per Thousand Inhabitants

Year	Births per 1,000 Jewish inhabitants	Births per 1,000 Muslim inhabitants
1939	23.0	46.42
1940	23.7	47.42
1941	20.7	49.22

Writers in the contemporary Hebrew press wondered at the intractability and persistence of the high Muslim birthrate despite the social, economic, and cultural changes that society was undergoing as it became exposed to European culture and enlightenment. These very factors, after all, had brought about a decline in the Jewish birthrate. How was it that the Muslim population in Palestine, unlike the peoples of other countries, remained unaffected by the zeitgeist? What explained this society's immunity to external influences when it came to having babies? The questions were largely rhetorical ones. *Hamashkif*, the organ of the Revisionist Movement, which fiercely opposed British rule, expressed skepticism about the data provided by the British administration. The data had not been put together sincerely and honestly, the newspaper charged, and were based on preconceptions and biased assumptions.[92]

The demographic gap between Palestine's Muslim majority and Jewish minority (the Jews constituted about a third of the population at the end of the 1930s) had political consequences. Both populations had national aspirations that clashed with each other and which had erupted in violence. At the end of 1944, Dr. Joseph Mayer, a physician and member of the Zionist leadership, declared: "The fact is that the Arabs do not even have to fight us, just continue with their birthrate as they have so far, and they will win."[93] Indeed, as the rest of this book will show, the disparity was the source of profound anxiety for Zionist leaders, who set out to battle it.

Abortions: The Major Means of Birth Control

"A mentality of barrenness is penetrating and spreading through the land; barrenness plain and simple. Deliberate barrenness of the woman's womb," warned the Yishuv's most widely circulated newspaper, *Davar*, published by the labor movement, in 1940.[94] The phrase "deliberate barrenness" was a reference to the phenomenon of abortion that had become commonplace in the Yishuv and which was the easiest, most important, and most widespread means of birth control.[95]

Bachi estimated in 1943 that a Jewish family in Palestine would naturally have an average of 5.9 children, given the community's marriage practices, if no artificial means were used. The decline, to just above two children per family, was attributable to a sharp rise in the use of birth control, but even more so to the rise in abortions. He stressed that, in the absence of preventive means and, especially, without abortions, the number of births in the Yishuv would be more than double what it was, and triple among Jews of European ancestry.[96] In 1945 Bachi declared categorically that "the future of the Jewish people is at risk more than perhaps it ever was . . . the prevention of pregnancy and abortions are so common among Jews that new births are not enough to make up for deaths."[97]

As I have already noted, it is difficult to determine a precise number of abortions in the Yishuv because of the lack of data, and because of the use in Hebrew of a single term for natural and induced abortions. We thus have detailed accounts of the numbers of births and pregnancy terminations at Hadassah hospital in Tel Aviv during the early 1930s.[98] But because the pregnancies that ended are not divided between miscarriages and abortions, we cannot derive statistics relevant to the current study. However, a report issued by the same hospital in the early 1930s states that the reduction in births should be a cause for great concern and that action had to be taken against abortions, which had achieved "major proportions."[99] This is evidence of the phenomenon even if it does not offer precise figures. Taken together, the varying kinds of evidence, among them physician testimonies, the press, and demographic data point to abortions being very common. These sources often use the word "thousands." A female pediatrician, Dr. Bilhah Puliastor, warned in 1931 that "the number of artificial abortions conducted in private and with emotional risk has increased throughout every country. The politics of hiding our heads in the sand has not helped."[100] A press item from 1934 accused women of acting lawlessly in having abortions.[101]

"A very large number of women come to request terminations of their pregnancies, without any medical reason to do so, and they take a refusal to do so as a huge tragedy and real catastrophe," described Dr. Leon (Arieh) Abramovitz, director of Hadassah hospital in Tel Aviv and the head of its maternity ward, in 1937. He added that Mizrahi women, who generally had high birthrates, were starting to come to Hadassah seeking abortions.[102] Here is evidence of a jump in the pervasiveness of abortions. "We frequently see flip attitudes toward abortions and a complete lack of responsibility," Dr. Shoshana (Rosa) Meyer, a specialist in pediatric medicine, wrote to the Jewish National Council, the Yishuv's executive body, in 1940.[103] In 1944, Prof. Abraham Halevi Fraenkel, a world-famous mathematician, rector of Hebrew University, and observant Jew, put it in a nutshell: for many years, he said, abortions "have been performed in the Yishuv not in the hundreds but rather in the thousands each year."[104]

Dr. Yossef Aschermann, founder of the maternity ward at Hadassah hospital in Tel Aviv, conducted a study at the beginning of the 1950s that examined 1,000 women of varying ages who had received care in recent years at private clinics. He found that a fifth of them, 210 women, had undergone a total of 369 abortions. Of these, 133 had had a single abortion, 40 had had two, and one woman had had nine. Half of the women were native-born or long-time inhabitants of the country, and half were new immigrants.[105]

Ze'ev (Wolfgang) von Weisl, a physician and journalist, estimated in 1947 that approximately 100,000 Jewish fetuses had been "exterminated," as he put it, "artificially, via abortions" over the previous twenty-five years. He accused mothers, in particular, of responsibility for this loss, "because Jewish mothers in Tel Aviv murdered them criminally by abortion."[106]

The available data do not provide a solid basis for making such estimates, but the anecdotal evidence sampled here was certainly part of the public discourse of the time. It shows that some people in the Yishuv were hugely concerned by the decline in the birthrate and sought to counter it. This anxiety no doubt led them to overstate the phenomenon and exaggerate their numbers. Yet the public debate certainly reflects the facts to some extent. The issue was engaged not only by intellectuals but also by doctors and demographers. While the public discourse does not constitute direct factual evidence of abortions, it certainly offers an indirect indication of the nature of the phenomenon, which was obviously common and notable enough to become a subject of public debate.

These sources indicate that abortions were a common method of birth control in the Yishuv. That is especially significant given that they were forbidden by law under the Mandate (just as they were throughout the West).[107] The law stated that "any person who intends to bring a woman to abortion, whether or not there is a fetus in her womb, and gives her medication in violation of the law, or caused her to drink poison or any other harmful substance, or used any other means, will be charged with a felony and subject to fourteen years in prison" (Criminal Code Ordinance 1936, section 175). Furthermore, "any woman who intends to bring herself to abortion, whether or not she has a fetus in her womb, and she drinks, in violation of the law, any poison or any harmful substance, or used force of any kind, or uses any other means, or who allows another person to give her such a substance or use such a means, will be charged with a felony and subject to seven years in prison" (section 176).[108] But the Yishuv was no different from other Western societies—abortions were illegal but very common.[109] One reason for this was the vague interpretation of the law. In 1940, Hadassah hospital inquired into the conditions under which the law permitted abortions. Among other things, the management wanted to know whether it was required to report every abortion or miscarriage, even one that occurred before the woman reached the hospital. Furthermore, it wanted to know the legal implications of not providing such information.[110] The reply it received from the attorney it consulted was ambiguous. Clearly, under English law, which Mandate law followed, if the abortion was conducted unlawfully by a person outside the hospital, that person "is guilty of a felony, and is liable to imprisonment for fourteen years."[111] But it was not quite clear what constituted an "unlawful" abortion. "This word is not defined in our code," the lawyer told Hadassah, and there were few precedents indicating what it meant, as the law had largely not been enforced. Until recently, the lawyer explained, there had been no court decisions involving the question of when and under what circumstances a medical practitioner could perform an abortion. It would seem, he noted, that a medical practitioner who encountered a case in which an abortion was ostensibly called for was required to ask himself whether the abortion was required for the sole permitted end of preserving the mother's life. This determination left room for a broad range of interpretation. The practitioner should take into account that he might be required to defend his action in court. In other words, the physician had to exercise his discretion. The lawyer further noted that the law did not require a physician or any other person to notify the authorities about a felony to which they were not an eyewitness. Such reporting was required only when a person was actively aiding an offender to avoid punishment. As such, granting medical care to a woman who had carried out an abortion on her own was not a violation of the law.[112] This legal opinion shows that the legal issues were not at all clear and that there was much leeway for the doctor to exercise his own judgment. As such, it helps explain the frequency of abortions in the Yishuv despite the formal legal prohibition against them, as well as the fact that most of the Yishuv's abortions were carried out by professional physicians in proper clinics, as is shown in chapter 4.

There are only scattered accounts of the enforcement of the anti-abortion law. Nearly all of them are cases in which the procedure ended in death or major medical injury to the pregnant woman. One of the few cases that came before a court was that of a Dr. Martha Tchernikovsky, in which the judge declared, according to newspaper reports, that "sufficient evidence has been brought before me to charge you with having arranged an abortion operation on March 18 [1936] on a young woman, Yonah Tzadok, in violation of section 192 of the Criminal Code Ordinance of 1927, and I therefore decide to send your case to be heard before the District Court in Jerusalem."[113]

Women throughout the Yishuv sought to avoid bringing children into the world, and as such abortions were performed throughout Palestine.[114] They were common in cities and towns, in farming villages and kibbutzim,[115] that is, among "our tillers of the land, the sector which for every healthy people is the forge of the generations to follow."[116] Yishuv authorities and institutions pursued extensive campaigns in urban and rural areas, in all kinds of settlements, and among all Zionist sectors, to encourage larger families and to fight abortions, as is covered in chapter 6. All this is evidence for the phenomenon's prevalence.[117]

Bachi noted that the frequency of abortions was higher in populations of higher socioeconomic levels.[118] But Dr. Helena Kagan, one of the pillars of pediatric medicine in Palestine and a member of the Zionist leadership, sounded the alarm on the spread of the fashion of birth control from the well-off to the poor.[119] Sidi Wronsky, a social worker who headed the Center for Children's Arrangement of the National Council, confirmed that abortions (she used the English word, rather than the ambiguous Hebrew term that can also mean a miscarriage) were common among the middle class and were documented because the women of this group had their procedures performed by doctors. Poorer women, in contrast, used more primitive means and thus went uncounted.[120]

Single women and girls in distress sought out abortions, but so did married women with children.[121] The latter, Bachi claimed, made "massive use" of the procedure.[122] A newspaper report claimed in 1938 that "married women see this thing [abortions] as a normal and natural matter."[123]

Both nonreligious and religious Zionist women had abortions. A journal put out by the latter community declared in 1944, regarding abortions, that "life in foreign lands has made an impression on us, even in circles that have not turned their backs on tradition."[124] It is hardly surprising, then, that the war against abortions included sermons in synagogues and other religious contexts.[125]

Abortions in the Yishuv were common, cutting across ethnic group, social sector, and socioeconomic level, and the transition from the pre–World War I high natural birthrate to a much lower one after the war was ultrarapid. While it was true that the Jews in the Diaspora were at the vanguard of limiting the births, in the Yishuv the transition from a high and low birthrate took place especially quickly.[126] Chapter 2 examines some of the reasons for this intensive pursuit of birth control, including abortion.

NOTES

1. Dr. Ze'ev von Weisl, "HaYeludah bein haYehudim Haitah haNemukhah beYoter," *Hamashkif,* July 18, 1941, 3.
2. Kanievsky 1944, 64.
3. Ba'al Heshbon, "Mah Garam leHafhatat Ahuz haUkhlusiah haYehudit," *Hamashkif,* Aug. 3, 1942, 2.

4. Alroey 2010, 89–90.

5. Report by Bachi, 1944, CZA J1/3717/3.

6. Emphasis in the original. Roberto Bachi, untitled document, Feb. 1945, CZA J1/31.393.

7. Roberto Bachi, "Maskanot Politiyot metokh Hakirotay 'al haHitpathut haDemografit shel haYehudim veha'Aravim beE"Y," Oct. 1944, CZA J1/3717/2, 1; Committee on the Birthrate Problems, "Tokhnit Shel Politikah le'Idud haImahut," apparently 1946, CZA A516/201.

8. Bachi 1944, 242–243. For more on the marriage age in the Yishuv, see Alroey 2010, 97–100.

9. Report by Bachi, 1944, J1/3717/3.

10. Economic Department of Jewish Agency, Palestine Facts and Figures, 48 (1947), in Alroey 2010, 91.

11. Kanievsky 1944, 66.

12. Memorandum from Hadassah's Statistics Department with regard to Dr. Rivlin's letter, 1939 (precise date not given), CZA J113/2312.

13. Kanievsky 1944, 64.

14. Katzenelson 1929, 18; Dr. A. Katzenelson, "Vital Statistics in Palestine," lecture delivered at the International Congress of Tropical Medicine and Hygiene, Cairo, Dec. 1928, CZA J1/33,045.

15. Report from Hadassah Hospital in Tel Aviv to the Hadassah management in Jerusalem, Dec. 11, 1924, CZA J1/1047/11.

16. Letter from Dr. Levontin, director of Hadassah hospital Tel Aviv, to the Hadassah management in Jerusalem, Dec. 8, 1926, CZA J113/401.

17. Dr. Ascherman and Dr. Levontin, letter to the Hadassah management in Jerusalem, Dec. 20, 1927, CZA J113/401.

18. Katzenelson 1929, 8, 18.

19. Chairman of the board of Hadassah city hospital in a letter to the municipal administration, May 2, 1932, TAA 4-4643a.

20. Bachi 1943a, 13.

21. Report on the activities of the Committee on Birthrate Problems, during its two years of existence (May 1943–Apr. 1945), Apr. 29, 1945, CZA J1/1974.

22. Elsewhere Bachi cites the figure 2.12. See Bachi and Matras 1962, 207; H. Myuzam, "Sekirah 'al haMegamot haDemografiyot haNokhehiyot ba'Olam, be'Am Yisra'el, uveYisra'el, 1964," CZA A516/276.

23. Yocheved Bat-Rachel, "De'agat HaImahut," Merkaz Kupat Holim, Jan. 1945, YTA, 15-36/4/4, 8; Bachi 1943a, 12–13.

24. Dr. Ze'ev von Weisl, "HaYeludah bein haYehudim Haitah vaNemukhah beYoter," Hamashkif, July 18, 1941, 3.

25. For more on Berman-Yeshurun, see Shehori-Rubin 2013.

26. Report by Dr. Tova Berman to David Ben-Gurion, May 10, 1944, BGA/correspondence/198564.

27. Roberto Bachi, "HaYeludah be Yisra'el uvaYishuv vehaDerakhim le'Idudah," apparently 1944, CZA J1/3717/3. I should clarify that in this chapter my aim is to describe and offer the facts about the birthrate. My account is based on Bachi's research and other sources. I address Bachi's interpretation of and personal opinion about these data in chapter 5.

28. Ibid.; Bachi 1944, 244.

29. Yocheved Bat-Rachel, "De'agat HaImahut," Merkaz Kupat Holim, Jan. 1945, YTA, 15-36/4/4, 8.

30. Roberto Bachi, "HaYeludah be Yisra'el uvaYishuv vehaDerakhim le'Idudah," apparently 1944, CZA J1/3717/3; Bachi 1944, 243.

31. List of the number of births, CZA J1/2717/3.

32. Program for a radio talk for a week devoted to birthrate issues, 1944, CZA J1/3717/2.

33. Roberto Bachi, "HaYeludah be Yisra'el uvaYishuv vehaDerakhim le'Idudah," apparently 1944, CZA J1/3717/3.

34. Tova Berman, "Ha'Emtza'im haDerushim le'Idud haYeludah baYishuv," Feb. 1945, CZA J1/3717/3; Roberto Bachi, "Be'ayat haYeludah BeYisra'el veHatza'ot leMediniyut haUkhlusiyah," undated, ISA 5588/2c; Committee on Birthrate Problems, "Tokhnit Shel Politikah le'Idud haImahut," 1945, CZA A516/201.

35. Ibid.

36. Ba'al Heshbon, "Hidat Tenu'at haUkhlusin haEretzyisraelit," *Hamashkif*, Sept. 8, 1946, 2.

37. Yocheved Bat-Rachel, "De'agat HaImahut," Merkaz Kupat Holim, Jan. 1945, YTA, 15-36/4/4, 9.

38. Roberto Bachi, "Be'ayat haYeludah BeYisra'el veHatza'ot leMediniyut haUkhlusiyah," undated, ISA 5588/2c.

39. L. Bein, "HaRibui haTiv'i veHishuvei he'Atid haKarov," *Hatzofeh*, June 8, 1945, 5.

40. Committee on Birthrate Problems, "Tokhnit Shel Politikah le'Idud haImahut," 1945, CZA A516/201.

41. Roberto Bachi, "Be'ayat haYeludah BeYisra'el veHatza'ot leMediniyut haUkhlusiyah," undated, ISA 5588/2c.

42. Kanievsky 1944, 69.

43. Roberto Bachi, "HaYeludah be Yisra'el uvaYishuv vehaDerakhim le'Idudah," apparently 1944, CZA J1/3717/3.

44. Bachi 1977, 196; Roberto Bachi, "Sekirah Ketzarah 'al haYeludah vehaTemotah beE"Y beTekufat 1939–1941," CZA J1/1957/2.

45. Hedwig Gellner, "Sekirah 'al 10 Shanim shel 'Avodah Sotziyalit beT"A," submitted to Mayor Rokach of Tel Aviv, Sept. 12, 1943, TAA 4-1427.

46. Dr. J[oseph] Mayer, "Havah veNa'aleh Otam leEretz Yisra'el," *Davar*, Apr. 10, 1946, 2.

47. Bein, "HaRibui haTiv'i."

48. Letters from Nurse Sternberg (no first name provided) of the Hadassah Preventative Medicine Service to Bachi, chairman of the Hadassah Prize Committee, Jan. 15, Jan. 22, 1945, CZA J113/1930.

49. B., "Limnoa' Ason," *Hatzofeh*, May 19, 1944, 2; L. Bein, "HaRibui haTiv'i veHishuvei he'Atid haKarov," *Hatzofeh*, June 8, 1945, 5.

50. Roberto Bachi, "HaYeludah be Yisra'el uvaYishuv vehaDerakhim le'Idudah," apparently 1944, CZA J1/3717/3.

51. H. Myuzam, "Sekirah 'al haMegamot haDemografiyot haNokhehiyot ba'Olam, be'Am Yisra'el, uveYisra'el, 1964," CZA A516/276; Bachi 1943b, 4.

52. Roberto Bachi, "HaYeludah be Yisra'el uvaYishuv vehaDerakhim le'Idudah," apparently 1944, CZA J1/3717/3; Bachi 1943b, 6.

53. H. Myuzam, "Sekirah 'al haMegamot haDemografiyot haNokhehiyot ba'Olam, be'Am Yisra'el, uveYisra'el, 1964," CZA A516/276.

54. Roberto Bachi, "Sekirah Ketzarah 'al haYeludah vehaTemotah beE"Y beTekufat 1939–1941," CZA J1/1957/2.

55. Bachi 1943b, 5; "HaYiten ha Yishuv leMi'ut haYeludah Livloa' et Hesegeinu be'Aliyah?" (no byline), *Davar*, Jan. 26, 1944, 4.

56. Bachi, 1943a, 13.

57. Jerusalem 3.5, Safed 4.8. Roberto Bachi, "Sekirah Ketzarah 'al haYeludah vehaTemotah beE"Y beTekufat 1939–1941," CZA J1/1957/2.

58. In the moshavot (farming villages) 4.2; Tova Berman, "'Al Be'ayot haYeludah," apparently 1943, CZA A516/100; Bachi 1943b, 5.

59. Roberto Bachi, Demographic Material for Mr. Kanievsky, Jan. 1944, CZA A516/201.

60. Roberto Bachi, "Sekirah Ketzarah 'al haYeludah vehaTemotah beE"Y beTekufat 1939–1941," CZA J1/1957/2.

61. Bachi 1943a, 13.

62. Roberto Bachi, "Sekirah Ketzarah 'al haYeludah vehaTemotah beE"Y beTekufat 1939–1941," CZA J1/1957/2; Roberto Bachi, "Be'ayat haYeludah BeYisra'el veHatza'ot leMediniyut haUkhlusiyah," undated, ISA 5588/2c.

63. Bachi 1943a, 13; Bachi 1943b, 6; Roberto Bachi, Demographic Material for Mr. Kanievsky, Jan. 1944, CZA A516/201; Roberto Bachi, "Be'ayat haYeludah BeYisra'el veHatza'ot leMediniyut haUkhlusiyah," undated, ISA 5588/2c.

64. Bachi 1944, 166.

65. Ben Bracha, "BeAspaklariyah," *Hatzofeh*, June 18, 1941, 2.

66. L. Bein, "HaRibui haTiv'i veHishuvei he'Atid haKarov," *Hatzofeh*, June 8, 1945, 5.

67. Shatil 1995, 379–380.

68. Roberto Bachi, "Be'ayat haYeludah BeYisra'el veHatza'ot leMediniyut haUkhlusiyah," undated, ISA 5588/2c.

69. Zehavah Uri, in Tsur, Zevulun, and Porat 1981, 77.

70. Idelson, in Tsur, Zevulun, and Porat 1981, 191.

71. Tsur, Zevulun, and Porat 1981, 290.

72. Tsur 2002, 154.

73. "BeMo'etzet HaKibbutz HaMe'euhad" (no byline), *Davar*, Nov. 6, 1944, 1.

74. "HaYiten ha Yishuv leMi'ut haYeludah Livloa' et Hesegeinu be'Aliyah?" (no byline), *Davar*, Jan. 26, 1944, 4.

75. Meir Orlian, "HaTipul haMeshutaf," *'Alonim*, Summer 1941, 7.

76. Ibid.

77. Meir O[rlian], "HaYeled haMe'ah," *'Alonim*, 1947, 19.

78. Bachi 1943b, 1.

79. Alroey 2010, 90.

80. Roberto Bachi, "Maskanot Politiyot metokh Hakirotay 'al haHitpathut haDemografit shel haYehudim veha'Aravim beE"Y," Oct. 1944, CZA J1/3717/2, 1.

81. Fraenkel 1944, 13; "Ne'um Rektor ha'Universitah, Professor A. H. Fraenkel beTekes haSiyum," *Hatzofeh*, May 5, 1940, 3.

82. Bachi 1977, 196. Gur Alroey parallels the Christian woman in Mandate Palestine to the Jewish Mizrahi woman. Their birthrates were similar, in the middle between Muslim women, who had many children, and Ashkenazi Jews, who had few. Alroey 2010, 103.

83. For example, Bachi compared the situation at the beginning of the twentieth century in Ukraine, where birth control was not practiced (as with the Arabs), with that of France, the home of birth control (who were thus like the Jews). Bachi 1943b, 3.

84. Mandate government figures, from Ba'al Heshbon, "Mah Garam leHafhatat Ahuz haUkhlusiah haYehudit," *Hamashkif*, Aug. 3, 1942, 2.

85. Tova Berman, "Al Be'ayot HaYeludah," undated (probably 1943), CZA A516/100.

86. Bachi 1943a, 16; "HaYiten ha Yishuv leMi'ut haYeludah Livloa' et Hesegeinu be'Aliyah?" (no byline), *Davar*, Jan. 26, 1944, 4; Bachi 1944, 245.

87. Bachi provides figures for 1942, CZA J1/3717/2. Unlike the Yishuv's case, Muslim rural locations also led with the highest birthrates, *Quarterly Bulletin of Vital Statistics*, Office of Statistics, Government of Palestine, Fourth quarter 1943, CZA J1/33,512.

88. Committee on Birthrate Problems, "Tokhnit Shel Politikah le'Idud haImahut," 1945, CZA A516/201.

89. At a young age her fertility was twice that of a Jewish woman, and at age thirty to thirty-five it was triple, at thirty-five to forty it was eightfold, and at forty to forty-five it was tenfold. Bachi 1943a, 18; Bachi 1944, 245. On births among Jews and Muslims, see Alroey 2010, 101–105.

90. Bachi 1943a, 18.

91. Roberto Bachi, "Sekirah Ketzarah 'al haYeludah vehaTemotah beE"Y beTekufat 1939–1941," CZA J1/1957/2; Bachi 1943a, 19.

92. Ba'al Heshbon, "Hidat Tenu'at haUkhlusin haEretzyisraelit," *Hamashkif*, Sept. 8, 1946, 2.

93. Letter from Dr. Meir to David Remez, Dec. 10, 1944, CZA J1/1974.

94. Yisrael Tunis, "Ha'Aliyah HaPnimit," *Davar*, Apr. 5, 4.

95. Report by Bachi, 1944, CZA J1/3717/3/.

96. Bachi 1944, 191, 235.

97. 324 Committee on Birthrate Problems, "Tokhnit lePolitikah Demografit," Apr. 22, 1945, CZA J1/2383.

98. List of diagnoses of patients at Hadassah hospital, maternity and gynecological ward, Oct.–Dec. 1935, Jan.–Mar. 1936, TAA, Hadassah Hospital, 4-4645, 4-4644.

99. Letter from the chairman of the board of directors of Hadassah municipal hospital to the municipal administration, May 2, 1932, TAA 4-4643.

100. Dr. Bilhah Puliastor, "HaHapalah ha Mela'akhutit," *Davar*, July 29, 1931, 3.

101. Dr. Lipman, "Mishmar HaBri'ut," *Davar*, Feb. 2, 1934.

102. Letter of Dr. A. Abramovitch, director of Hadassah municipal hospital, to A. Perlson, chairman of the board, May 28, 1937, TAA, Hadassah hospital, 4-4645.

103. Letter from Dr. Shoshana Meyer to the Health Department of the National Council, May 20, 1940, CZA J1/3717/1.

104. Fraenkel 1944, 28.

105. Dr. Y. Asherman, "Hapalah Mela'akhutit Mehabelet BePirion HaIsha," *Eitanim*, Nov. 11, 1952, 266.

106. Dr. Ze'ev von Weisl, "Mea'et haElef she'Avdu Lanu laNetzah," *Hamashkif*, Oct. 10, 1947, 3.

107. Hoffer and Hull 2010, 11–12, 49–50.

108. Criminal Law Ordinance, 1936, RZA PA/16/4/2 (translated from the Hebrew). For more details regarding the law, see Triger 2014, 87–88, 99; see also Amir and Shoshi 2007, 777–808; Rimalt 2010, 138.

109. Hoffer and Hull 2010, 11–12, 49–50.

110. A letter from S. Horowitz & Co., Advocates, to Hadassah Medical Organization in Jerusalem, Apr. 5, 1940, CZA J113/1914.

111. Section 175 of the Criminal Code Ordinance 1936; letter from S. Horowitz & Co., Advocates, to Hadassah Medical Organization in Jerusalem, Apr. 5, 1949, CZA J113/1914.

112. Letter from S. Horowitz & Co., Advocates, to Hadassah Medical Organization in Jerusalem, Apr. 5, 1940, CZA J113/1914.

113. "Mishpat Dr. Martah Tschernikovsky," *Do'ar Hayom*, Apr. 16, 1936, 8; 'Edutah haDramatit shel Yonah Tzadok," *Do'ar Hayom*, Apr. 5, 1936, 4.

114. Thousands of women who chose to have an abortion were interviewed by Dr. Tova Berman between the years 1934 and 1944. Letter from Tova Berman to Ben-Gurion, May 10, 1944, CZA J1/3717/3.

115. David Ben-Gurion, "Shalosh He'arot," *Hapo'el Hatza'ir* 27, Mar. 18, 1947, 2; for example, the testimony given by Pelah Yitzhaki, resident of Kibutz 'Evron, in Shechter 2011, 255.

116. Yisrael Tunis, "Ha'Aliyah HaPnimit," *Davar*, Apr. 5, 4.

117. Report of the Committee on Birthrate Problems, Apr. 29, 1945, CZA J1/1974.

118. Bachi 1944, 191.

119. Minutes of a meeting of the Committee on Birthrate Problems, June 22, 1943, CZA J1/3717/1.

120. Ibid.

121. Margalit-Stern 2011, 193.

122. Bachi 1943a, 15.

123. Binah Velfish, "'Al 'Inyan she'ein Medabrim Bo," *Davar*, Apr. 27, 1938, 3.

124. B., "Limnoa'Ason," *Hatzofeh*, May 19, 1944, 2.

125. Minutes of a meeting of the Committee on Birthrate Problems, June 22, 1943, CZA J1/3717/1.

126. Roberto Bachi, "Maskanot Politiyot metokh Hakirotay 'al haHitpathut haDemografit shel haYehudim veha'Aravim beE"Y," Oct. 1944, CZA J1/3717/2, 1.

CHAPTER TWO

THE PARENTS' REBELLION

Economic Factors

The Causes of Abortion and the Yishuv's Low Birthrate

"ALMOST ALL WOMEN MARRY," DECLARED THE Yishuv's senior statistician, Roberto Bachi, in 1943, adding that "the marriage age is low." That being the case, he wondered, how was it that the final number of children produced by each Yishuv family was so small?[1] The question cannot be answered with a single, unequivocal sentence. A host of factors affect birthrates everywhere and always—time, place, movements of people, socioeconomic and ethnic affiliation, values, perceptions, historical events, and personal circumstances. The Yishuv was no exception. The small number of children born to the Jews of the Yishuv and the large number of abortions performed there have multiple interlocking causes. Some of the factors are universal, others specifically Western, and still others unique to the Yishuv. Some of them were very influential and operated throughout the period under discussion; the impact of others was felt at specific points in time.

In this chapter I discuss these many factors and consider each one in isolation so as to examine its particular significance. It is important to keep in mind, however, that only rarely did any one factor function alone. Most of the time several causes operated simultaneously, interacting with, impinging on, and amplifying or suppressing one another. Thus, while I present each separately, the discussions are interwoven and sometimes overlap.

"The causes of a family's unwillingness to have a large number of children are many and complex," wrote Berman in 1945.[2] A Yishuv physician active in encouraging larger families, Berman divided these causes into two groups, the first being economic and the second everything else. In other words, Berman believed that money was the central determinant, as it was in the Western world, and that ameliorating families' financial woes would lead them to have more children.[3] Economics is certainly important, but to understand it in the context of the Yishuv it is necessary first to understand immigration and its effect on the birthrate. For this immigrant society, the fact that most of its members came from other lands was the starting point for everything. It affected the Yishuv's perceptions, values, and socioeconomic profile.

IMMIGRATION AND ITS IMPLICATIONS

Immigration was key to the development of Jewish society in Israel, both before and after the establishment of the state.[4] The Yishuv was built out of waves of immigrants, who faced many challenges. Most of the Jewish immigrants who arrived in Palestine under the British Mandate came from a traditional milieu in Europe. The family stood at the center of that culture, as it did for Jews who arrived from Asia and North Africa.

In the nineteenth century Jewish communities around the world underwent huge transformations, including swift population expansion. The traditional Jewish family was predisposed to high fertility, but toward the end of the nineteenth and at the beginning of the twentieth century this changed. Secular education, urbanization, emancipation, modernization, and secularization all had a dampening effect on the Jewish birthrate, an effect that became particularly evident in the interwar period.[5]

At the dawn of the twentieth century, about half of the world's Jews lived in Russia and Poland.[6] Tens of thousands of them had begun to emigrate to Western Europe and to North America, where they found themselves in a new world that challenged them on many fronts.[7] Bachi maintained that this migration was a major factor in the drop in the birthrate that characterized the Jews of Western and Central Europe and the United States.[8]

The decline in the birthrate characteristic of Europe at the end of the nineteenth century spread at the beginning of the twentieth century to other areas peopled by immigrants from Europe, among them the United States, Canada, Argentina, and Australia, all of which were popular destinations.[9] Furthermore, the immigration process itself reinforced the process of reducing the birthrate, as the newcomers encountered economic instability and had to adjust to new conditions. Immigration also affected the family, as it resulted in intergenerational tensions and often led to changes in gender roles.[10]

Sometimes just thinking about emigration from the old country prompted Jews to restrict the size of their families. The birth of a baby could delay plans to leave, as Marion Kaplan has shown in her work on Jewish life in Nazi Germany. Women, disinclined to have children because of their concerns for the future, were further motivated to use birth control and have abortions so as to expedite emigration.[11]

When they arrived at their destinations, Jews encountered further incentives to keep their families small. A number of studies have demonstrated that the birthrate of US immigrants at the beginning of the twentieth century declined precipitously, especially among Eastern European Jews, and abortion was a common remedy for an unwanted pregnancy.[12]

Frequent pregnancies caused distress and despair among immigrant Jewish women. They encountered a new world with priorities different from those they had known. Largely ignorant of birth control methods, many sought abortions, the only effective means they knew to prevent the birth of another child. The abortion rate among Jewish immigrants to the United States reached huge proportions. Some endured as many as twelve or thirteen abortions, this at a time when the procedure could lead to disaster.[13]

The results soon became evident. The average Eastern European Jewish immigrant family in the United States in the first decade of the twentieth century had five children. In the 1930s the average was under two children. That figure was tiny compared to the large size of Jewish families in the preceding generation, and was also small compared to non-Jewish families in the country.[14] In fact, Jewish immigrants tended to have smaller families than other groups of immigrants. It may be that, unlike members of these other groups, Jews brought with them from their former countries the concept of restricting family size.[15]

But the major means of preventing babies that the Jews resorted to was abortion, and most of these were done at home, at great risk to women. It is hardly surprising, then, that the leading American advocates of birth control, Margaret Sanger, Emma Goldman, and Rose Pastor Stokes, focused their efforts in immigrant neighborhoods in New York, in particular among the Jews.[16] Jewish doctors and organizations played a role in founding and staffing birth control clinics in such neighborhoods, many of the patrons of which were Jews—immigrants themselves or the daughters of immigrants.[17] A pamphlet that Sanger published in 1912, *What Every Girl Should Know*, was translated into Yiddish, to be issued and reissued many times.[18] The reverberations of the birth control practiced by Jewish immigrants to the United States reached as far as Palestine. "No population group is so characterized by abortions and birth control as the Jews," Bachi wrote in 1944 with regard to the Jews of America.[19]

Jewish immigrants to Palestine faced any number of difficulties, some that every immigrant everywhere faces—economic uncertainty, social disruption, cultural change—and some unique to the Yishuv, in particular, Arab hostility. Coping with these challenges, and the desire to establish themselves in their new country, prompted the newcomers to keep their families small. At a mock trial held in Tel Aviv in 1943 (about which I write more in chapter 6), the defendant was a typical Yishuv woman who had had an abortion. When she was asked by the prosecutor why she had waited five years after her marriage to have her first child, she replied that after she and her husband came to Palestine they wanted to "establish [them]selves" and "put down roots" in the new land.[20] Sarah L., who came to Palestine from the United States in 1948, was "proud to bear [her] second child . . . here in the land of Israel."[21] But the difficulties of adjusting to the new country at an especially difficult time, during the War of Independence, led her to seek an abortion, an act to which she was fundamentally opposed. But circumstances won out. "Although the idea of abortion was entirely repugnant to my own moral principles," she wrote, "I had no choice in the matter."[22]

But, as in the case of immigrants to the United States, adjustment difficulties were not the only factors leading families to have fewer children. Immigrants, and especially the women among them, also found themselves facing a window of opportunity. Women emigrating from traditional societies encounter new prospects in their new country. They can work outside the home, receive education, and encounter members of the opposite sex, all of which lead to changes in gender roles. They are also able to establish new gender relations.[23] For many of the women who immigrated to Palestine, childbirth and motherhood were not the only or even the most important things in their lives. Even intimate relations changed, especially among the younger immigrants. Women and men paired up without marriage,[24] often leading to unplanned pregnancies. This led to efforts to prevent pregnancies and, when that did not succeed, women sought abortions.

Furthermore, the Yishuv was a young society. Young immigrants arrived in Palestine without their parents, leaving behind what one newspaper called "the ancient tradition of the Hebrew family," and the very centrality of the family to Jewish society.[25] Moreover, they lacked the extended family that could have offered emotional and practical support for a young family. This was a real hardship for young mothers. The Tel Aviv municipality reported in 1935 with regard to the maternity wards in local hospitals that it was important to take into account "that most of the mothers are new immigrants, whose relatives are still overseas." Were that not the case, the report said, these women would have preferred to give birth at home and would thus have been saved the indignity of the overcrowded hospital wards.[26] The lack of support from an extended family had postpartum consequences as well. "These mothers cannot be left at home without any help," the report asserted, "at least during the first week following birth, at a time when the father must go to work so as not to lose his livelihood."[27]

Another aspect of the problem was noted by Chaya Yisraeli, a member of Kvutzat (Kibbutz) Kinneret, who gave birth to her daughter in 1917 under harsh conditions, without any guidance or oversight from an experienced mother. "Our entire community is young," she noted. "There are no mothers, no grandmothers, no experience or knowledge of childcare."[28] "Psychologically," another kibbutz member wrote in 1941, "you can understand the young mother who enters into her new situation without experience and without the assistance she would have been given overseas by neighbors and relatives. The women of our land left their parents' home at the age of seventeen or eighteen without having learned the issues involved in family life."[29]

The immigrants brought with them the prevailing views and values of their countries of origin. The decline in births in the Yishuv during the 1920s and 1930s was thus part and parcel of the reduction in the birthrate among European Jews.[30] Many immigrants from Eastern Europe were influenced by Soviet society, which permitted abortions until 1936.[31] While there is little firsthand evidence of this because of the decrease in immigration from that country following the Bolshevik Revolution, the Yishuv was much influenced by newspaper articles that described events and daily life in the Soviet Union.[32] The wave of migration that came from Central Europe in the 1930s led to a change in the Yishuv's ethnic makeup and the German influence became pronounced. Particularly influential was the German view that a small family was an ideal, not simply the product of circumstances.[33] The German bourgeoisie had come to use abortion as a means of birth control before World War I, and the phenomenon widened under the Weimar Republic and even more so after the Nazis came to power, when Jews became anxious about their survival.[34] Echoes of the prevalence of abortions in Germany appeared in the Hebrew press.[35] For example, in 1934 a physician reported in *Davar* that in Berlin "women are entirely irresponsible when it comes to self-aborting."[36] Jews who came from countries of low fertility continued to produce few children in Palestine. Woman immigrants born in Austria or Germany had an average of 1.5 children in the 1930s, less than the Yishuv average.[37] Such immigrants, Bachi complained, continued the demographic practices of their countries of origin. Their participation in the enterprise of building the Yishuv did not encourage them to have more children.[38]

Eastern European Jews also used birth control and practiced abortion.[39] In Poland, home to a large Jewish population, the percentage of Jews living in the cities declined between the world wars as a result of the low birthrate.[40] Abortion was a popular method of keeping families small,[41] especially among assimilated and nonreligious Jews of this region. Moshe Brezniak, a member of the Zionist HaShomer HaTza'ir youth movement in Rovno in the 1930s, was surprised at the frequency of abortions among the women in the agricultural training commune he belonged to there. Living expenses at the commune were high, the major expenses being electricity, telephones, and abortions. "The abortion industry was quite developed at our kibbutz," he recalled in his memoirs.[42] Evidence of how common they were is provided by the public mock trials held in Jewish communities centering on the practice of abortion, usually with a woman as defendant. One such trial was held in Grodno (in Poland) in 1933.[43] The pervasiveness of abortions apparently led some women pioneers of the Yishuv to travel to Poland specifically to "get rid of an unwanted pregnancy," as the writer Alona Frankel relates about one Dr. Fischler, a family friend, in her memoir. "Dr. Fischler scraped no few zygotes of gifted Sabras [native-born members of the Yishuv or Israelis] out of the wombs of hard-working Palestinian pioneers, who shared my mother's ideals. They would come to Poland to have an abortion, and my mother helped them and hosted them—to her displeasure, it should be said, as they stained her embroidered silk nightgowns and the delicate, fine bed linens with blood."[44]

The tendency toward small families that had become the norm in the countries of origin became even more pronounced in the Yishuv in the face of local conditions. "Economic, social and psychological conditions all have an especially strong impact against fertility," Bachi argued in 1940.[45] Furthermore, the immigrants had already become accustomed in Europe to restricting births, and this attitude became part of Sabra culture, as well as of some parts of the Mizrahi community. Bachi saw it as especially characteristic of what he called the progressives, those who believed that the way to address the neglect of children and difficult family life that economic hardship brings was to practice birth control.[46] The assimilation of the European immigrants into "other types of population" (that is, the Mizrahim) was, Bachi argued in 1943, bringing a tragedy of low natural increase on the Yishuv.[47]

The immigrants of the 1930s included no small number of physicians. By 1935, some 1,700 Jewish doctors lived in Palestine, meaning one for every 174 inhabitants of the Yishuv—a world record. By 1939, the number of doctors had risen to 1,987, and in 1947 the Yishuv had 2,650 doctors.[48] Many of them came from Germany, where Jews flocked into the medical profession.[49] They, with other physicians who came from Europe, brought with them a liberal attitude toward abortions. In the 1930s, Dr. Haim Yassky, Hadassah's director in Palestine, received complaints about Dr. Arieh (Leib) Sadowski, chief of the maternity ward at Hadassah hospital in Jerusalem, for carrying out abortions for socioeconomic reasons and because of what Dr. Yassky called "excessive liberalism."[50]

These physicians were influenced by eugenic ideas—a theory advocating the improvement of the human species via controlled reproduction, favoring those considered to have "good" genes.[51] They advocated planned parenthood, with the intent that healthy mothers should bring healthy infants into the world and bring them up in stable family environments so that they would grow up to be robust adults. Some Yishuv doctors linked these ideas with the aim of shaping a new, vigorous Jew, the "exact opposite" of the Jew of the Diaspora.[52] They thus supported abortions carried out for social and economic reasons. Sarah L. related in 1948 that a doctor she consulted recommended that she have an abortion, justifying it on the grounds of her difficult mental state after immigrating, brought on by adjustment and financial difficulties.[53] Any number of testimonies tell of doctors advising women to have abortions during the difficult times that followed the outbreak of World War II. Immigrant doctors brought with them the tools and practice of abortion, which had advanced considerably in medical terms. That women were able to place themselves in the hands of professionals also encouraged them to have abortions.[54]

Immigration was thus a major influence on the Yishuv's diminished birthrate. It can be considered the starting point for several other factors.

Economics

In every culture around the world, fertility is affected not only by biology but also by social and economic context. In many countries, poverty and difficult living conditions make raising children an arduous task. In such environments, women often choose to end their pregnancies.[55] Such was the case in France and in the Soviet Union in the 1920s and 1930s,[56] as well as in Germany, where the abortion rate increased in times of economic crisis, falling wages, and rising unemployment. Abortions were the last resort for despairing women who, for economic reasons, had to keep their families small.[57] For immigrant women from Germany to Palestine, it was a familiar and common practice that they knew from their previous lives. One such woman, coping with economic hardship, spoke of making this choice: "I became pregnant at the age of almost forty. Carrying through the pregnancy meant losing my job, on which we were dependent for our livelihood. We therefore, with heavy hearts, decided on an abortion, which at that time was against the law."[58]

The economic situation is often cited in a variety of sources from the Yishuv period as the primary reason for the low birthrate in general and for abortions in particular. The "economic situation" is a general term that contains within it a variety of issues: income insufficient to cover even modest expenses, inadequate housing, high rents, and unemployment. These were all prevalent in the Yishuv, and became much more acute in times of crisis. When that happened, it brought on "fear of children, a symptom that has spread at an alarming rate," as one newspaper reported.[59] Furthermore, many believed that the Yishuv as a whole and its women in particular had positive fundamental attitudes towards having children. That meant that if women were having abortions, the cause was economic hardship.[60]

Data from the 1940s show that the source of the decline in the birthrate was the lack of social security and the low standard of living for most members of the Yishuv, who had to work extremely hard to make their livelihoods.[61] Most of the families included on a list of those in need of assistance compiled by the Tel Aviv municipal social services department at the beginning of the 1940s were families with large numbers of children. In almost all these cases the parents were having difficulty supporting their families and, as a result, the children were poorly nourished and weak.[62] Large families collapsed under the pressure. "A young women of a Mizrahi community was blessed with seven children," the economist Yitzhak Kanievsky wrote. "Her face and her entire body are emaciated like that of a seventy-year-old woman, even though she is only twenty-eight. Also her young husband, thirty years old, who works as a porter. Their strength is waning because of their search for a livelihood and the difficulties of raising children. The woman is crumpling from her suffering and the children are weak because of a shortage of food and sufficient care."[63]

"Men kill themselves and women abort the fruit of their womb," screamed a newspaper headline in 1946.[64] The article recounted the lives of the inhabitants of the poor neighborhoods on the Tel Aviv–Jaffa border, where families were typically large, with six children on average. It told of despair, suicide, and the spread of abortions. "The depth of the abyss they have sunk into," the article relates, is evident in the fact that "these women, who have been blessed with the fruit of their womb, have recently begun to go to specialists who take their fetuses from them."[65]

Unemployment, low wages, and a tax system that weighed especially heavy on large families all made life especially difficult for working-class families.[66] A Yishuv family of this type could not allow itself the luxury of multiple children even if the parents were inclined in that direction, wrote Lilia Bassewitz, a member of the Council of Women Workers, in 1933.[67]

Tova Berman asserted in 1944 that more than 30 percent of the thousands of Yishuv women who underwent abortions in the previous decade had done so because of their shaky economic situation. These women needed to work outside the home to support their families and had no one to take care of their babies while they were at work. "My husband doesn't earn enough" and "my husband is ill" were common claims.[68] This can also be considered a manifestation of prevailing gender perceptions, which viewed men as breadwinners and women as caregivers. The challenge to this division of labor was a dead end when it came to the size of families. When the man of the house was unable to support his wife and children, the family found itself in dire economic straits.

Women who left or were abandoned by their husbands faced an unbearable plight.[69] Often, to get out of an intolerable marriage, women assumed responsibly for economic support for their children, resulting in great hardship,[70] wrote Hedwig Gellner, head of the Tel Aviv municipality's social welfare department. During grave economic crises, more and more of the city's families fell apart. "Hundreds of fathers have left their children," Gellner reported for the period 1936–1939,[71] leaving families in already difficult circumstances without a primary breadwinner. Bassewitz wrote in the 1930s that "fathers are not acknowledged by their children and mothers lack the economic wherewithal to educate them."[72] Many families thus sought help from the social services department.[73] Bassewitz maintained that abortions should be allowed when a woman is not interested in bringing up a child alone because of separating from her husband.[74] The Union of Hebrew Women for Equal Rights, founded in 1919,[75] documented a large number of examples demonstrating that economic hardship was the lot of a woman who had been left to raise her children alone. The union argued that this was a major reason for the decline in the birthrate.[76]

Unmarried women who became pregnant often opted for abortions, even in cases where they wanted the child, simply because they did not know how they could support it. No few proved willing to carry their pregnancies to term if they were promised childcare, which would enable them to keep their jobs to support themselves and the child.[77] Another reason women decided to abort was their fear of public opinion.

In a mock trial on the low birthrate and abortions held in Tel Aviv in 1943, a mother, played by an actress, was the principal defendant. Her testimony covers several pages, whereas only a few lines record the testimony of her codefendant, the father. The court clearly considered the father a secondary figure, even though the issue is one that involves couples. When the prosecutor asks him, "Why did you decide to have only one child?" the father's response is "My wife already explained." When he is asked what his position had been, he answers: "I left the final decision to my wife—after all, all the burden of childcare would fall on her."[78] This was the common wisdom at the time, that women bore primary responsibility for bearing and raising children. That may be the reason women sometimes decided to have abortions on their own, without involving their partners. One woman who did so was the mother whom the novelist Shulamit Lapid, who grew up in Tel Aviv in the 1930s and 1940s, tells about in her book.[79] Yonah Tzadok concealed her 1936 abortion from her boyfriend and her family. She told them she was being operated on for appendicitis.[80]

But it was not uncommon for the man to decide on the abortion, persuading or compelling his wife or partner to end her pregnancy against her will. The men did not want the financial burden of a child.[81] Sarah L. was one such case: "Hence, when I became pregnant again, my husband insisted that I interrupt this pregnancy."[82]

In not a few cases does "the husband forces the wife to have an abortion simply because the burden of one or two children is enough for him," as a radio program devoted to the birthrate reported.[83]

"There is the influence of the husband, the surroundings, society,"[84] Abraham Fraenkel wrote of abortions in 1944. Sometimes women found themselves blamed for the pregnancy, explicitly or implicitly. As Miriam Kimmelman related: "In addition to all the mental anguish, Yehuda blamed me for the pregnancy . . . , and said that I should have been careful and used birth control. That made me depressed."[85]

Economic considerations also influenced doctors who performed abortions. Many of them found themselves without jobs. Searching for independent means of supporting themselves,[86] some began to perform illegal abortions, "in exchange for bright and shiny coins," as one woman told her doctor in 1942.[87] The fact was, claimed Dr. Mordechai Albrecht in 1947, "that many physicians [of the Yishuv], especially in Tel Aviv, perform hundreds of abortions a year, in exchange for a bit of money."[88]

THE SECOND CHILD DILEMMA

For more than a few families with a single child, money was a critical factor in deciding whether to have another child or whether to have an abortion in the case of a second pregnancy. Economic problems "made it difficult to see how we could adequately care for an additional child," Sarah L. explained regarding her decision to abort her second pregnancy.[89]

With rare honesty, Miriam Kimmelman recalled her situation in 1942 as the mother of a small child. "And here a new tribulation came upon us— pregnancy. Another child was beyond our means. I knew that I had to end the pregnancy no matter what. I made inquiries and received the address of a good doctor. It all passed. But in my soul, and visibly, a painful wound remained . . . , and again I am pregnant, and again an abortion."[90]

In many circles, and especially in the working public, the addition of a child to the family added a further burden to an already difficult life. "We hear from time to time that another child might mean a dearth [of resources] for the previous child," wrote Yocheved Bat-Rachel of the Council of Women Workers.[91] The "defendant" in the mock trial of 1943 testified that she decided to abort because of she and her husband had low salaries, which were not even enough to properly provide for their only child. "How can I think of a second child?" she wondered.[92] In her novel *Maybe They Were Not*, Shulamit Lapid tells of parents, new immigrants with a young daughter who lived in Tel Aviv in the 1930s in great privation. When the mother discovered that she was pregnant for a second time, she panicked. "How could she bring another child into the world when she did not have bread for her small daughter?" Lapid wrote.[93]

Deficient Housing and Its Implications

The housing shortage was one of the major obstacles to a higher birthrate. It is often cited as a direct cause of small families, and affected both established families and young couples preparing to start a family.[94] In Tel Aviv, which attracted thousands of immigrants in the 1930s, the housing shortage broke all records. In the first half of that decade the economy prospered and well-accoutered shops sold luxuries, hotels and cafés did a brisk business, and industry flourished. But the supply of housing did not meet the high demand. Many families found themselves living in substandard conditions.

In those days it was common for more than one family to share single apartment. In 1934, about a tenth of the Jewish population in both cities and villages lived in housing unfit for human habitation—metal or wooden huts or dilapidated stone structures. Some lived in one-room apartments in which they shared a bathroom with several other families. Aside from the over-crowding, the sanitary and hygienic conditions in these homes, in the Mediterranean climate, presented a health danger.[95] Workers in the city suffered the worst—thousands of them lived in bad hygienic conditions. This also had direct implications for the reduced birthrate. Young people found it hard to build an independent life and to have families when they had to live with parents or relatives.[96] Furthermore, as the Tel Aviv municipality reported in 1935, "From a social and health point of view it is indescribable and inexcusable that a mother give birth in a tiny home in the presence of other children who are sometimes in the very same room."[97]

The situation in the Yishuv in the years 1936–1939 was very bad. These were the years of the bloody Arab Revolt. Fearful of Arab violence, thousands of Jews fled Jaffa and crowded into neighboring Tel Aviv, which was already congested because of the large number of immigrants who had settled there earlier in the decade. An economic crisis brought on by the security crisis worsened the housing situation and enlarged the numbers of the needy. The situation grew even worse when World War II broke out. The market for exports dried up, factories stopped producing, and the tourism industry collapsed.[98]

Even though the construction of new housing had not met the growing demand caused by the swelling Jewish population, housing starts plummeted when the war broke out and the lack of adequate housing became even more acute.[99] Working-class families, most of whom lived in single rooms, bore the brunt of this.[100] The lack of steady jobs also made it hard for workers to make the financial commitment involved in purchasing a home.[101] The files of the Tel Aviv municipality Social Assistance Department from the years 1939–1944 show that many families from all sectors, social strata, and ethnic groups required housing assistance.[102] According to Hedwig Gellner, the department's director in 1943, "stress and poverty have grown in broad swathes of the public, of a type we have not before known."[103] Kanievsky offered a comparison. In few countries, he said, did the housing shortage and the suffering it caused affect as broad a cross-section of the population as in the Yishuv.[104] Thousands of young couples were not having children because they could not afford homes, the press reported in 1945.[105]

Neither was renting a home a solution. With housing in short supply, rents rose. Families paid exorbitant sums for a single room with no light, ventilation, or comfort. Furthermore, with demand so high, many landlords refused to rent their property to families with children.[106] "The landlady almost would not agree to rent me a room because of the child," claimed the defendant in the mock trial, adding that "had I had two children I would have had to vacate the room." That was why she had an abortion.[107]

A young couple, refugees from Romania, immigrated in 1944. They had been married for seven years but were childless. They endured concentration camps, labor camps, and cellars during the five years of the war. Malnourished, wandering from country to country, they could not think of bringing children into the world. "Now they have come to the homeland they longed for," wrote Joseph Mayer in 1944. They were lucky—the husband found a job with a monthly wage of thirty Palestine pounds (P£)—a fairly high salary at the time. Now they wanted to have their first child. But the family paid P£15 in rent each month—half their monthly income—and that for a room and half a kitchen. Even though the woman was thirty-five years old, "and soon her age will be too high to have a first child," the couple was debating what to do. They wondered if they could provide the child with his minimal needs. Even if they skimped on food for themselves to provide for the child, they worried about "whether the owner of the apartment would evict them when the first signs of pregnancy appeared."[108]

Substandard hygienic conditions made for unhealthy children. Dr. Benno Gruenfelder, director of pediatrics at Hadassah hospital in Jerusalem, offered an account of the high morbidity among children and high infant mortality rate, caused in part by poor housing conditions, which were "very bad . . . creating conditions similar to those that prevailed at the end of the last century in barracks housing throughout Europe."[109] Joseph Mayer linked the high birthrate among Yemenite Jews in Tel Aviv's neighborhoods and substandard living and housing conditions, where there were puddles, filth, sewage, and stench in yards and streets. The huge overcrowding in these neighborhoods was a cause for concern about the health of the children who lived there. "In such conditions and in such ethnic groups, overcrowding inevitably means a high infant mortality rate," Mayer wrote.[110] The message was that, when housing was of this sort, having multiple children put their lives at risk.

The link between large families and inferior housing was often extended to identify this combination as typical of Mizrahi families. The Yishuv's Assembly of Representatives resolved in 1943 that "distress is especially high in Mizrahi communities, which have large families."[111] Even though the Yishuv sought to encourage larger families, its leaders and writers looked askance at large Mizrahi families. High Mizrahi birthrates led, it was argued, to negative social phenomena such as neglect, delinquency, and nonproductivity among Mizrahi youth.[112] Under the difficult conditions in Palestine that made the burden of raising children heavier, it was only natural, Bachi argued in April 1943, that the Mizrahim would begin to emulate the childbearing patterns of Western communities.[113]

ECONOMIC AND HOUSING PROBLEMS IN RURAL SETTLEMENTS

Difficult economic conditions and housing issues suppressed the birthrate not only in the city but also in rural settlements built on land purchased by the Zionist movement. Rafael Eitan (Raful), who would become the eleventh chief of staff of the Israel Defense Forces, described the hardship and poverty his family suffered in Tel Adashim, the moshav (semi-cooperative farming village, pl. *moshavim*) where he was born in 1929. His family was "miserably poor." There were four children and his father was unable to provide for all their needs. When his mother became pregnant again, they decided on an abortion, so as not to bring a new baby into a world where he would suffer poverty and want. But they were so poor that his parents could not obtain the sum needed to pay a doctor to perform an abortion. The father offered to pay in two installments but the doctor refused. As no credit was available, Raful related, "a person was born."[114]

In these rural settlements, especially in the first years after each one was founded, the inhabitants lived in tents or huts. When permanent housing was built, the homes were modest and small. In moshavim a family home typically consisted of a single room and a tiny kitchen. Homes were identical for all residents, no matter how many children they had. "Is it surprising that such housing conditions make the settlers terrified of having another child?" Kanievsky exclaimed.[115] In fact, the settler organizations, which promoted the establishment of new settlements, told settlers not to have families until permanent homes were built and the village had established itself economically.[116]

The Labor Battalion, one of the legendary organizations that operated in the Yishuv in the 1920s, was made up of thousands of Zionist pioneers scattered around the country. They performed a range of labor, and lived communally, with a common kitty. Among other projects, the Labor Battalion founded settlements. Pregnancy was frowned on. The members of the battalion lived in difficult conditions where babies could not be cared for properly, and infant death was not rare.[117] In one case, a couple kept the woman's pregnancy secret for as long as they could. "How dare she have a baby," some members told another pregnant comrade in December 1925.[118]

Living conditions at kibbutzim were especially difficult. Housing at a young kibbutz "does not encourage a normal birthrate," the press reported, with considerable understatement.[119] In the twenties and thirties many kibbutznikim lived in tents, barns, or huts. Overcrowding was legion. "We slept two to a single bed. There was nowhere else to put a bed," women from Kvutzat Kinneret recalled in the 1920s.[120] Up until the mid-1930s, a kibbutz member generally waited between ten and fifteen years, and sometimes longer, before he could move into a constructed room of very modest proportions— between ten and twelve square meters (110 and 130 square feet).[121]

Often separate housing was not granted to couples. The housing shortage at kibbutzim included a phenomenon nicknamed the "primus," after the three-legged kerosene cooking stove, or the "third," meaning a single man or woman who was housed in the same room or tent with a couple. A tent for four, housing a couple and one or two single men or women was not unheard of.[122] "The crowding in apartments grew worse," Lilia Bassewitz wrote in 1934, under the pseudonym Rachel.

> They brought tents, and raised the number of people in each room. They had already added a "third" to each family. "There is no other way," everyone says. . . . We are three in a room, I, he—my boyfriend—and she, my neighbor, the third member of the family. Only a thin cloth divider separates us from her. We have lived this way for two years already, and I have still not gotten used to it, I will never get used to it."[123]

Obviously this limited the intimacy that a couple could enjoy and thus delayed the arrival of children, as Bassewitz acknowledged with unusual candidness when she recounted the difficulty of wanting to be with her lover and her inability to do so because of the additional person in the tent. "Sometimes, as I sleep, I feel the touch of a hand on my face, a stroking, inviting hand, and he comes to me. I wake up from a deep sleep in alarm. I hold my breath and whisper to him: 'Quiet, quiet,' and get mad at him for not being careful with his movements." But she acknowledged that there were members of the commune who did not let this situation disrupt their intimate relations. "There is intimacy that takes place in view of others. Out of habit, we take such instances of intimacy lightly, asking: what's the big deal? What is so tragic and horrible about it? But I cannot accept it."[124] Bassewitz concludes by presenting a dilemma she was torn between—on the one hand, she understood the need to absorb immigrants and to bring new people into her tent, as the national effort required, but on the other hand she felt this was, as she put it, a desecration of her love. Why, she wondered, was she required to make such a great sacrifice?

When she published this account in the organ of the United Kibbutz Movement (HaKibbutz HaMe'uhad), it set off a storm. Single men and women fled from the rooms they shared with couples and slept out in the open.[125] Kibbutz children, while receiving the best housing available, also suffered from tough conditions. The children's homes at Kibbutz Ein Harod in the 1920s were "one large black hut, as if it had been painted with soot." It was furnished with beds for adults. "Babies were tied to them with rope so as not to fall off," one kibbutz woman later recalled.[126]

When beds were lacking, babies were sometimes placed in crates that had previously contained sugar. The proposal to purchase a crib for a baby girl led to a fiery debate at one kibbutz. Some members saw it as an indulgence. But Yitzhak Tabenkin, one of the leaders of the kibbutz movement, thought otherwise. "We must realize that it is our job to raise a healthy generation in this land," he wrote, "and how can we do that if we do not create the most elementary conditions for doing so?"[127] By a majority vote, the kibbutz decided to reject the purchase of the crib. In this case the ideological commitment to frugality was allied with economic constraints. Together, these overcame basic physical needs.

Kibbutzim were for the most part founded in peripheral regions where they suffered from climactic extremes and what one kibbutznik euphemistically termed "special" conditions that made life extremely difficult.[128] Chaya Yisraeli of Kvutzat Kinneret gave birth to her daughter in 1917. World War I was raging and "there is no sugar, no rice, no vegetables." Conditions were especially difficult at Kinneret, where the summers were fiercely hot and dry and the winters cold and wet.[129]

In the 1920s and 1930s, many kibbutzim lacked the most basic living conditions. Sir John Campbell, commissioner of refugees for the League of Nations, visited several kibbutzim in 1927 and reported on the harsh conditions he saw there. Outlays for food, clothing, and personal needs were extremely low, he found, and at many kibbutzim people lived in real poverty.[130] "Kinneret stood out for one thing," women who lived there in the 1920 later related. "It knew how to not provide the most basic of needs. It was concerned with the farm. The idea. So who needs hot water?"[131]

Kibbutznikim suffered also from bad and insufficient food. "A long and grueling twelve-hour work day does not ward off hunger," a kibbutz man wrote in 1927.[132] A woman named Sonia related in the 1930s that "exhausted and famished, we went straight into the dining room. The kitchen was dark, there was nothing to cook, and not even a crumb of bread was to be found."[133] The situation improved somewhat at the end of the 1930s, but the standard of living at kibbutzim remained low.[134] "I read and also heard about the difficulties faced by pioneers in Palestine," recounted a visitor to the Kibbutz Kfar Giladi dining room in the 1930s, "but I never in my worst dreams imagined anything so primitive."[135]

Illnesses were brought on and exacerbated by the harsh conditions. Chaya Yisraeli of Kvutzat Kinneret gave birth to her daughter after a severe bout of malaria during her pregnancy.[136] A woman from Kibbutz Hulata, founded in 1936, became pregnant several times and aborted the fetus on each occasion. Her reason was that she suffered from frequent attacks of malaria.[137]

The babies' and children's houses at kibbutzim were run under the supervision of physicians who visited them frequently.[138] But, inevitably, the tough conditions led children to fall ill and sometimes even led to death.[139] The death of children was tantamount to an indictment of the pioneers. Infant mortality cast doubt over their entire enterprise—their ideological decision to immigrate to Palestine and make do with little for the sake of the nation. Sometimes they even asked if they had a right to bring children into the new world they had created. They thus, unsurprisingly, sought to keep the death of children quiet.[140] Kibbutz members knew, writes Muki Tsur, based on his research of the movement, that if they wanted to prove that "Zionism does not kill babies," they had to bring about a significant reduction in infant mortality by observing advanced health protocols, providing proper food, and other such measures. Kibbutzim thus resolved to give the best housing they had available to children, better than that assigned to adults. "Members are evacuating their homes for the children, and moving into huts and tents," Meir Orlian of Tirat Zvi wrote in 1947.[141] Children had their own dining room and received the best food available. But this cost a lot of money. Furthermore, women had to be assigned to childcare, it being a given that this work was by nature women's work. Yet the kibbutzim suffered from a shortage of working hands, and of women in particular. During the period under study here, women were a notable minority of the kibbutz population and were needed for a variety of service positions. Children were thus a further and significant economic burden on the communes.[142] In many cases, a temporary and deliberate limit on the number of children born seemed unavoidable.[143]

"We have in the recent period reached a situation in which we must give up everything, we do without letters, without books," a member of Ein HaHoresh reported in the 1930s. Some thus thought that "we must also deny ourselves children."[144] The first child born at this kibbutz was a surprise no one was prepared for, and was perceived as something that only "two people wanted," in opposition to the commune's position.

Teddy Kollek, a founder, in 1937, of Kibbutz Ein Gev, on Lake Kinneret's eastern shore, later related that he suggested at a kibbutz assembly that the birth of children be postponed. "We have to live in accordance with our abilities," he said. "The problem was not having children, but how to live in the framework of our earnings. We had great hopes . . . but the reality was harsh. I argued at the assembly that all sorts of requirements needed to be put off for a year or two, and that it was possible to put off having children."[145]

At the beginning of the 1940s young kibbutzim were still claiming that their shaky finances and low standard of living meant that they could not afford to support children and their members thus refrained from having any.[146] "Provisions do not even meet the minimum," Kanievsky exclaimed. "What chance is there for natural increase at such a kibbutz? When it is clear in advance that every new soul may cause a further decline in what are already harsh conditions?"[147]

With money too short to provide more than the most minimal standard of living and with rains fickle, kibbutzim told their members to avoid pregnancy, whether by passing a formal decision or through informal persuasion. If pregnancy ensued, it was not to be brought to term.[148] Chava, a founding member of one kibbutz, recounted how her commune resolved "that we cannot permit ourselves to bear children."[149] Sometimes, even in the absence of such an official rule, members were so anxious about their community's survival that they took childlessness upon themselves. One example was Shenke, who chose to abort her pregnancy in the 1940s even though her kibbutz had made no final decision on the matter. She recounted that she identified with the need to avoid having children at that time so as not to impose a burden on community.[150]

In the early 1930s, kibbutzim founded by the radical socialist HaShomer HaTza'ir movement decided how many children each family could have and for what length of time to halt all childbirth in each kibbutz.[151] In the decade that followed, couples living at these kibbutzim who wished to have another child were required to bring their request before the membership, who decided whether the commune could afford another mouth to feed.[152] Sometimes, couples who did not abide by the decision were forced to leave the kibbutz.[153] Sarah, another founding member of a HaShomer HaTza'ir kibbutz, recalled three assemblies at which babies were proscribed. People argued then, she reported, that "we are not yet in a situation in which we can permit having children." One young woman who became pregnant was ordered to have an abortion, Sarah related. But she also said that the woman refused to obey and that the baby was born.[154] In other words, kibbutz decisions on this matter were not always enforced. Most kibbutzim accepted the premise that the number of children had to be limited,[155] but each community made its own decisions.[156] Members sometimes obeyed and sometimes did as they wished. But presumably the very fact that such a decision was made kept the birthrate low and the abortion rate high.

Yocheved Bat-Rachel lived at a large kibbutz, Ein Harod. In 1945 she related that, from the time it was founded in the 1920s, it was difficult to have big families because of the particular difficulties presented by local conditions, "which no working woman in any other country had ever experienced." These included poverty, substandard housing, "and a sense of larger responsibility to the next generation, which were seen as the object of all our efforts."[157] It was part of kibbutz ideology to raise the next generation properly, and when that proved difficult, kibbutzim preferred to reduce the number of children rather than the level of care, education, and services it provided to them.

The religious kibbutzim were a case unto themselves. Their dedication to the Zionist cause sometimes prompted them to delay the establishment of families and the birth of children until their communes were well-established. But their religious ideology and their commitment to a life conforming to Jewish religious law, halakhah, required them to be fruitful and multiply, and without delay. Furthermore, halakhah forbade abortion, except in special cases of danger to the woman (see more in chapter 5). The rabbinic ruling that was generally accepted in the religious community of the time was that so long as a man had not produced at least one son and one daughter he and his wife were not permitted to use birth control, even on an ad hoc basis. Furthermore, the earlier fulfillment of the command to reproduce was taken to be of sublime spiritual value.[158] Nevertheless, as religious families in Central and Western Europe had limited their births regardless of these strictures, the religious kibbutz movement did not see itself as bound to obey them without question. Its communities discussed the need to delay childbirth in the 1930s because of the tenuous security situation, malaria, and economic conditions that made child rearing difficult.

Some argued that "large numbers of children are a burden on the farm, exhausting the working woman." Others countered that "a religious kibbutz must discuss [such issues] in accordance with Jewish law."[159] The Religious Kibbutz Movement thus found itself in a complex position. It wanted to fulfill its national mission by placing its settlements on firm foundations, but on the other hand also wanted its communities to live according to the halakhah.[160] It found itself torn between the imperatives brought on by the security threat, harsh climate, lack of housing, and economic distress, all of which militated against having large numbers of children, and its religious ideal of large families.

During World War II, one member of Sde Eliyahu, a religious kibbutz in the Beit She'an Valley, asserted that, under the circumstances, children were out of the question.[161] In 1943, at neighboring Tirat Zvi, the membership acknowledged that they all wanted large families, but that it was necessary to grapple with how this could be done in the framework of communal life.[162] Most couples and members at religious kibbutzim believed that they should have children and rejected abortion.[163] But, given the harsh conditions in which they lived, the issue did come up, largely in the form of the question of whether women who already had a son and a daughter could use birth control (rabbinic rulings then forbade men to take measures to prevent pregnancy).[164] Formally, deliberate abortion was out of the question in these kibbutzim. But given the great hardship, even members of religious kibbutzim sometimes had abortions. Ruth, the daughter of a couple who had joined Tirat Zvi in 1943, recounted that her parents had five children, "more children than it was possible for them to devote themselves to."[165] On religious principle, the kibbutz refused to pay for abortions. But the mother had two such procedures anyway, one paid for by her in-laws in the city, after they understood what distress she was in.[166] As a general rule, however, the religious kibbutzim did not make decisions to terminate pregnancies, because of the halakhic prohibition and because of their traditional view that Jews should have large families. Nevertheless, the issue came up for discussion and sometimes decisions were made to postpone the birth of children because of the difficult living conditions. This in and of itself was a revolutionary innovation in religious society.

THE HOSPITALIZATION PROBLEM

With economic distress prompting a surge in abortions in the 1930s, Dr. Leon (Arieh) Abramovitz of the Tel Aviv municipal hospital (formerly Hadassah hospital) wrote a report on the issue. He related that, from the first day of her pregnancy, a woman found herself putting out considerable sums of money. Visits to pregnancy clinics and the treatments and care offered there cost money. Giving birth cost money. On top of this, he reported, "there is nowhere to give birth; to get into a hospital you need to be a special case, or be in a pathological condition, or homeless."[167] All these factors constituted further economic incentives to have an abortion.[168]

When the British took control, Palestine entered a new era when it came to medical care. In 1918, after the defeat of the Turks, the British army began organizing medical services, which then became, in 1920, the Health Department of the Mandate administration.[169] The department oversaw twenty-six hospitals and thirty-one clinics distributed around the country, most of which belonged to religious and philanthropic organizations.[170] It also operated eleven government hospitals, which for the most part served the Arab population.[171] The Yishuv developed health services of its own, under the aegis of the National Council's Health Department, headed by Dr. Avraham Katznelson. It coordinated the health organizations that operated in cities, towns, and farming communities and represented them to the British administration.[172] Local authorities also provided health services. The Hadassah Medical Organization founded hospitals in Jerusalem, Tel Aviv, Haifa, Safed, and Tiberias. Medical service organizations called Kupat Holim also operated, and the largest of them, the Histadrut's Kupat Holim Clalit, founded a hospital in the Jezreel Valley in 1923 and Beilinson hospital in Tel Aviv in 1936. Kupat Holim Amamit was founded by Hadassah in 1931, Kupat Holim Leumit was founded by the Revisionist Zionists in 1933, and Kupat Holim Maccabi was founded by a group of German immigrant physicians in 1941. Branches of European medical organizations also operated in Palestine.[173] Furthermore, private hospitals came into existence in the 1920s and 1930s, charging relatively large sums for hospitalizations and other treatments, such as operations and births.[174]

But the care available for pregnant women and maternity care did not meet the Yishuv's needs, which grew rapidly as more and more immigrants arrived. Pregnancy clinics were overburdened, to the point that in the 1930s they were described as "catastrophic."[175] There was also a shortage of midwives for home births. Doctors feared that pregnant women would not receive the care and treatment they needed.[176]

The number of women who gave birth at home declined over the years. Hadassah's nurses campaigned to convince women to have their babies in sterile hospitals.[177] Substandard housing further contributed to this trend. "If in the summer one can somehow compel women to give birth at home, in the winter, and especially in the rainy season, it is simply impossible because of bad housing conditions, which become even worse in this season," reported Hadassah's director, Dr. Mechulam Levontin, in the 1920s.[178] The move toward having babies in hospital was a positive one from a medical point of view, but was a mixed blessing. Hospitals charged fees that poor women could not afford to pay.[179]

Furthermore, maternity wards were overcrowded and thus could not accept all the women who needed or sought their care. "To my chagrin," a physician wrote in 1933, "the question of providing space for births in hospitals remains unresolved. The small number of beds designated for births in the country's hospitals is by no means sufficient to meet the huge demand from women who seek to have hospital births."[180] The delivery rooms and maternity wards at Hadassah hospital in Tel Aviv were overtaxed and it could not offer women what was then the standard stay of eight days.[181] In years of financial crisis, the shortage was felt even more acutely in municipal hospitals. Hadassah Tel Aviv's maternity ward reported in 1936 that "the pressure in this ward, heavy in normal years, has intensified in the past year because of the worsening economic situation in the city."[182] At a meeting of the board of the Tel Aviv municipal hospital in 1940, Tel Aviv's mayor, Israel Rokach, stressed the dearth of maternity beds.[183] As a result, hospitals began, paradoxically, to encourage women to give birth at home, taking in only women who had special medical needs—that is, women with pathological indications or women whose socioeconomic situation was so bad that home birth would be risky.[184]

Women were packed into rooms in the wards, making the experience stressful even for those who found room in hospitals. The suffering was not limited to the women in the wards. People living near Hadassah hospital complained that screaming women were disturbing their sleep and making it impossible for them to get the rest they needed to prepare for the hard labor expected of them the next day. "It has a very bad effect on our health," some of these neighbors said in a letter to the Tel Aviv Health Department.[185] The citizenry accepted that it was natural for women to be in pain in childbirth, but found it difficult to believe that there was no medication that could prevent "unnatural, feral, unrestrained screams." They claimed that these "exaggerated, unending screams have no physiological justification, but surely break out because of superstition and can be reduced by admonishment from the doctors and nurses."[186] Such an attitude toward the ostensible bad behavior of women in labor—women forced to give birth in overcrowded and unpleasant conditions—certainly did not encourage them to have more children.

In the 1930s and 1940s some twenty private hospitals were opened, mostly in the large cities. Given the need, they functioned mostly as maternity hospitals, while also offering gynecological surgery. An increasing number of women chose the private option. Kupat Holim Clalit referred many of its members to private hospitals because of a shortage of beds in its own facilities. In such cases it subsidized some, but not all, of the cost.[187] In 1945, the number of births in private hospitals nearly equaled those in public hospitals,[188] and this despite the fact that only a relatively small part of the population could afford private care.[189]

Giving birth in a private hospital in Tel Aviv cost, in 1943, P£10–P£23; if complications ensued that required lengthy hospitalization, the cost was much higher.[190] Mayor Rokach protested that year that the rates charged by one of these hospitals, Asuta, were excessive.[191] Outside Tel Aviv charges were sometimes lower, but still much more than most people could afford. It cost P£5 to have a baby at a private hospital in Hadera. That may seem reasonable, but it was high by contemporary standards, and many patients ended up paying it in installments.[192]

To grasp the magnitude of these rates, they need to be compared to earnings. The monthly wage earned by a nurse in a private hospital on the eve of World War II was about P£8; during the war years it reached P£20.[193] At the beginning of the 1940s, a monthly income of P£25 was considered almost princely for a family; most families brought in less.[194] At the beginning of the 1930s, the monthly earnings of a Jewish laborer ranged between P£3 and P£7.5, and that assuming that he or she was employed continuously throughout the month. Many laborers earned a daily wage and it was quite common for work not to be available every day.[195] A working-class woman earned even less, an average of P£2 per month.[196] About two-thirds of the working-class families who belonged to Kupat Holim Clalit lived, until 1939, off about P£6 a month.[197] With these figures in mind, the cost of hospitalization in a private maternity ward was obviously prohibitive for most of the Yishuv's population. Yet, at times, such women had no other choice. The costs then became "a huge burden on a family that sometimes has to pay off the cost of a birth over many months or even years," Tova Berman reported.[198] Yocheved Bat-Rachel of the Council of Women Workers related: "Each member who has encountered a lack of space in a [public] hospital and has had to find a place in a private institution knows the huge agony and suffering this involves. It costs her blood and money that she does not have. In such cases she is compelled to borrow money, and her family must repay the debt over the space of a year or two."[199] If this was the case with normal births, it was all the more so when there were complications, "in which case the family goes deep into debt that weighs on it for a long period of time."[200] At some maternity hospitals charitable subsidies were available to defray the cost for poor women.[201]

A private abortion by a qualified physician was inexpensive by comparison. At the end of the 1930s one could be obtained in Tel Aviv for about P£6.[202]

While even this was beyond the means of many families, it was still much cheaper than having a baby.

Pregnant women found themselves in a trap. Home birth was problematic; public hospitals were overcrowded and overtaxed, not to mention expensive; fees were even higher in private facilities, beyond what most in the Yishuv could afford. Abortion was thus a reasonable and economical alternative.

The centrality of economics to the birthrate issue is proved from the opposite direction as well. When the economy grew, the birthrate went up. For example, three years after the outbreak of World War II, in 1942–1943, the Palestinian economy enjoyed a substantial upturn.[203] This prosperity raised the demand for labor, unemployment fell significantly—and the birthrate rose.[204] Similarly, the birthrate recovered throughout the West beginning in 1943, and especially after the war was over. The baby boom was, in part, a consequence of economic growth.[205]

NOTES

1. Roberto Bachi, "HaYeludah be Yisra'el uvaYishuv vehaDerakhim le'Idudah," apparently 1944, CZA J1/3717/3.
2. Tova Berman, "Ha'Emtza'im haDerushim le'Idud haYeludah baYishuv," Feb. 1945, CZA J1/3717/3.
3. Tova Berman, "Al Be'ayot HaYeludah," undated (probably 1943), CZA A516/100.
4. Morag-Talmon and Atzmon 2013, 10.
5. DellaPergola 2009; DellaPergola 2002.
6. Altshuler and Mendelson 1984, 53.
7. Weinberg 1988, 43–63; Hyman 1998(b).
8. Bachi 1943a, 8.
9. Coale, Anderson, and Harm 1979, 3.
10. Hyman 1998(a).
11. Kaplan 1998, 82.
12. Cotts Watkins 1991; Coser, Anker, and Perrin 1999, 52; Exler 2000, 53.
13. Exler 2000, 55; Weinberg 1988, 219–221; Rosenbaum 2011, 253; Cotts Watkins 1991, 270.
14. Weinberg 1988, 220; Exler 2000, 1; Coser, Anker, and Perrin 1999, 49–50.
15. Cotts Watkins 1991, 470, 479; Coser, Anker, and Perrin 1999, 4, 7, 50.
16. Goldman 1931.
17. Moran Hajo 2012, 126.
18. Exler 2000, 14–15; Rosenbaum 2011, 251–265.
19. Roberto Bachi, "Maskanot Politiyot metokh Hakirotay 'al haHitpathut haDemografit shel haYehudim veha'Aravim beE"Y," Oct. 1944, LI IV-243-3-59.
20. Tova Berman, text for the mock trial on birthrate problems, 1943, CZA J1/3717/1.
21. Letter from Sarah L. to Tel Aviv Mayor Israel Rokach, Feb. 18, 1949, TAA 4-4643.
22. Ibid.
23. Margalit-Stern 2013, 116.
24. For example, Rosenberg-Friedman 2012.
25. Pinhas Shifman, "Shinu'yei Mivne baHinukh," *Hatzofeh*, Aug. 14, 1942, 3.

26. Letter from the deputy mayor of Tel Aviv, in the name of the municipality council, to the commissioner of Negev district, Jaffa, Mar. 28, 1935, TAA 4-4644.

27. Ibid.

28. Tsur and Yisra'eli 1985, 129.

29. Meir Orlian, "HaTipul haMeshutaf," 'Alonim, Summer 1941, 8.

30. Bachi 1977, 199.

31. Kozma 2010, 99; Burton 2000; Avdeev, Bloom, and Troitskaya 1995; Bernstein 2007.

32. For example, Dr. Bilhah Puliastor, "HaHapalah ha Mela'akhutit," Davar, July 29, 1931, 3; "She'elot haMishpahah vehaImahut beUSSR" (no byline), Davar, June 11, 1936, 9.

33. Roberto Bachi, "Maskanot Politiyot metokh Hakirotay 'al haHitpathut haDemografit shel haYehudim veha'Aravim beE"Y," Oct. 1944, LI IV-243-3-59.

34. Bachi 1944, 174; Frevert 1997, 111; Kaplan 1998, 82.

35. "Pehitat haLeidot Le'or haNitu'ah haMarksisty," (no byline), Davar, July 13, 1934 (n.p.).

36. Dr. Lipman, "Letahlu'ei haNashim," Davar, Feb. 2, 1934, 7; Dr. Bilhah Puliastor, "HaHapalah ha Mela'akhutit," Davar, July 29, 1931, 3; Keta Bachar, "Tahanot ha'Eitzah leNashim veTinokot," Ha'em Vehayeled, 1935, 32.

37. Roberto Bachi, "Sekirah Ketzarah 'al haYeludah vehaTemotah beE"Y beTekufat 1939–1941," CZA J1/1957/2.

38. Bachi 1943a, 15.

39. Bachi 1944, 174–175.

40. Mendelson 1976, 183.

41. Exler 2000, 55.

42. Brezniak 2004, 21.

43. YIVO NY, Poster Collection P/413.

44. Frankel 2004, 96, 99.

45. Roberto Bachi, "Yeridat haTeludah—Sakanah Le'umit," Ha'aretz, 1940 (no specific day, n.p.).

46. Roberto Bachi, "Maskanot Politiyot metokh Hakirotay 'al haHitpathut haDemografit shel haYehudim veha'Aravim beE"Y," Oct. 1944, CZA J1/3717/2, 1; Roberto Bachi, "Be'ayat haYeludah BeYisra'el veHatza'ot leMediniyut haUkhlusiyah," undated, ISA 5588/2c; Roberto 1943b, 5.

47. Roberto Bachi, radio talk, 1943, CZA J1/3717/1.

48. Golz 2013, 33; Levy and Levy 2008, 20, 27; Ben-Gurion Diaries 1, Feb. 11, 1952, BGA K218888, 8.

49. Levy and Levy 2008, 37.

50. Dr. Haim Yassky, memorandum of discussion with Prof. Bernhard Zondek, Dec. 22, 1935, CZA J113/7487.

51. Zalashik 2008, 82; Hashiloni-Dolev 2013, 71–75.

52. Shvarts and Stoler-Liss 2011, 90–91; on the "new Jew," see Biale 1992, 231–267.

53. Letter from Sarah L. to Tel Aviv Mayor Israel Rokach, Feb. 18, 1949, TAA 4-4643.

54. Roberto Bachi, radio talk, 1943, CZA J1/3717/1.

55. Moran Hajo 2012, 136–139.

56. Alpern Engel 2004, 162.

57. Frevert 1997, 187; Usborne 2007, 10.

58. Proskauer 1989, 86–87. I thank Dr. Dorit Yosef for this source.

59. P. SH., "HaBerihah Mipnei haYeled," Davar, Mar. 2, 1934, 8; Tova Berman (no title), Davar, Jan. 1, 1945.

60. Letter from Dr. Halperin to Hadassah administration, Feb. 13, 1939, CZA J113/2312; Dr. Joseph Mayer, radio program, apparently July 1944, CZA J1/3717/2; Binah Velfish, "'Al 'Inyan she'ein Medabrim Bo," Davar, Apr. 27, 1938, 3.

61. Kanievsky 1944, 20.
62. Letter from Hedwig Gellner to Tel Aviv Mayor Rokach, Sept. 5, 1940, TAA 4-1426.
63. Kanievsky 1944, 20.
64. "BiKronot haMavet Shel T"A ha'Atikah" (no byline), *Yediot Aharonot*, Feb. 15, 1946, 3.
65. Ibid.
66. Bachi 1943a, 15.
67. Lilia [Bassewitz], "Isha, Em Vayeled," *Mibifnim*, Apr. 1933, 15.
68. Tova Berman, Reasons for termination of pregnancy, Table 1, Jan. 1944, CZA A516/181; Tova Berman-Yeshurun, "Hapalah Mela'akhutit," *Eitanim* 7, 4–5 (Apr.-May 1954), 138; report by Dr. Tova Berman to David Ben-Gurion, May 10, 1944, BGA/correspondence/198564; Tova Berman, "Ha'Emtza'im haDerushim le'Idud haYeludah baYishuv," Feb. 1945, CZA J1/3717/3; Tova Berman, "Vitur 'al haYeled," *Devar Hapo'elet*, July 31, 1934, 17.
69. On the reasons for abandonment (often economic, but also a legal situation that did not see abandonment as a crime deserving punishment, and the lack of legal ability to force the fathers to acknowledge paternity and bear responsibility for their children) and its implications, see Razi 2009, 86–90.
70. Hedwig Gellner, "Sekirah 'al 10 Shanim shel 'Avodah Sotziyalit beT"A," submitted to Mayor Rokach of Tel Aviv, Sept. 12, 1943, TAA 4-1427.
71. Ibid.
72. Lilia [Bassewitz], "Isha, Em Vayeled," *Mibifnim*, Apr. 1933, 15.
73. Report on organizations' members, who are supported by the Social Welfare Department of the Tel Aviv municipality, 1939–1941, TAA 4-1426.
74. Lilia Bassewitz, a meeting of women on women's hygiene issues, July 1933, YTA 15-28/14/1, 5–6.
75. Shilo 2013.
76. Letter from the Union of Hebrew Women for Equal Rights to the Committee on Birthrate Problems, 1940s, CZA L75/3.
77. Letter from Dr. Tova Berman to David Ben-Gurion, May 10, 1944, CZA J1/3717/3; report by Dr. Tova Berman, Feb. 16, 1945, CZA J1/3717/3.
78. Tova Berman, text for the mock trial on birthrate problems, 1943, CZA J1/3717/1.
79. Lapid 2011, 83.
80. "Edutah haDramatit shel Yonah Tzadok," (no byline) *Do'ar Hayom*, Apr. 5, 1936, 8.
81. Report by Dr. Tova Berman to David Ben-Gurion, May 10, 1944, CZA J1/3717/3; report by Dr. Tova Berman, Feb. 16, 1945, CZA J1/3717/3; Tova Berman, program for a radio talk for a week devoted to birthrate issues, July 1944, CZA J1/3717/2.
82. Letter from Sarah L. to Tel Aviv Mayor Israel Rokach, Feb. 18, 1949, TAA 4-4643.
83. Program for a radio talk for a week devoted to birthrate issues, July 1944, CZA J1/3717/2; Cohen 2001, 129.
84. Fraenkel 1944, 29.
85. Kimelman 2003, 37, 40, 119.
86. Golz 2013, 33.
87. "Rofeh Mesader Hapalot Mela'akhutiyot," (no byline) *'Iton Meyuhad*, Oct. 10, 1941 (n.p.).
88. Dr. Mordekhai Albrekht, "Neged haHashmadah Shel ha'Aliyah haPnimit," *Davar*, Jan. 6, 1947, 3.
89. Letter from Sarah L. to Tel Aviv Mayor Israel Rokach, Feb. 18, 1949, TAA 4-4643.
90. Kimelman 2003, 37, 40, 119.
91. Yocheved Bat-Rachel, "De'agat HaImahut," Merkaz Kupat Holim, Jan. 1945, YTA, 15-36/4/4, 7, 14.
92. Tova Berman, text for the mock trial on birthrate problems, 1943, CZA J1/3717/1.
93. Lapid 2011, 82.

94. Sh. Zeevi, a proposal to the National Council, May 21, 1944, CZA J1/34358.

95. Kanievsky 1944, 171.

96. Ibid.

97. Letter from the deputy mayor of Tel Aviv, in the name of the municipality council, to the commissioner of Negev district, Jaffa, Mar. 28, 1935, TAA 4-4644.

98. Hedwig Gellner, "Sekirah 'al 10 Shanim shel 'Avodah Sotziyalit beT"A," submitted to Mayor Rokach of Tel Aviv, Sept. 12, 1943, TAA 4-1427.

99. Kanievsky 1944, 171.

100. "HaYiten ha Yishuv leMi'ut haYeludah Livloa' et Hesegeinu be'Aliyah?" (no byline), Davar, Jan. 26, 1944, 4; Dr. Mayer, program for a radio talk for a week devoted to birthrate issues, July 1944, CZA J1/3717/2.

101. Tova Berman, text for the mock trial on birthrate problems, 1943, CZA J1/3717/1.

102. Report on diverse populations receiving support from the Tel Aviv municipality's Social Welfare Department, 1939–1941, TAA 4-1426.

103. Hedwig Gellner, "Sekirah 'al 10 Shanim shel 'Avodah Sotziyalit beT"A," submitted to Mayor Rokach of Tel Aviv, Sept. 12, 1943, TAA 4-1427.

104. Kanievsky 1944, 171.

105. L. Bein, "HaRibui haTiv'i veHishuvei he'Atid haKarov," Hatzofeh, June 8, 1945, 5.

106. Hedwig Gellner, "Sekirah 'al 10 Shanim shel 'Avodah Sotziyalit beT"A," submitted to Mayor Rokach of Tel Aviv, Sept. 12, 1943, TAA 4-1427.

107. Tova Berman, text for the mock trial on birthrate problems, 1943, CZA J1/3717/1.

108. Dr. Mayer, program for a radio talk for a week devoted to birthrate issues, July 1944, CZA J1/3717/2.

109. Dr. B. Grinfeld, lecture for the Mother and Child Committee, Feb. 1934, CZA J1/3081.

110. Dr. J[oseph] Mayer, "Havah veNa'aleh Otam leEretz Yisra'el," Davar, Apr. 10, 1946, 2.

111. Decisions of the 13th session of the Assembly of Representatives, Sept. 29, 1943, CZA J1/7220.

112. Roberto Bachi, "Maskanot Politiyot metokh Hakirotay 'al haHitpathut haDemografit shel haYehudim veha'Aravim beE"Y," Oct. 1944, CZA J1/3717/2, 1.

113. Bachi 1943a, 16.

114. Eitan 1985, 20.

115. Kanievsky 1944, 20.

116. "Le'inyanei haSha'ah" (no byline), Hatzofeh, Oct. 5, 1944, 2.

117. Interview with Zviya Harit, conducted by Roni Azati and Sarash Erez, Aug. 25, 1989–Feb. 20, 1990, YTA 16-12/26/2.

118. Ibid.

119. Ema Levin, "HaHaverah baKibbutz, baMeshek uvaTenu'ah," 'Al Hamishmar, Dec. 14, 1945, 3.

120. Tsur, Zevulun, and Porat 1981, 153.

121. Shatil 1995, 209, 211–212; Nir 2008, 139; conversation with Muki Tsur, Aug. 1, 2015.

122. Z. Dor-Sinai, in Tsur, Zevulun, and Porat 1981, 190.

123. Rachel, in Tsur, Zevulun, and Porat 1981, 286.

124. Ibid., 287.

125. Conversation with Muki Tsur, Aug. 1, 2015.

126. 'Atara Shturman, in Tsur, Zevulun, and Porat 1981, 191.

127. Z. Dor-Sinai, in Tsur, Zevulun, and Porat 1981, 185.

128. Meir Orlian, "HaTipul haMeshutaf," 'Alonim, Summer 1941, 8.

129. Tsur and Yisra'eli 1985, 129.

130. Shatil 1995, 204.

131. Ibid.

132. Tsur, Zevulun, and Porat 1981, 170.
133. Ibid, 302.
134. Shatil 1995, 204, 206–209; Nir 2008, 67, 137–138.
135. Tsur, Zevulun, and Porat 1981, 302.
136. Tsur and Yisra'eli 1985, 129.
137. Cohen 2001, 129.
138. On the 1920s, see Eva Tabenkin, in Tsur, Zevulun, and Porat 1981, 189. On the 1930s, see Tsur, Zevulun, and Porat 1981, 290.
139. Sinai 2013, 189–198.
140. Ibid.
141. Meir Orlian, "HaYeled haMe'ah," 'Alonim, 30, 1947, 20. See also: Tsur, Zevulun, and Porat 1981, 187; Conversation with Muki Tsur, Aug. 1, 2015.
142. Shatil 1995, 202, 212; Sheffer and Fogiel-Bijaoui 1993, 28–29.
143. Tsur 2014, 58.
144. Tsur, Zevulun, and Porat 1981, 289.
145. Zameret 1987.
146. Letter from Dr. Tova Berman to David Ben-Gurion, May 10, 1944, CZA J1/3717/3.
147. Kanievsky 1944, 20.
148. Lilia [Bassewitz], "Isha, Em Vayeled," Mibifnim, Apr. 1933, 15; Shechter 2011, 255; Margalit-Stern 2011, 195; conversation with H. from Kibbutz Negba and Y. from Kibbutz Bet-Alfa, Feb. 23, 2015; Tsur 2014, 58–59; Sheffer and Fogiel-Bijaoui 1993, 20–21.
149. Lamdan 2004, 59.
150. Ibid., 58.
151. Lilia [Bassewitz], "Isha, Em Vayeled," Mibifnim, Apr. 1933, 15.
152. Ze'ev (Wolfgang) von Weisl, "Me'et ha'Elef She'avdu Lanu LaNetsah," Hamashkif, Oct. 10, 1947, 3.
153. Sheffer and Fogiel-Bijaoui 1993, 20–21.
154. Lamdan 2004, 58.
155. Tsur, Zevulun, and Porat 1981, 290.
156. Lamdan 2004, 58.
157. Yocheved Bat-Rachel, "De'agat HaImahut," Merkaz Kupat Holim, Jan. 1945, YTA, 15-36/4/4, 5.
158. Feldman 1998.
159. Donash, "BaTirah," Hatzofeh, Apr. 12, 1940, 3.
160. Report towards the Third Council of the Religious Kibbutz Movement (on the years 1941–1944), Oct. 1944, RKMA 3-M1, 63.
161. Sheshar 1991, 107.
162. Meir Orlian, "'Al HaTipul haMeshutaf," 'Alonim, 13, June 1943, 17.
163. Letter to the Religious Kibbutz administration, Aug. 2, 1941, RKMA B1479.
164. Shimshon, "'AL She'elat haYeludah," Dapim 7. Aug. 25, 1939.
165. Netzer 2012, 11.
166. Ibid.
167. Letter of Dr. A. Abramovitch, director of Hadassah municipal hospital, to A. Perlson, chairman of the board, May 28, 1937, TAA, Hadassah hospital, 4-4645.
168. Yocheved Bat-Rachel, "De'agat HaImahut," Merkaz Kupat Holim, Jan. 1945, YTA, 15-36/4/4, 10.
169. Levy 1998, 198.
170. Ibid., 199.
171. Golz 2013, 22; Levy and Levy 2008, 25.
172. Levy 1998, 238.

173. Ibid., 209–237; Golz 2013, 32.

174. Golz 2013, 31.

175. Letter from Dr. Haim Yassky to Tel Aviv Mayor Israel Rokach, May 21, 1935, TAA 4-4644.

176. Report from Dr. Haim Abarbanel—Hadassah Tel Aviv to the Executive Committee of the Clinics for pregnant women in Tel Aviv, May 1935, TAA 4-4644.

177. Dr. Avraham Yehuda Levy, "Matzav haBri'ut ba'Aretz biShnat 5693," *Do'ar Hayom*, Sept. 20, 1933 (n.p.).

178. Letter from Dr. Levontin, director of Hadassah hospital Tel Aviv, to the Hadassah management in Jerusalem, Dec. 8, 1926, CZA J113/401.

179. Letter from Dr. Haim Yassky to Rabbi Yitzhak Herzog, July 25, 1937, CZA J113/8087; correspondence between Mr. Brumberg—Hadassah and Ha'ezra in Jerusalem, June 3, 1938, June 23, 1938, CZA J113/8087; correspondence between Israel Rokach and activists in Ha'ezra in Australia and South Africa, 1939–1940, TAA 4-1426.

180. Dr. Avraham Yehuda Levy, "Matzav haBri'ut ba'Aretz biShnat 5693," *Do'ar Hayom*, Sept. 20, 1933 (n.p.).

181. Report from Hadassah hospital in Tel Aviv to the Hadassah management in Jerusalem, Dec. 11, 1924, CZA J1/1047/11; letter from Dr. Levontin to the Hadassah management in Jerusalem, Dec. 20, 1927, CZA J113/401; memorandum on the issue of hospitalization in Tel Aviv, Dec. 16, 1933, TAA 4-4644; memorandum of a meeting on work of midwives at Hadassah hospital in Jerusalem, June 14, 1935, CZA J113/7487.

182. Annual report of Hadassah hospital in Tel Aviv, 1936, TAA 4-4645.

183. Minutes of the meeting of the executive committee of the municipal hospital in Tel Aviv, Jan. 10, 1940, TAA 4-4686.

184. Report from Hadassah hospital in Tel Aviv to the Hadassah management in Jerusalem, Dec. 11, 1924, CZA J1/1047/11; annual report of Hadassah hospital in Tel Aviv, 1936, TAA 4-4645.

185. Letter from residents to the Health Department of the Tel Aviv Municipality, July 7, 1936; letter from Mr. Yaccobovsky to Tel Aviv Municipality, Sept. 8, 1936, TAA 4-4645.

186. Letter from residents to the Health Department of the Tel Aviv Municipality, July 7, 1936, TAA 4-4645.

187. Golz 2013.

188. Tova Berman, "Ha'Emtza'im haDerushim le'Idud haYeludah baYishuv," Feb. 1945, CZA J1/3717/3; Yocheved Bat-Rachel, "De'agat HaImahut," Merkaz Kupat Holim, Jan. 1945, YTA, 15-36/4/4, 11.

189. Dr. Ascherman and Dr. Levontin, letter to the Hadassah management in Jerusalem, Dec. 20, 1927, CZA J113/401.

190. For more information on the cost of births in private hospitals, see Golz 2013, 62, 109, 134.

191. Ibid., 126.

192. Ibid., 210.

193. Ibid., 62.

194. Program for a radio talk for a week devoted to birthrate issues, July 1944, CZA J1/3717/2.

195. Bernstein 2003, 83–84.

196. Rene Varshaviak, "haVikhu'ah shel haPe'ulah haTarbutit vahaSotziyalit," *Davar*, Feb. 19, 1932, 3.

197. Dr. Tova Berman, minutes of a meeting of the Committee on Birthrate Problems, June 22, 1943, CZA J1/3717/1.

198. Tova Berman, "Ha'Emtza'im haDerushim le'Idud haYeludah baYishuv," Feb. 1945, CZA J1/3717/3.

199. Yocheved Bat-Rachel, "De'agat HaImahut," Merkaz Kupat Holim, Jan. 1945, YTA, 15-36/4/4, 11.

200. Ibid.

201. Golz 2013, 73.

202. "'Edutah haDramatit shel Yonah Tzadok," (no byline) *Do'ar Hayom*, Apr. 5, 1936, 8.

203. Hedwig Gellner, "Sekirah 'al 10 Shanim shel 'Avodah Sotziyalit beT"A," submitted to Mayor Rokach of Tel Aviv, Sept. 12, 1943, TAA 4-1427.

204. L. Bein, "HaRibui haTiv'i veHishuvei he'Atid haKarov," *Hatzofeh*, June 8, 1945, 5; Ba'al Heshbon, "Hidat Tenu'at haUkhlusin haEretzyisraelit," *Hamashkif*, Sept. 8, 1946, 2.

205. Roberto Bachi, "He'arot 'Al haMeganot haDemografiot ba'Olam uve'Artseinu, ve'AL haMediniyut haDemografit beYisra'el," apparently 1957, CZA A516/210.

CHAPTER THREE

THE PARENTS' REBELLION
Social and Psychological Factors

WHILE THE YISHUV'S LOW BIRTHRATE AND high abortion rate cannot be understood without reference to economic factors, many Jews in Palestine decided to have only one child at least in part for other reasons as well. The "parents' rebellion," as Tova Berman referred to it, had deeper social and psychological roots. She noted that a large proportion of the population simply preferred not to have even a single child, without any connection to their economic position. This lack of interest in children was decisive, the substrate on which all the reasons for the low birthrate could develop.[1]

This claim that the economic factor was not primal is supported by the fact that the better-off a couple was, the fewer children they had.[2] "High-level officials, professionals, and Jews of whatever stripe belonging to the middle class have fewer children than workers living on very little," Berman remarked. She added that even during periods in which the rent was low, "there were no more children than there are now."[3] The same argument was made at the kibbutzim. "Don't say that the principal cause of abortions is the economic situation," a woman living at a kibbutz declared in 1940. The primary cause, in her view, was social pressure.[4]

But whatever the other reasons for avoiding pregnancy and birth, money was what many women cited as the final straw when asked to explain their abortions.[5] It may well be that they saw it as an objective and legitimate justification they could offer; one that pinned the blame on the government and administrative bodies responsible for the Yishuv and the welfare of its members. Nevertheless, other factors were clearly in play. "There are two kinds of people," Joseph Mayer said, "those who are able to support children but do not want to have them, and those who want children but who are unable to properly support and educate them."[6]

Psychology

The psychology of motherhood is especially convoluted and complex, wrote the psychologist and educator Dr. Yisra'el Rivkai in 1935. The major reason for the complexity was the clash, as he called it, between the joy and fear that accompanied the act of bringing a child into the world. It was even more complicated among Jews in Palestine than elsewhere, he said, because of the unique nature of the Yishuv's struggle to create, out of thin air, a society in which men and women were equals. Children were seen as an obstacle to this goal, with the result that motherhood became a matter of profound anxiety.[7]

In his encounters with many women who had abortions, Dr. Arieh Sadowski said the "psychic factor had been critical" in their decisions.[8] But that term is a very general one that subsumed a large number of factors behind the gut feeling and profound fear many women had of having children. "Our women are overcome with dread of bringing children into the world," Dr. von Weisl wrote in 1947. "They are happy childless and tremble at the greatest blessing of all, the fruit of their wombs."[9]

The word "fear" was also used by Lilia Bassewitz, who recounted how much time, worry, and thought a woman spent on a child before being born. The child lived in her thoughts and inner experience for many years before he or she actually appeared in physical form. Sometimes, she said, such thoughts were full of anticipation and hope. But in other cases, she acknowledged, they were anxious and fearful, a fear that takes control of a woman's life.[10]

What sort of fear were they talking about? It may have come out of a sense of being unprepared for motherhood. Some women, notably kibbutz women, stated explicitly that they were not psychologically prepared to be mothers.[11] When a woman unexpectedly found herself pregnant, it felt like a catastrophe, Bassewitz related, plunging her into sometimes suicidal despair. "Anyone who knows how a child can be prayed for and the quivering anticipation the desire for a child can bring, the joy and happiness that the expectation of a wanted child brings, can comprehend the depression and despair that the anticipation of an unwanted child can bring on," she said.[12]

Furthermore, Rivkai asserted, anxiety was a product of the inexperience of many new mothers who lacked "a family environment including elderly women able to guide her with the benefit of their experience and dispel her needless fears."[13]

Fears were doubtless also a product of the disparity between a mother's dreams about how she would like to raise her child and the difficulty of living up to those standards, for any number of reasons of which economics was one. A mother who could not provide her child with a banana or apple, Berman said, who could not walk her baby on the beach or along an avenue, feels that she is not proper mother. No wonder she does not want another child.[14]

Another cause of anxiety might well have been mothers' lack of energy, as the "defendant" in the mock trial of 1943. When asked why she had an abortion following her first birth, she answered: "The boy was still small, and I didn't feel I had the strength to care for toddlers. I was always irritable."[15] Doctors reported hearing similar sentiments from many women. "Completely healthy women claim that they are weak and bad-tempered and that they don't have the strength to care for even a single child, much less two or more," Berman complained in a letter to Ben-Gurion.[16]

Yocheved Bat-Rachel described the plight of the young mother who, returning home with her newborn, had to immediately "enter into a work routine" at home and outside it. She desperately needed rest, but the housework had been neglected in her absence and she had to care both for her baby and for the rest of the family. In most cases, Bat-Rachel remarked, the mother felt exhausted, especially during the period she nursed. Her health was tenuous, and it would be a long time before her strength returned to her. She thus lost any interest in another pregnancy.[17] In many cases, Berman claimed, women put off another pregnancy "simply because of their apprehension about the tough period that would follow the birth."[18]

The documentation shows that women's decisions about abortions depended no little on the public atmosphere.[19] "When they see a woman with a baby in her arms, and she is pregnant again," Berman explained, "few of her acquaintances and neighbors will refrain from making a crack that she is 'pregnant again!' It is hardly surprising that a woman who encounters such an attitude from the public will not wish to have another child."[20] There was no respect for pregnant women, she wrote. Young people did not give her their seats on the bus and workplaces dismissed expectant women.[21] Berman maintained that all these phenomena served as incentives not to get pregnant and to have a baby.

What Berman called "a lack of connection to the child" was seen by others, as well, as a cause of low birthrates and high abortion rates, especially among the better-off.[22] She was seconded by Dr. Helena Kagan, a towering figure in pediatrics in the Yishuv, who feared that the phenomenon would become "a fashion that would spread to the poorer strata."[23] It was clear to Berman that the conjunction of poverty with the "prevailing psychology of the better-off" led to a low birthrate among a wide variety of social groups.[24]

The economic factor affected both women and men, but psychological birthrate issues were seen as women's issues. It was taken as a given that the burden of childcare rested almost completely on women, and women were stereotyped as emotional, easily affected, and making decisions based largely on their feelings. But, in fact, women's identities and functions in the Yishuv had changed and often challenged the stereotypical model.

The New Woman's Identity and Birth Control

A woman's freedom to choose and make her own decisions about her fertility is a litmus test of women's standing in a society. In the nineteenth century women began to demand their bodies for themselves and control over childbirth. Beginning at the end of the nineteenth century, fertility was a focus of feminist interest. Feminists viewed motherhood as a limitation on women and the source of their inferior status. After 1918 a growing number of women sought to take control of their bodies. Feminists made reproductive rights a top priority.[25] Since they believed that control of their own reproduction was a fundamental right and a means of liberating themselves from the biological destiny that constrained them, these feminists campaigned to legalize abortion.[26] Furthermore, as recent studies have shown, abortion maximized women's control of childbirth.[27] Traditional birth control methods were the man's responsibility or required the cooperation of both partners. Abortion lay solely in the purview of the woman, and could even be done without the male partner's knowledge. Women thus saw abortion as a means of taking control of their reproduction.[28] But this campaign had the negative consequence of focusing feminism's opponents on preventing women from gaining sole control of the decision to have children, and in particular of preventing abortions.[29]

Feminism, however, was not the only force changing views of reproduction and abortion. The dramatic transformation of women's status in Western society in the twentieth century, and the educational and employment opportunities that this opened up for them, had a direct effect on the birthrate and on birth control.[30] As women increasingly sought personal fulfillment, they had fewer babies.

Women's work outside the home was a notable cause of the increasing practice of abortion in Europe.[31] The Yishuv was no different.[32] Families in which the wife and mother did not work outside the home had more children, Bachi found in 1943. But he noted that the correlation could mean a cause in either direction—it could be that having more children kept women from seeking work outside the home.[33]

The Yishuv labor market was stratified according to traditional gender standards. Men were the principal breadwinners, and women who entered the labor market almost always worked at jobs seen as women's work—food preparation, sewing, and nursing. Women had a harder time finding employment than men did.[34] But wages were low and men often could not support families on their own, impelling women to bring in earnings with part-time jobs. In some families, women were the main wage earners, usually working in housekeeping in other homes.[35] When both parents were away from home most of the day, they had little time or attention for raising and educating their children, Hedwig Gellner reported.[36]

Furthermore, there were few childcare facilities where children could be placed while their mother worked.[37] "Mothers wait for many months before they can get their children into an institution—and this privilege only comes in especially tragic circumstances or for health reasons,"[38] Berman wrote. On the one hand, women needed to work to support their families, while on the other hand, working meant that they could not care for babies and children.[39] As Lilia Bassewitz noted, this was a disincentive to have children. Due to the necessity of working outside her home, "a woman must agree, perhaps gritting her teeth, that her body will be a grave for the child who could have been born, and to suffocate the maternal instinct beating within her."[40]

A woman reluctant to leave her job, or fearful of losing it, thought more than twice about allowing herself to get pregnant, and if she did, about whether to have the baby come to term. In a survey conducted in January 1944, more than 10 percent of the women who had undergone an abortion in the previous decade offered this reason. Women who worked as housekeepers, farmers, factory workers, and seamstresses, or in other professions, wanted to remain employed and thus had abortions.[41]

"I wanted to work in my profession as a preschool teacher, and I knew that with two small children I would not be able to do so," testified the "defendant" in the mock trial of 1943. "I was afraid of losing my job," she said.[42] In an era in which social benefits and labor laws protecting working women were nonexistent, women had few options. As the "defendant" said, "Who wants to employ a pregnant woman?"[43] Berman presented data showing that public institutions indeed laid off pregnant women.[44]

Women did not only work outside the home because finances compelled them to. Some women viewed having a career as a value in and of itself, a part of their new identities. Furthermore, women's entry into the workforce offered them an opportunity for personal development. They adopted values that were not always consistent with traditional gender roles, according to which a woman's primary responsibility was the home and family. The Yishuv offered a new model of womanhood not centered on having children. "The Jewish mother's motivation to have children" has changed, Berman said.[45] In a survey conducted by Dr. Yisra'el Rivkai, a vast majority of women (73 percent) responded that they were disinclined to have children because it would "interfere with public activity." Almost as many (62 percent) reported that they had delayed having their first child for this reason.[46]

Changes in gender conceptions were evident in the kind of education women received and the kind of work they did, and both affected the birth-rate. "There is hardly a young woman today who doesn't aspire to economic independence, to earn all her own needs and those of her family," wrote journalist Hemda Nofech in 1937. The implications for the birthrate were clear, she noted: "Given the many burdens of her work, a woman cannot devote herself solely to her family as mothers of the last generation did. The result is a decline in the birthrate."[47]

In particular, work was an ideal for women of the labor movement. It was more than a way of making a living—labor was a means of liberation from their traditional role as tenders of the home. It made them partners in the nation-building enterprise. "We admire women not just as mothers but also as workers, learners, participants in social life, fighting hand in hand with men for our ideas," one pioneer woman wrote in the 1930s.[48] "The woman's immense desire to be a partner in the realization of pioneer objectives," meant that large families were problematic in pioneer society, Yocheved Bat-Rachel noted.[49] Some pioneer women deliberately eschewed family life and motherhood so as to devote themselves to the pioneering Zionist ideal.[50]

According to Dr. Rivkai, the Yishuv's idealistic women feared that motherhood would interfere with their public activity.[51] This perception was evident especially in the kibbutzim. "The kibbutz woman must also live outside her child," insisted Batya of Givat HaShlosha in 1931.[52] She protested the idea that children should be the priority of a mother "with a public connection," that is, a woman interested in acting outside the home. Yet these women, she said, absented themselves from kibbutz assemblies and gave up reading books for their children's sake. Even so, they felt that they were not giving their children enough. "It is our heritage to be overwrought about motherhood," Batya declared. She blamed a tradition of many generations, but expressed cautious optimism that this emotional overdrive would gradually lessen over the years.[53]

The repudiation of traditional motherhood was especially strong in the kibbutzim, in which the very concept of the private home was abolished. Meals were eaten communally and children were brought up in children's houses. Both these practices were meant to liberate women and permit them to devote themselves to the commune on a par with men. But that was not how things were at first. Kibbutz life at its very beginning presented a dilemma for mothers, who were torn between continuing their farm work and devoting themselves to their children. When Miriam Baratz, the first mother at the first kibbutz, Degania, had her child in 1913, she feared that she would lose her job in the dairy. She thus took her day-old baby with her to work there, to the disapproval of the other members, who feared that the baby would fall ill and believed that Miriam ought to stop working and devote herself to her baby.[54] The opposite happened to Chaya Yisraeli of Kvutzat Kinneret, who gave birth to a baby in 1917. Most of her comrades objected to her devotion to her baby's care at a time when her working hands were needed and the commitment to the ideal of manual labor central. Kibbutz members gossiped that "Chaya isn't working." Chaya's transformation from devotion to the farm to devotion to her own child was difficult for her comrades to accept. She was known as a devoted and faithful worker, and her fellows asked, "And if Chaya does not carry out our aspiration to be like mothers in Russia and Germany, to raise her child alongside her farm work, what will happen to our movement?"[55]

In the years during which the first kibbutzim were being established, "it was still not commonly recognized by most comrades that childcare was a branch of the commune's work."[56] Later, the concept of communal education would crystallize in the kibbutzim, designed partly to free women from having to care for their individual children. But most women ended up working at traditional feminine jobs. These were largely in services (cooking, washing, cleaning, and childcare) rather than in what was perceived as productive branches that brought in money. While they did not care for their biological children, they cared for all the children of the kibbutz. It was tantamount to an expansion of their roles as mothers. While the image was otherwise, there was a notable disparity between the talk of gender equality and how it was, or was not, put into practice.[57] Nevertheless, women worked outside of the home, as part of an operation included in the commune's work roster. It was limited to specific hours and was recognized as work in every sense of the word. As such, the kibbutz woman was a full partner in building the farm, while having children was dropped down to a lower rung of women's priorities.

Kibbutz women viewed devotion to one of their commune's work branches and involvement in its social life as more important than having children.[58] An assembly of women workers held at Degania Bet in the 1930s resolved unanimously that they were "liberated" from the burdens of motherhood. With humor shaded by more than a bit of longing, they declared to the men of the kibbutzim that "if all is in your hands—the farm, initiative, security—then take this, too. You give birth to children, and we will be for the wide open spaces, the green meadows, the fresh air under blue skies, under the sun's golden rays. We are weary of this yoke, the legacy of the ages."[59] Some kibbutz women chose to do this in practice—they had abortions so they could continue to work.[60] Lilia Bassewitz of Ein Harod thought that women who wanted to participate in the commune's work but had trouble doing so because of closely spaced pregnancies should be allowed to have abortions.[61]

For the Religious Kibbutz Movement it was also clear that women should be freed from housework and take part in the commune's labor roster. This clearly meant thinking in new ways about the family. "[Women] cannot shut themselves up within the bounds of the family at a time when general areas of activity touching on the entire commune and its society await both men and women," Meir Orlian wrote in 1941.[62]

True, many members of religious kibbutzim continued to view motherhood as the woman's most important role.[63] But not everyone agreed. Tzila, of Tirat Zvi, protested: "Why is it so clear that the woman's principal role is motherhood? . . . Let us hope that we can carry out the task that nature has placed on us, but also the other roles that society, the commune, and the security situation demand of us."[64] She did not reject motherhood, but refused to see it as her only role. She wished to devote herself also to the building of the nation. But her voice was a lone one. Unlike quite a few women in the secular kibbutzim—such as Miriam Baratz, Devorah Dayan, and Eva Tabenkin—who refused to renounce motherhood but claimed that motherhood alone was not enough, for most religious kibbutz women it went without saying that motherhood needed to be their top priority, for both traditional and national reasons.[65]

As it became more and more common for women to work outside the home, criticism of women who did so increased. The most prominent argument against it was the small families it engendered. "Women have begun to search for new areas of activity outside the family, out of an 'inferiority complex' that the roles filled by men are more important and superior," said one writer, who said that the result was the collapse of the family.[66]

Some charged that women delayed having families and gave birth to fewer children not out of feminist ideals of entering the workforce and participating in the building of the nation, but simply because such a life was easier and left them more time for leisure and intellectual activities. When what hung in the balance was, on the one side, having another child, and on the other the freedom to work, social activities, and an easier life, the latter won, Berman said.[67] Bourgeois city women were depicted as self-indulgent, spoiled, and addicted to comfort. Their low birthrate, Yocheved Bat-Rachel of the Council of Women Workers maintained, was the "result of pampering."[68] David Ben-Gurion, who criticized the low birthrate in the 1940s, stated forthrightly that women were evading their ancient responsibility, motherhood, because they wanted easier lives.[69]

No matter what the reason, Lilia Bassewitz said, women of her generation, even those who wanted children, could not permit themselves to have a baby every year or two. The physical and psychological burdens she faced were too great. She needed a longer time to rest up from each birth. It was hard to believe that a woman "would consent to having one child after another as their grandmothers had."[70]

Nevertheless, while many pioneer women, kibbutz women, and bourgeois city women did not see motherhood as the center of their lives, many others continued to devote themselves to their homes, either because they continued to hold by traditional gender roles or because the British administration, faced with high unemployment, promulgated legislation mandating that only one member of each family could enter the labor market. Of course, this was almost always the man. Women whose husbands worked were thus by law forbidden to so. But many married women nevertheless worked informally, at jobs that the administration could not easily keep track of. But this did not necessarily encourage larger families. The father's work was seen as active participation in the building of the land, and thus won him high prestige. Fathers were also perceived as having active and varied social lives, whereas mothers shouldered housework and childcare. "Diapers, cooking, laundry, and raising children" comprised "many little labors that crushed thought and made it impossible to concentrate," complained Yehudit of Kfar Yehoshua.[71] Such tasks were exhausting and debilitating and won women no social prestige. As opposed to previous generations, in which the work of motherhood was valued, at this time mothers had lost the crowns they once wore, the same woman lamented.[72] "The mother of children is looked on with some scorn. People see her as behind the times. She has no time to be an activist or to devote herself to a profession," Berman related.[73] Mothers who were not active in public life were valued less, she said in a letter to Ben-Gurion.[74] As mothers were not esteemed, women preferred not to be tied down to motherhood.

The ideal of the new woman—an educated woman who made her own livelihood, who sought time to pursue her own interests—required a reduction in the birthrate. But even women who accepted their traditional roles did not necessarily have more children.

Women were caught in a trap, one they find themselves in to this day. "In recent decades we have witnessed a process of women's emancipation and her entry into the workplace," Mayer said in 1944. It was "a very important process in and of itself—but we know very well how difficult it is to put the two things together—the woman as a professional and the woman as a mother."[75] The problem of how to combine motherhood and a career, still familiar today, was all the more acute then, in the absence of social programs to help women, such as maternity leave and day care. In the 1940s "we have yet to find a method that permits married women to integrate their work and home duties," Bachi wrote.[76] It was only natural that the direct result was ever-diminishing birthrates.

Did the pioneer imperative for women "to wear pants, shovel gravel, milk cows, and hoe the crops" come at the expense of childbirth, which was "the central artery of our lives, the soul of the people?" wondered Yehudit from Kfar Yehoshua.[77] The liberation of women was an important value in its own right, she maintained, but it impinged on another central value, that of child-birth. Mayer also saw the entry of women into public life as a blessing, but one injurious to natural increase, "because the proper tools and means needed for this change of values" had not yet been put in place.[78] In other words, the Yishuv found it difficult to incorporate changing gender roles. It had not prepared the ground for the transformation of women's lives. Women thus had to choose between work and family, between having several children and having abortions.

Pregnancy outside of Marriage

Pregnancy outside of marriage was a major reason women in the West had abortions.[79] European Jewish society was no different. From the beginning of the twentieth century, the number of abortions brought on by such pregnancies grew.[80] This was true of the Yishuv, too, where, as in the West, women also had abortions when marriages went bad, or when men abandoned women with children or partners during their first pregnancies.[81] In such cases, obviously, the lack of financial security was also a factor.[82]

Hedwig Gellner, head of the Tel Aviv municipality's social services de-partment, described the plight of unwed mothers, who required her office's assistance. It was difficult to locate fathers so that the burden of support could be placed on their shoulders as well she said, and when they could be found they often denied paternity.[83] There were other cases in which the man acknowledged that he and the woman were both responsible, but refused to be involved in raising the child. "I will never move to Hulata and will not es-tablish a family with you," one Shaul informed Gerda Cohen, a single woman from Kibbutz Hulata, when she notified him that she was pregnant. He told her to end the pregnancy.[84]

On top of this, the Yishuv remained conservative as a whole and frowned on premarital and extramarital relations. This is evident in the fact that such pregnancies and the children born of them were termed "illegal," even though there was no law on the books that forbade such liaisons.[85] Jewish law opposed sexual relations outside marriage, the Yishuv's chief Ashkenazi rabbi, Yitzhak Herzog, told Bachi and Abraham Fraenkel in a conversation about fighting against abortions. But he also said that "if a girl becomes preg-nant, it is a serious crime for her to have an abortion." She was required to have the child.[86] In other words, according to halakhah, an abortion was a worse crime than having a child outside marriage. But the Yishuv's attitudes were not based on Jewish law; rather, they grew out of conservative social attitudes and traditional attitudes toward the family and birth. "Society does not permit a single woman to raise a child, and she thus faces difficult conditions, leading to large numbers of abortions," Bachi wrote.[87] Relatively older women who had not married but became pregnant sometimes wished to have the child but nevertheless decided to abort, out of fear of what people would say.[88]

Henia Pekelman, a single woman worker, had very little money. She was raped and conceived. When the doctor informed her she was pregnant, it was a blow to her. "If it is true, I will kill myself," she wrote in her diary. She thought of drowning herself in the sea and tried to bring about an abortion by immersing herself in what she called "strong drugs," but without success.[89] Two voices debated inside her. One said: "You have no sanction to live. You have gone off the straight path. You have dishonored yourself, your women's honor. You are about to have a child against the faith of Moses and Israel." But the second voice argued that she had done no one any evil. "How can you murder the soul living within you? And who knows whether your child will not do more good in his life than a child born in accordance with the faith of Moses and Israel? You are still young and you must not end your life. What evil have you done? Why kill yourself? Because a despicable man abused you? If you die, the guilt will fall only on you. If you live, you will be able to take revenge. You must live only in order to seek vengeance."[90] With her mother's encouragement she decided to go through with the pregnancy. But the baby girl she gave birth to died a short time later.[91]

But many other women in this position sought abortions. "I was pregnant and wanted an abortion because I did not want my mother and sisters to hear about it," testified Yonah Tzadok, a nineteen-year-old single woman who became pregnant twice in the space of eight months, at the trial of the doctor who had performed two abortions on her and injured her in the process. "I was ashamed and frightened," she confessed. "I became pregnant to my boyfriend, Adel, an Arab driver."[92] She hid the pregnancy from him, too. In this case, the fact that the pregnancy resulted from premarital relations was further complicated because the liaison was between a Jewish woman and an Arab man, a relationship which the Yishuv decried for both moral and national reasons.

With abortions available, very few babies were born outside marriage.[93] Frankel noted that if the number of abortions were reduced, the number of babies born outside of marriage would increase.[94] But such cases seem not to have been a major cause of the Yishuv's low birthrate.[95]

Secularization

For centuries the Jewish people lived in accordance with halakhah and tradition. For this reason, Bachi argued, in the nineteenth century the Jews multiplied at a rate several times that of other European populations.[96] He considered religion to be the prime explanation for the high Jewish birthrate of the time. Having children is indeed an important and central Jewish precept. Jewish law forbids abortion except in extreme cases in which the mother's life is at risk.[97] But the secularization characteristic of that same century meant that halakhah's influence on the ways many Jews lived, and in particular on the number of children they had, diminished steadily. "As long as traditional values prevailed," Berman declared in one of her lectures, births outstripped deaths. But "now that those values have been destroyed, the birthrate is declining."[98]

The accelerating secularization of the nineteenth and twentieth centuries, in both Western and Eastern Europe, brought the Jewish birthrate down and the abortion rate up.[99] Having many children seemed to many Jews to be less important than it once had been, especially given that women were especially drawn to secular culture because it subverted traditional gender roles. It was the women who were the vanguard of assimilation in Eastern Europe.[100] Jews came to feel less bound by tradition as they increasingly received one or another level of secular education. According to a study conducted in England in 1947 that was widely reported in the Hebrew press, the more educated parents were, the fewer children they had.[101] Immigration also speeded up secularization, and was an important cause of the decline in the Jewish birthrate among European Jews who settled in the United States.[102]

In Palestine at the beginning of the twentieth century, Jews of European origin displayed a high fertility rate, mostly because of their adherence to religious tradition.[103] But this began to change quickly.[104] New immigrants arrived who were cut off from the communities in which they had grown up and from their extended families. They sought to create a new society, one quite different from that of the Diaspora. Jewish law no longer dictated how members of the Yishuv lived their lives, and as such the birthrate declined and, in particular, the abortion rate rose.[105]

Religious belief, wrote one newspaperman, was a source of optimism. A traditional Jew did not calculate how many children he could support with his income. He put his faith in his creator to help him. "But with the growth of critical thinking and a material view of the world, the bastion of faith has collapsed," the writer proclaimed. The secular Jew felt detached from community and insecure. He did his numbers, figuring his income and out-lays, and thus had fewer children.[106]

The demographic data offer proof of religion's effect on the birthrate. Pious Haredi Jews had, on average, more than five children during the Mandate period.[107] Men who worked in religious professions—for example, ritual circumcisers and slaughterers—had larger families.[108] Religious Zionists, on the other hand, who were full participants in the Zionist effort in the cities as well as in religious moshavim and kibbutzim, had fewer children.[109] In both religious and secular agricultural settlements, families had an average of two children in the 1940s.[110] This clearly shows that secularization was not the only cause of small families. Rather, the religious precept of having many children did not trump all other considerations even among religious Jews.

Nevertheless, despite rapid secularization, traditional views of the family's centrality and importance remained strong.[111] It was evident, for example, in the unquestioned assumption that couples should have children. I have found no evidence of any kind that men and women in long-term relationships sought not to have any children at all. Frankel could thus declare that "the nation's future does not depend on when a mother has her oldest (and perhaps only) child, but rather on how many children she has in total."[112]

The Modern Family

Modernization in all its aspects has also been credited with bringing the Yishuv birthrate down. First, it brought with it medical and technological developments that reduced the infant and child mortality rate, while also making it easier to avoid pregnancy and birth. Birth control devices became more effective and less expensive,[113] at the same time that abortions came to be done more professionally and thus became less risky. As one newspaper headline put it: "The benefit of less mortality has been overtaken by fewer births."[114] Scientists, it was charged, had not only refrained from battling the declining birthrate; they had actually encouraged it.[115]

The modernization of medicine came along with the adoption of modern ideas about society, and in particular about childbirth. The control of fertility came to be viewed as an expression of a person's control of his destiny, life, and future. The individual's ability, and responsibility, to shape his personal future is fundamental to modern culture.[116] For members of modern societies, birth control and family planning were ideas whose time had come.

Modernization also brought with it a new concept of the family. Social, economic, and cultural transformations during the nineteenth century created a new concept of the ideal family—one that included two children. This view of the family became a hallmark of modern Western society.[117]

The family with two children was the norm in Weimar Germany, and this was achieved in part by means of abortions.[118] The model was first adopted by the upper urban classes, then spread to lower classes, and then to rural areas. It was also taken up by Western European Jews. "The great majority of Jews, especially in Western countries, belong to those social classes that adhere most to the familiar standard of a pair of children (at most!)," wrote Katzenelson in 1929.[119] The ideal spread to Eastern Europe as well. In her memoir about her childhood, Alona Frankel wrote of how her mother, in Poland in the 1930s, underwent an abortion to remove twin fetuses from her womb. "My mother, as befit a salon-communist intellectual, condemned uncontrolled reproduction," Frankel related, "and like many in her milieu, preferred a single child."[120]

The concept that a modern family was a small family and that large families are primitive made its way into the Yishuv as well.[121] While the Yishuv sought to build a nation, it also aimed to establish a new and modern society. "The current fashion of the one or two-child system [*Ein/Zwei Kindersystem*]," as Bachi put it, was widespread in the Yishuv.[122] "The social *bon ton* of a maximum of two children is becoming the standard in this land, and disgracefully among the working public as well and in all our organizations, urban and rural," wrote a kibbutz woman in 1940.[123]

This fashion was a driving factor behind the rising abortion rate, as Berman showed in a survey she conducted.[124] It could be seen in cities and farming villages, as well as kibbutzim. Lilia Bassewitz of Ein Harod complained in 1934 about what she saw as the nefarious influence on her kibbutz of the bourgeois standard of small families. "May modernity not find expression among us," she wrote, "in the form of being dismissive of having children."[125]

Couples who had three, four, or more children, Bachi claimed, were considered "not modern."[126] The Yishuv's modern sector, the Committee on Birthrate Problems declared in April 1945, was that sector which used birth control and abortion to avoid having children.[127] The members of the committee, like many in the Yishuv, viewed modernity as a synonym for European culture. The modern family of no more than two children was thus a feature of the modern part of the Yishuv, that is, Jews who had come from Europe.[128]

While having few children was considered modern and European, having many was viewed as "uncultured" and characteristic largely of the Mizrahi community.[129] In the 1940s, observers like Bachi claimed that, while Mizrahim had in the past been known for their "unchecked fertility," they were increasingly emulating cultured Westerners when it came to keeping their families small. There was a natural phenomenon, Bachi thought, of "the assimilation of the primitive communities into more cultural ones," which brought about a drop in the birthrate.[130]

As far as the critics of birth control were concerned, the concept of the modern family was based on a desire for a higher standard of living and greater convenience. In the past, Berman remarked, people dressed differently, did not expect to have running hot water and central heating, and made do with simple furniture. In the 1940s, though, the standards had become much higher. Providing a child's needs cost a lot of money, meaning that a family who had an additional child would not be able to have the lifestyle they desired.[131] Convenience was a consideration even for those of means, Bachi maintained, who chose to have only one child "because it is easier."[132] It was the pursuit of pleasure that characterized many in the Yishuv that was keeping the birthrate low, some charged.[133] "We must openly express the concern about that European decadence regarding the birthrate that is eating away at us here as well," said a writer in the Zionist-religious daily Hatzofeh: "It unravels all that is natural and healthy in human beings, in the pursuit of vacuous, bogus, and distorted social and human ideas."[134]

Women were the main targets. They were accused of preferring pleasure over the motherhood that was their principal vocation, a vocation of critical national importance. "Will we ever become a majority in this land," asked a writer for Hamashkif in 1947, "or are we doomed to national oblivion— because of our women's desire for pleasure, passion for indulgences, and immorality?"[135] Modern mothers, the writer charge, "forget their duties and prefer a trouble-free lifestyle at the expense of the lives of their as-yet unborn children."[136]

Modernity also transformed the position of the child in the family. The twentieth century was to be the century of the child, notes sociologist Göran Therborn. During that century, children became rarer, more precious, more highly valued, and more powerful.[137] The drop in the birthrate in the West was caused in part by a desire to provide children with better educations.[138] Jews who left Europe for the United States—Jewish mothers in particular— wanted to grant their children the educations and other advantages that they had not received themselves in their large and poor families. They used birth control and abortion to achieve this.[139] This was not just a bourgeois phenomenon. Socialists also maintained that every child had the right to be born into a world in which he could grow up well. They thus advocated family planning in the name of ensuring equal opportunities to every child.[140]

In the Yishuv, too, the child became the focus of attention. Parents wanted to ensure that their children had everything. They wanted to grant "*fewer* children *greater* opportunities in life."[141] "The common view," Bachi wrote in 1943, "is that the child is the center of family life, and the requirements of his education are so inflated that parents have no way of bringing up more than one or two children." Indeed, many parents were concerned that the more children they had, the less they would be able to provide for each one.[142] This desire, Berman claimed, led families to make do with a single child, even "at the cost of his loneliness in the absence of a brother or sister and at the cost of the fate they impose on the only child to be a member of a nation that has always been an oppressed minority."[143] Here the child's standing as a minority in his family was explicitly paralleled to the Jewish people's status as a minority wherever they lived.

Insecurity

War can bring about demographic changes and shake the family, both while it is in progress and in the years that follow. "War destroys the best part of the population from a demographic point of view," Kanievsky wrote in 1944.[144] He meant the most fertile part of the population. In wartime, young men of fertile age (18–45) are away from home, often for years. Second, many of the victims of the war are young people, which affects the birthrate for years after the war ends. The absence of men, their loss, and the resulting surplus of women that results from war mean there are fewer marriages and fewer births. The two world wars, which killed tens of millions of people, also hugely depleted Europe's population. World War I led to a drastic plunge in the birthrate and a high abortion rate in Britain, Germany, Russia, and France.[145] One of the reasons for this may have been that people were unwilling to bring children into a world of want and violence.[146]

The Jewish population in Mandate Palestine felt physically insecure on both a communal and personal level. The national conflict between the Jews and Arabs intensified during this period, which was marked by outbreaks of violence. As a result, members of the Yishuv were apprehensive about having children.[147] A composition authored by a participant in a seminar in 1945 on the plummeting Yishuv birthrate stresses the effect of the security situation. She listed years and their crises: "1935—dark year. 1937—riots. 1939—war. 1940— tense situation on the El Alamein front." The Jews felt insecure, she wrote, while the mood among the Muslims was the opposite—they enjoyed political and economic confidence, which caused an increase in their birthrate.[148]

The disturbances of 1936–1939, the period of the Arab Revolt, are often cited in contemporary sources as a cause of the decline in the Yishuv birthrate,[149] exacerbating the already-low birthrate that began years before.[150] Toward the end of 1936, when the disturbances began, the Auerbach Maternity Home, a private hospital founded by Dr. Leo Arie Auerbach in Ramat Gan, just outside Tel Aviv, suddenly found itself with fewer patients.[151] Shoshana Bart, the daughter of the founder of a maternity home in Hadera, later recalled that the facility had empty beds during the disturbances.[152]

"Scary nights of attacks during the disturbances," Orlian wrote after Tirat Zvi was attacked by Arabs. "The evacuation of families with their children . . . , and the severing of family life for half a year" increased anxiety among young mothers and affected the fertility rate.[153] The decline in the number of children enrolling in first grade in Tel Aviv's schools in 1943 was a direct result of the contraction of the birthrate in 1937, during the Arab insurrection.[154]

The end of the disturbances segued into the beginning of World War II, meaning no letup in anxiety for many years. The birthrate reached a nadir.[155] A German invasion of Palestine seemed quite possible until the Germans were defeated in North Africa in the autumn of 1942. Italian airplanes bombed Tel Aviv at the start of the war. The Yishuv's Jews reacted by not bringing children into the world, and by having abortions when pregnancy occurred.[156] In 1939–1941, fertility among Jewish families of European origin was so low that Bachi feared that the future of the Yishuv was at stake.[157]

An organization, apparently the Ezra Association: Maternity Aid for Palestine, reported in 1940 about the dilemma. On the one hand, the need to assist women bearing children increased because of the growing number of refugees reaching Palestine's shores. Some of these were pregnant women who had managed to get to Palestine after losing their husbands. On the other hand, the capacity for helping them had weakened, as fewer donations from overseas were coming in after the war broke out.[158]

In 1943, when the front moved away from Palestine and people felt secure again, the birthrate recovered somewhat—a process evident in the next two years, and influenced by the return of soldiers to their families after long service in the British army.[159] However, the war was, as Bachi put it, but a side effect in a process that had begun long before. Security was only one factor affecting the birthrate.[160] The recovery was thus short lived.

Nationalism and Socialism as Depressors of the Birthrate

Increasing the birthrate was a national imperative. Restricting it was seen as an injury to the nation and an obstacle to achieving the goals of the Zionist movement, which aspired to create a Jewish majority in Palestine. On the other hand, the building, settlement, and development of the country were vital national missions, of unequaled importance, which required the mobilization of all available forces. Having children, which demanded devotion and effort, was shunted to the sidelines by that part of the Yishuv that sought to realize national goals that it saw as the top priorities. As Yehudit, a moshav woman put it, many young people had come to Palestine. They were fired up "with desire to build the land. They are all young, enthusiastic, the family has been ejected . . . from its top position, and in its stead has come idealism."[161] This view was primarily common among the socialist-Zionist pioneers who sought to settle the far corners of the land.

Even before World War I some pioneers who had recently arrived announced their opposition to marriage and the establishment of families which, they maintained, would tie them down and interfere with their total devotion to the national mission they had taken upon themselves.[162] They saw the establishment and stabilization of kibbutzim as the primary national goal, and the path by which the country would be built. They thus sought to put off the establishment of families. When couples formed, the communes demanded that they not have children, or restrict their number.

"It was clear to both of us that we would be a family," wrote Chaya Yisraeli, a founder of Kvutzat Kinneret. But, she noted, she and her lover each lived their own lives. The harsh conditions and the desire to strengthen the kibbutz pushed aside their personal desires.[163] After he was wounded during the war, the two of them decided that they had to have a child, but they did all they could to keep the pregnancy a secret, knowing that the commune would oppose it.[164]

Such opposition to the birth of children grew out of both ideology and the difficult physical conditions I have portrayed, and continued in the 1920s. "I was not all that happy to receive the news of Bella's pregnancy," one kibbutznik recounted. "I felt uncomfortable with the commune, and accused myself of a kind of betrayal of the idea. Could it really be that a dedicated and loyal pioneer like me would impose additional concerns on the collective?"[165] He, too, tried to keep his partner's pregnancy a secret, fearing how it would be received by his friends. "It was contrary to the accepted mores of those times."[166]

The pioneers were utterly committed to the project of building a new Jewish nation, but they were also ideological socialists, especially those who chose kibbutz life. Their socialism meant subordinating the good of the individual to that of the collective, and this too depressed the birthrate. Establishing a family, they worried, would impinge on the consolidation of the collective. Couples with children would focus on the needs of their children rather than the imperatives of the collective. Furthermore, their brand of socialism proclaimed that the traditional nuclear family was a bourgeois, hierarchical institution that oppressed women and stood in the way of the establishment of a new collective, egalitarian, and moral society.[167] For this reason the kibbutzim deliberately dismantled the traditional family. Children belonged to the entire collective and were raised in children's houses rather than in their parents' homes. All decisions about their care and education were made by the commune. The commune also made the decisions about whether and when to bring children into the world. In the view of the pioneers, the kibbutz as a whole needed to make such decisions in accordance with the common kibbutz and national needs.[168]

But socialism, with its stress on the liberation of the individual from established social convention and constraints, could also lead in the other direction. A socialist pioneer could thus declare that "every man and every woman has the right to determine freely not only *when* they wish to have a child but also *with whom* they wish to have the child."[169] Thus, even though they accepted that the collective could place its interests over those of its individual members, the pioneers also believed that a woman had full rights over her own body. It was this right that also granted legitimacy to abortion.

Socialists and revolutionaries advocated for a woman's right to abort not just in the Yishuv but around the world. In Germany, the campaign against the law forbidding abortion "is not just the battle of the working woman in general, but the battle of the movement of socialist working women," Dr. Rivkai wrote.[170] Socialist and anarchist leaders of the early twentieth century pointed to the double burden that women bore as workers and mothers and demanded that they have access to effective and inexpensive means of birth control. This was a precondition of the emancipation of women, they claimed.[171] But even more central to this battle was the disparity between the availability of abortions to different classes. Socialists condemned the upper classes' monopoly over the means of controlling birth, which left the working class in an inferior position.[172] They viewed legal restrictions on abortion as a form of class oppression. Well-off women could afford safe abortions but their poor counterparts could not. Feminists viewed the ban on abortions as patriarchal oppression, while for socialists it was a form of class oppression, an injustice that had to be removed in order to achieve social equality.[173]

Socialist women in the Yishuv's cities and kibbutzim took this position and advocated the legalization of abortion. First, they argued, women had the sovereign right to make decisions about their own bodies; second, abortions had to be equally available to the bourgeoisie and the working class. In the 1930s, working class women demanded the repeal of the law that imposed sanctions on a woman who ended her pregnancy and demanded that, instead, the law explicitly legitimize abortions. "Is it right that a woman worker who earns P£2 per month has to borrow money to enable herself to end a pregnancy?" asked one such worker in the early 1930s.[174] The abortion law, she and others like her argued, imposed a burden on thousands of women. Rather than preventing them from seeking abortions, it forced them to seek out nonprofessionals to perform them.[175]

Women workers looked first at their needs and proclaimed that legal abortions were necessary to ensure equal rights for women. They also decried all external pressure imposed on women in this regard, whether by their male partners or by society. A woman writing in *Devar Hapo'elet*, the organ of working class women in the Yishuv, asserted that a woman who wished to end her pregnancy "has the right to determine her fate and her life. But it must be *her internal* decision and society must not make rules about it. No legal code determines how much time should pass between one birth and another and what the right number of children is for a 'cultured' family."[176] Each woman needs to be trusted to make this difficult decision for themselves. After all, the psychological and physical pain involved will be felt by her, not others.

Lilia Bassewitz took the same position. "It is clear that a woman has the right to decide when she will have a child," this kibbutz woman maintained. "No man will determine or decide that for her."[177] Women should not permit anyone, not even the public as a whole, to decide this for her, Bassewitz maintained, because "who knows when a woman needs a child and what psychological factors operate within her during different periods of her life and which make a child a necessity in her life."[178] In other words, she placed the woman and her feelings at the heart of the issue.

The complexities of Yishuv socialism, which demanded on the one hand devotion to the collective while on the other hand advocated individual freedom led to situations in which, for example, a kibbutz might order a woman member to end her pregnancy and encounter her refusal to do so. Arela Lamdan tells what happened when her mother, a founder of her kibbutz, became pregnant. The commune's administrator informed her that the commune had decided that there should be no births at this time and that she thus must get an abortion. "Mother told me that she heard him out politely and decided to continue with the pregnancy."[179] Nor did all socialist-Zionist women see abortion in a positive light. Rachel Katznelson-Shazar, a founder of the Council of Women Workers and one of the Yishuv's leading advocates of women's rights, maintained that the decision to have an abortion was an intimate one that a woman should make on her own, but also termed abortion "a woman's violence against herself."[180] Lilia Bassewitz also opposed abortions in principle, but she nevertheless campaigned for their legalization.[181]

For members of the Religious Kibbutz Movement the issue was even more complex. Rather than rejecting tradition, they sought to integrate it into their revolutionary new lives. "To speak of tradition in family life at a time when we have shattered tradition in economic life," wrote Meir Orlian, "is like breaking the barrel and keeping the wine."[182]

The Holocaust

The Holocaust's effect on the Yishuv and its birthrate was unlike any other. The murder of millions of Jews, including family members and friends of many Jews living in Palestine, caused enormous personal and collective pain. Beyond that, it threatened the achievement of the Zionist project, which had seen European Jewry as a reservoir of immigrants who would bring about a Jewish majority in Palestine. In its wake, Yishuv leaders began to use harsh language to condemn birth control and abortion. Yet, at the same time, the Holocaust also had the effect of lowering the birthrate.

The Holocaust decimated world Jewry and made its demographic future look problematic in the extreme.[183] The Yishuv, built largely on immigration from Europe, feared for its future. In the decade from 1935 to 1945 very few Jewish children were born in Europe, and most of those who were born were murdered by the Nazis. In April 1945, as the war was coming to an end, the Committee on Birthrate Problems estimated that the birthrate among survivors of the Holocaust would be very low.[184] "If the adults who have survived manage to establish a new generation before they reach old age," Bachi said, "it will be a miracle, one that will not happen of its own accord."[185]

The Yishuv assumed that the survivors would be physically broken and psychologically shattered.[186] "If it were possible to bring the remnants to Palestine soon," one newspaper argued in the summer of 1945, "there would be a chance of quickening their recovery. But we should not place any hopes in them regarding natural increase."[187]

But this forecast turned out to be only partially correct. On April 18, 1945, at the displaced persons camp into which the Bergen-Belsen concentration camp had been converted following liberation, two first post-Holocaust children were born. The mothers, one from Vilna and the second from Kovno (Kaunas), had spent the war years in ghettoes and concentration camps. While both children were born orphaned of their fathers, who had not survived, everyone in the camp rejoiced.[188] The long process of the rehabilitation of the survivors had begun, and part of it was a large wave of new babies.

Most of the displaced persons camps, or DP camps, in Europe were located in the American zone of occupation in Germany (although Bergen-Belsen was in the British zone), and it was at these camps that many of the survivors lived initially after the war. The marriage rate was high. Most of the survivors were single men and women in their twenties and thirties, whose families had been murdered. Couples began to form at the DP camps. Finding a partner and starting families was a way for them to cope with the loss they had experienced and to extricate themselves from the depression that followed the war. They saw these new families as in some sense a replacement for the families they had lost and a foundation for a new life. They expected not to find eternal love but rather to establish a family, and to have children quickly before it was too late.[189]

Some sources describe a large measure of sexual freedom in the camps, following years of oppression and suffering. Many women became pregnant after refusing to accept the birth control devices offered them by American soldiers.[190] But other sources paint a very different picture. "The young boys and girls," recounted a survivor, Sabina Shweid, "who had been left alone, without parents, siblings, or other family, longed for closeness. They did not seek only physical closeness, not just sex, but rather family closeness." The result was "wedding fever."[191] Religious survivors viewed establishing a family as a religious duty and social imperative so as to ensure the survival of tradition.[192] "They are delighted to amuse a baby in their arms and to see that the chain of their physical being has not been severed," wrote Dr. Walter Falk, a leading Yishuv and Israeli pediatrician.[193]

In fact, the survivors in the DP camps had one of the highest birthrates in the world in the years 1946–1948. By the end of 1946, some thousand Jewish babies had been born in the British zone of occupation in northwestern Germany, some 200 of them in Bergen-Belsen.[194] In February 1947 the birthrate at the DP camps in Germany was 60 per 1,000 people, "and that is today the record high birthrate for all of Europe," *Davar* reported.[195] In November 1947 *Hatzofeh* reported that some 660 babies were being born each month in the DP camps in the American zone.[196] By the beginning of 1948, 1,000 babies had been born at the Bergen-Belsen DP camp,[197] and that same year the birthrate among survivors in the American zone reached 35.8 per 1,000, the highest rate in the West at that time.[198]

The birthrate was also high at the detention camps in Cyprus, where survivors who had tried to get into Palestine only to be turned away by the British were held. In 1947, it was sixty babies per month, wrote the pediatrician Dr. Falk in his letters from these camps. The baby houses there are very crowded and the conditions in them harsh, he noted.[199]

"People are observing the precept of life," wrote one Yishuv newspaper, viewing the high birthrate in the camps as a manifestation of the huge powers of the survivors.[200] "Having children is the greatest and most persuasive demonstration of Jewish vitality," another newspaper declared.[201]

But the high birthrate among survivors in the DP camps did not necessarily translate into large families. The opposite is the case. The birth statistics relating to Holocaust survivors in Israel, collected some fifteen years after the war ended, showed that "there are only two children for every 3.75 adults, such that every survivor couple, after their death, will leave behind only a single descendant."[202] A survey of a sample of survivor families in Israel showed that half of them had had two children and 9 percent had had just one.[203]

There were a variety of reasons for this phenomenon. "The survivors of the Holocaust, the embers saved [from the fire] who gathered from all the torture camps and places of destruction, were mostly male, because all Jewish women, like Jewish children, were eliminated in the early stages of the annihilation as 'unproductive elements,'" *Davar* reported, noting this fact's implications for the birthrate.[204] Indeed, mothers were often murdered with their children. The loneliness of survivors left without families was exacerbated by the gender imbalance among them. That also led to intermarriage with non-Jews. Fewer Jews were born because of the gender imbalance, and given that Jewish religious law does not recognize as Jewish the child of a mother who is not Jewish.[205]

In the ghettoes, the Germans had forbidden births, and for many women pregnancy was tantamount to a death sentence.[206] Some of them tried to have an abortion under harsh conditions. Gisele Perl, a Jewish gynecologist incarcerated at Auschwitz-Birkenau, testified that she performed abortions secretly to save the lives of women.[207] As a girl during the war, Sabina Shweid absorbed this dread of pregnancy. After reaching Palestine, it reappeared. "My life was no longer as it had been. I knew for certain that I did not want children. A child would be a catastrophe, I wept in my heart! What would I do if, God forbid, I became pregnant? . . . Mother had an abortion during the war . . . I do not want to become pregnant, have a child, or have an abortion."[208]

Those women who did survive were sometimes, by the time the war ended, close to or after their fertile years. Others were young but some of them had undergone "medical" experiments in the camps that left them sterile.[209] Most of these women were unable to become pregnant and give birth.

Harsh living conditions, first in the DP camps and then in Palestine, made life difficult for many survivors. Bachi tempered his elation at the high birthrate with skepticism about whether the trend would continue once the survivors left the camps "and would have to earn their livings in normal conditions."[210] A number of welfare organizations, such as the UN Relief and Rehabilitation Association, or UNRRA, operated in the camps and did their best to assist the survivors. When people left the camps they had to fend for themselves, even as their journey into a peaceful and secure life had not yet ended. Survivors who went to Palestine in the years following the end of the world war obdurately chose an exhausting and dangerous path. When they arrived, they quickly encountered economic and security threats in their Promised Land, a situation that continued after Israel was established.

Life was difficult in the Yishuv after the war and in Israel's early years, and this, too, depressed their birthrate. Furthermore, for many in the Yishuv, not just the survivors, the Holocaust served as a warning sign against having too large a family. The more children a family had, the harder it was to flee, hide, and feed them in times of crisis. For reasons of pure survival, better to have fewer children.[211]

The Holocaust also had another effect. Yishuv families often stood alone. Their extended families had in many cases been annihilated. Tova Berman wrote about the plight of mothers buckling under the heavy burden of keeping house and raising children after coming home following a hospital birth. This was especially difficult in lone families where there were no grandmothers, mothers, or other relatives who could take over some of the work from the mother in the period following the birth.[212] The absence of support from an extended family also encouraged a rise in the abortion rate.[213]

Europe and the United States experienced a baby boom after the war. In the United States the Holocaust spurred Jewish families to have more children, beginning in the 1940s and lasting through the 1970s.[214] In the Yishuv the response was different. After a brief recovery in the birthrate, it again dropped in response to difficult conditions and political and military uncertainty. "We look for an enhanced birthrate because our lives depend on it," Yocheved Bat-Rachel wrote in 1945.[215] It had never been truer.

Conclusion

"The birthrate question is highly multifaceted," the Committee on Birthrate Problems stated in a report to the National Council in April 1945. "A variety of factors, health-related and demographic, social and economic, moral and religious, affect it."[216] This chapter has shown that that was indeed the case, both with regard to the birthrate and with regard to abortions. Some of the factors were universal, common to the entire West, while others were local and unique. But only rarely did any of these causes operate in isolation. In general, several causes acted simultaneously in determining specific decisions to restrict reproduction. Furthermore, the factors were mutually interdependent and operated on each other. Immigration affected the economic situation and brought Western concepts to Palestine, which developed and intensified against the local background. The security situation affected the economy; secular education and secularization, which caused the birthrate to decline, led to a change in the status of women, which itself affected the birthrate. Bachi summed it up best: "It could be said that the economic difficulties in the Land of Israel, the tragic situation in the Diaspora, the disturbances [in Palestine] and the [world] war further constrict an already constricted birthrate."[217]

It is not simple to determine whether any single cause was dominant. Bachi admitted as much in 1943, when he wrote that "the factors leading to a decline in natural increase along national lines are not sufficiently clear. Several of them can be enumerated, but it cannot be said with certainty that one or another factor is the determining and decisive one."[218] Berman maintained that the birthrate had declined principally because of abortions, which were motivated, in the Yishuv as in the rest of the world, primarily by economic issues.[219] The second most important reason, Berman believed, was women's desire to live freely and participate in public life, rather than being tied to her home.[220] But Bachi believed that the principal reason for the ongoing decline in the Yishuv birthrate lay in "the multiplication of the number of people in the less fertile social strata who arrived in Palestine in the mass immigration from Europe in the years 1932–1940."[221] In other words, he blamed intensive immigration from Western Europe during the 1930s.

Some other factors were clearly less influential. For example, Jewish religious practice and religious law did not have a great effect. The effect of trends from the West was very clear, and the Yishuv was quick to adopt the mores of the modern world. But in the Yishuv a unique set of extreme circumstances, among them immigration, the local conflict, and the trauma of the Holocaust, came together in a way that made the birthrate crisis far more intense and complex than it was elsewhere in the West.[222]

"The difficult conditions in which the country is being built," Bachi related, "the lack of any social assistance to encourage births, and a general atmosphere opposed to large families . . . have had their effect. The new Land of Israel has not only failed to make a contribution to the Jewish people's demographic rehabilitation; it has actually exacerbated it."[223]

But, according to Bachi, there was another reason for the low birthrate, beyond those discussed in this chapter. "There was no public opposition to the mass use of abortions by married women," he noted.[224] That is the subject of the next chapters.

NOTES

1. Tova Berman, "Ha'Emtza'im haDerushim le'Idud haYeludah baYishuv," Feb. 1945, CZA J1/3717/3; Tova Berman in a program for a radio talk for a week devoted to birthrate issues, July 1944, CZA J1/3717/2; minutes of a meeting of the Committee on Birthrate Problems, June 22, 1943, CZA J1/3717/1.

2. Dr. Sadowski, minutes of a meeting of the Committee on Birthrate Problems, June 22, 1943, CZA J1/3717/1.

3. Program for a radio talk for a week devoted to birthrate issues, July 1944, CZA J1/3717/2.

4. Kibbutz member, "Lo Zo haDerekh," *Devar Hapo'elet*, 7:1, Mar. 31, 1940, 27.

5. Dr. Sadowski, minutes of a meeting of the Committee on Birthrate Problems, June 22, 1943, CZA J1/3717/1.

6. Program for a radio talk for a week devoted to birthrate issues, July 1944, CZA J1/3717/2.

7. Dr. Y. Rivkai, "LaPsikhologiyah Shel ha'Imahut Etzleinu," *Ha'em Vehayeled*, 1935, 47–48.

8. Minutes of a meeting of the Committee on Birthrate Problems, June 22, 1943, CZA J1/3717/1.

9. Ze'ev (Wolfgang) von Weisl, "Me'et ha'Elef She'avdu Lanu LaNetzah," *Hamashkif*, Oct. 10, 1947, 3.

10. Lilia [Bassewitz], "Isha, Em Vayeled," *Mibifnim*, Apr. 1933, 13.

11. Letter from Dr. Tova Berman to David Ben-Gurion, May 10, 1944, CZA J1/3717/3; Dr. Tova Berman, Lecture on the Politics of Births, June 17, probably early 1940s, CZA A516/165.

12. Lilia [Bassewitz], "Isha, Em Vayeled," *Mibifnim*, Apr. 1933, 17–18.

13. Dr. Y. Rivkai, "LaPsikhologiyah Shel ha'Imahut Etzleinu," *Ha'em Vehayeled*, 1935, 48.

14. Program for a radio talk for a week devoted to birthrate issues, July 1944, CZA J1/3717/2.

15. Tova Berman, text for the mock trial on birthrate problems, 1943, CZA J1/3717/1

16. Letter from Dr. Tova Berman to David Ben-Gurion, May 10, 1944, CZA J1/3717/3; Yocheved Bat-Rachel, "De'agat HaImahut," Merkaz Kupat Holim, Jan. 1945, YTA, 15-36/4/4, 7.

17. Yocheved Bat-Rachel, "De'agat HaImahut," Merkaz Kupat Holim, Jan. 1945, YTA, 15-36/4/4, 11–12.

18. Tova Berman, "Ha'Emtza'im haDerushim le'Idud haYeludah baYishuv," Feb. 1945, CZA J1/3717/3.

19. Kibbutz member, "Lo Zo haDerekh," *Devar Hapo'elet*, 7:1, Mar. 31, 1940, 27.

20. Program for a radio talk for a week devoted to birthrate issues, July 1944, CZA J1/3717/2.

21. Tova Berman, "Ha'Emtza'im haDerushim le'Idud haYeludah baYishuv," Feb. 1945, CZA J1/3717/3.

22. Dr. Tova Berman, Lecture on the Politics of Births, June 17, probably early 1940s, CZA A516/165; program for a radio talk for a week devoted to birthrate issues, July 1944, CZA J1/3717/2.

23. Minutes of a meeting of the Committee on Birthrate Problems, June 22, 1943, CZA J1/3717/1.

24. Ibid.

25. Abrams 2002, 164, 167, 172–173; Klapper 2013.

26. On the feminist approach to abortion and its complexity, see Ir-Shai 2008, 423–428; Moran Hajo 2012, 2; Rimalt 2010, 138–142.

27. Rosenbaum 2011, 253; Abrams 2002, 110.

28. Coser, Anker, and Perrin 1999, 7.

29. Reagan 1997, 110.

30. Maloy and Patterson 1992; Gantz 2003; Andorka 1978; McRae 1991; Jungho 2010.

31. Taylor Allen 2008; Grossmann 1995, 6.

32. For example, Katvan and Halperin-Kedari 2011.

33. Bachi 1944, 163.

34. Bernstein 2013, 87.

35. Hedwig Gellner, "Sekirah 'al 10 Shanim shel 'Avodah Sotziyalit beT"A," submitted to Mayor Rokach of Tel Aviv, Sept. 12, 1943, TAA 4-1427.

36. Ibid.

37. Tova Berman, "Ha'Emtza'im haDerushim le'Idud haYeludah baYishuv," Feb. 1945, CZA J1/3717/3.

38. Tova Berman, "'Al Be'ayot haYeludah," apparently 1943, CZA A516/100.

39. Dr. B. Grinfeld, lecture for the Mother and Child Committee, Feb. 1934, CZA J1/3081.

40. Lilia [Bassewitz], "Isha, Em Vayeled," *Mibifnim*, Apr. 1933, 15.

41. Tova Berman, Reasons for termination of pregnancy, Table 1, Jan. 1944, CZA A516/181.

42. Tova Berman, text for the mock trial on birthrate problems, 1943, CZA J1/3717/1.

43. Ibid.

44. Dr. Tova Berman, lecture on the politics of births, June 17, probably early 1940s, CZA A516/165.

45. Ibid.

46. Dr. Y. Rivkai, "Lapsikhologiyah shel ha'Imahut Etzleinu," *Ha'em Vehayeled*, 1935, 50.

47. Hemda Nofech, "Mah Hen Sevurot beShe'elat ha'Ishah haModernit beE"Y," *Tesha' Ba'erev*, 7, Apr. 22, 1937 (n.p.).

48. Polia, "Be'Ikvot Reshimah Ahat," *Devar Hapo'elet*, Aug. 25, 1935, 124.

49. Yocheved Bat-Rachel, "De'agat HaImahut," Merkaz Kupat Holim, Jan. 1945, YTA, 15-36/4/4, 5.

50. Sinai 2013, 151.

51. Dr. Y. Rivkai, "LaPsikhologiyah shel ha'Imahut Etsleinu," *Ha'em Vehayeled*, 1935, 48.

52. Batya, (no title), *Mibifnim*, 52, Nov. 23, 1931, 5.

53. Ibid.

54. Sinai 2003, 79–80.

55. Tsur and Yisra'eli 1985, 130.

56. Ibid.

57. Fogiel-Bijaoui 1991.

58. Letter from Dr. Tova Berman to David Ben-Gurion, May 10, 1944, CZA J1/3717/3.

59. Rivka Liss, in Tsur, Zevulun, and Porat 1981, 280.

60. Tova Berman, Reasons for termination of pregnancy, table 1, Jan. 1944, CZA A516/181.

61. Kaminski 2012; Lilia Bassewitz, a meeting of women on women's hygiene issues, July 1933, YTA 15-28/14/1, 5-6.

62. Meir Orlian, "HaTipul haMeshutaf," *'Alonim*, Summer 1941, 10.

63. Gdalya, (no title), *Batirah*, 27, May 20, 1938 (n.p.).

64. Tsila, "Leshe'elat haTilboshet," *Batirah*, 31, June 24, 1938, 8. Women writing in kibbutz publications typically used only their first names.

65. Sinai 2013, 153.

66. H. Sh. Halevy, "'Al Medukhat haYeludah haYerudah," *Hamashkif*, July 18, 1943, 2.

67. Letter from Dr. Tova Berman to David Ben-Gurion, May 10, 1944, CZA J1/3717/3.

68. Yocheved Bat-Rachel, "De'agat HaImahut," Merkaz Kupat Holim, Jan. 1945, YTA, 15-36/4/4, 7.

69. David Ben-Gurion, "Shalosh He'arot," *Hapo'el Hatza'ir* 27, Mar. 18, 1947, 2.

70. Lilia [Bassewitz], "Isha, Em Vayeled," *Mibifnim*, Apr. 1933, 16–17.

71. Yehudit, "LeShalosh He'arot Shel Ben-Gurion," *Hapo'el Hatza'ir* 47, Aug. 12, 1943, 25.

72. Ibid.

73. Program for a radio talk for a week devoted to birthrate issues, July 1944, CZA J1/3717/2.

74. Letter from Dr. Tova Berman to David Ben-Gurion, May 10, 1944, CZA J1/3717/3.

75. Program for a radio talk for a week devoted to birthrate issues, July 1944, CZA J1/3717/2.

76. Bachi 1943a, 15.

77. Yehudit, "LeShalosh He'arot Shel Ben-Gurion," *Hapo'el Hatza'ir* 47, Aug. 12, 1943, 25.

78. Ibid.

79. Hoffer and Hull 2010, 49–50.

80. Ruppin 1934, 160–63.

81. Binah Velfish, "'Al 'Inyan she'ein Medabrim Bo," *Davar*, Apr. 27, 1938, 3; minutes of a meeting of the Committee on Birthrate Problems, June 22, 1943, CZA J1/3717/1; Margalit-Stern 2011, 195. On the increase in the abandonment of spouses, see Razi 2009, 86–90.

82. Miriam Aharonova, "'Uvdot meHadar 'Avodatah shel Rofah," *Devar Hapo'elet* 9, Nov. 27, 1934. For more information, see Shvarts and Stoler-Liss 2011.

83. Hedwig Gellner, "Sekirah 'al 10 Shanim shel 'Avodah Sotziyalit beT"A," submitted to Mayor Rokach of Tel Aviv, Sept. 12, 1943, TAA 4-1427

84. Cohen 2001, 129.

85. Dr. Arieh (Leib) Sadowski, minutes of a meeting of the Committee on Birthrate Problems, June 22, 1943, CZA J1/3717/1; minutes of a meeting of the Committee on Birthrate Problems, Sept. 21, 1943, CZA J1/3717/2.

86. Memorandum from a meeting with Rabbi Yitzhak Herzog, Prof. Abraham Fraenkel, and Prof. Roberto Bachi, 1943 (no specific date), CZA J1/3717/2.

87. Minutes of a meeting of the Committee on Birthrate Problems, Sept. 21, 1943, CZA J1/3717/2.

88. Letter from Dr. Tova Berman to David Ben-Gurion, May 10, 1944, CZA J1/3717/3; report by Dr. Tova Berman, Feb. 16, 1945, CZA J1/3717/3.

89. Pekelman 1935, 121.

90. Ibid., 122.

91. Ibid., 123, 143.

92. "Edutah haDramatit shel Yonah Tzadok," (no byline) *Do'ar Hayom*, Apr. 5, 1936, 4, 8.

93. Minutes of a meeting of the Committee on Birthrate Problems, Sept. 21, 1943, CZA J1/3717/2; Bachi 1944, 111.

94. Minutes of a meeting of the Committee on Birthrate Problems, Sept. 21, 1943, CZA J1/3717/2.

95. Dr. Avraham Katzenelson, in ibid.; Tova Berman, Reasons for termination of pregnancy, Table 1, Jan. 1944, CZA A516/181.

96. Roberto Bachi, radio talk, 1943, CZA J1/3717/1.

97. Ir-Shai 2008, 437–439.

98. Dr. Tova Berman, lecture on the politics of births, June 17, probably early 1940s, CZA A516/165.

99. Weeks 1999; Chatterjee and Riley 2001; Mendelson 1976, 178, 190.

100. Hyman 1997, 49–63.

101. Eli'ezer Levinshtein, "Be'ayot Sotsiyaliot Hadashot," *Davar*, Feb. 25, 1947, 2.

102. Exler 2000, 82–84; Bachi 1943a, 8. On Jewish immigrant women and their attitude to religion and secularization, see also Hyman 1997, 123; Stahl Weinberg 1988, 17.

103. Roberto Bachi, "He'arot 'Al haMegamot haDemografiyot ba'Olam uveArtseinu, ve'al ha-Mediniyut haDemografit beYisra'el," apparently 1957, CZA A516/210.

104. Rosenberg-Friedman 2012.

105. "Be'ayat haYeludah baYishuv" (no byline, apparently Bachi), Apr. 12, 1943, *Ha'aretz* (n.p.), CZA J1/3737/1.

106. H. Sh. Halevy, "'Al Medukhat haYeludah haYerudah," *Hamashkif*, July 16, 1943, 4.

107. *Lu'ah ha'Aretz LiShnat Tashad* (1944), 184; Bachi 1941, 14.

108. Bachi 1943a, 15.

109. P. I., interview with the author, Apr. 10, 2012; Bachi 1944, 242; Rosenberg-Friedman 2013, 62–65.

110. "HaYiten haYishuv leMi'ut haYeludah Livloa' et Hesegeinu be'Aliyah?" (no byline), *Davar*, Jan. 26, 1944, 4.

111. Razi 2010.

112. Fraenkel 1944, 18.

113. H. Sh. Halevy, "'Al Medukhat haYeludah haYerudah," *Hamashkif*, July 18, 1943, 2.

114. "HaYiten ha Yishuv leMi'ut haYeludah Livloa' et Hesegeinu be'Aliyah?" (no byline), *Davar*, Jan. 26, 1944, 4.

115. H. Sh. Halevy, "'Al Medukhat haYeludah haYerudah," *Hamashkif,* July 18, 1943, 2.
116. Therborn 2004, 241.
117. Woycke 1988; Andorka 1978, 18–20.
118. Grossmann 1995, 70.
119. Katzenelson 1929.
120. Frankel 2004, 33.
121. Memorandum from Hadassah's Statistics Department with regard to Dr. Rivlin's letter (from Jan. 1, 1939) Mar. 1939 (precise date not given), CZA J113/2312.
122. Bachi 1943a, 6.
123. Kibbutz member, "Lo Zo haDerekh," *Devar Hapo'elet* 7:1, Mar. 31, 1940, 27; letter from Dr. Shoshana Meir to the Health Department of the National Council, May 20, 1940, CZA J1/3717/1.
124. Report by Dr. Tova Berman, Feb. 16, 1945, CZA J1/3717/3.
125. L. B., "Isha, Em Vayeled," *Ha'em Vehayeled,* 1933–1934, 177.
126. Bachi 1943a, 15.
127. Committee on Birthrate Problems, "Tokhnit lePolitikah Demografit," Apr. 22, 1945, CZA J1/2383.
128. For example, Tova Berman expressed this perception when she referred to Kupat Holim's well-baby clinics, which were patronized mostly by Ashkenazi women. These women, she said, were on a "higher cultural and economic level" than the Mizrahi sector. Dr. Tova Berman, lecture on "HaTipul haMonea' ba'Em uvaYeled, 1949–1954," at a gathering of Kupat Holim pediatricians, (no date), CZA A516/175.
129. Roberto Bachi, "Be'ayat haYeludah BeYisra'el veHatza'ot leMediniyut haUkhlusiyah," undated, ISA 5588/2c.
130. Bachi 1943a, 19.
131. Program for a radio talk for a week devoted to birthrate issues, July 1944, CZA J1/3717/2.
132. Bachi 1943a, 20.
133. Dr. Ze'ev von Weisl, "HaYeludah bein haYehudim Haitah vaNemukhah beYoter," *Hamashkif,* July 18, 1941, 3.
134. Ben Bracha, "BeAspaklariyah," *Hatzofeh,* June 18, 1941, 2.
135. Ze'ev (Wolfgang) von Weisl, "Me'et ha'Elef She'avdu Lanu LaNetsah," *Hamashkif,* Oct. 10, 1947, 3.
136. Ibid.
137. Therborn 2004, 227.
138. Dr. Tova Berman, lecture on birthrate politics, June 17, probably early 1940s, CZA A516/165.
139. Weinberg 1988, 183, 222, 224; Coser, Anker, and Perrin 1999, 52.
140. Spargo 1914, 13.
141. Emphasis in original. "Be'ayat haYeludah baYishuv" (no byline, apparently Bachi), Apr. 12, 1943, *Ha'aretz* (n.p.), CZA J1/3737/1.
142. Bachi 1943a, 15; L. B., "Isha, Em Vayeled," *Ha'em Vehayeled,* 1933–1934, 177.
143. Program for a radio talk for a week devoted to birthrate issues, July 1944, CZA J1/3717/2.
144. Kanievsky 1944, 18, 44–47.
145. Van De Kaa 1999, 18–19; Abrams 2002, 306; Alpern Engel 2004, 161; Bridenthal, Grossmann, and Kaplan 1984; Reggiani 1996.
146. Taylor Allen 2008, 17.
147. "Be'ayat haYeludah baYishuv" (no byline, apparently Bachi), Apr. 12, 1943, *Ha'aretz* (n.p.), CZA J1/3737/1.

148. Havah M., composition written in a seminar for kibbutz movement emissaries at Kibbutz Givat Hashloshah, 1945, YTA 2-23/32/7.
149. Memorandum from Hadassah's Statistics Department with regard to Dr. Rivlin's letter (from Jan. 1, 1939) Mar. 1939 (precise date not given), CZA J113/2312; Fraenkel 1944, 21.
150. Tova Berman, "'Al Be'ayot haYeludah," apparently 1943, CZA A516/100.
151. Golz 2013, 146.
152. Ibid., 211.
153. Meir Orlian, "HaTipul haMeshutaf," 'Alonim, Summer 1941, 8.
154. "Rishumam Shel Yemei haMe'ora'ot" (no byline), Hamashkif, Sept. 19, 1943, 4.
155. Fraenkel 1944, 21.
156. Hedwig Gellner, "Sekirah 'al 10 Shanim shel 'Avodah Sotziyalit beT"A," submitted to Mayor Rokach of Tel Aviv, Sept. 12, 1943, TAA 4-1427.
157. Roberto Bachi, "Sekirah Ketzarah 'al haYeludah vehaTemotah beE"Y beTekufat 1939–1941," CZA J1/1957/2; Roberto Bachi, "He'arot 'Al haMeganot haDemografiot ba'Olam uve'Artseinu, ve'AL haMediniyut haDemografit beYisra'el," apparently 1957, CZA A516/210.
158. Letter from 'Ezer Yoldot' (apparently Ezra association, founded 1908) to the Social Welfare Department of the National Council, Nov. 27, 1940, CZA J113/2312.
159. Havah M., composition written in a seminar for kibbutz movement emissaries at Kibbutz Givat Hashloshah, 1945, YTA 2-23/32/7.
160. "Be'ayat haYeludah baYishuv" (no byline, apparently Bachi), Apr. 12, 1943, Ha'aretz (n.p.), CZA J1/3737/1.
161. Yehudit, "LeShalosh He'arot Shel Ben-Gurion," Hapo'el Hatza'ir 47, Aug. 12, 1943, 25.
162. Tsur, Zevulun, and Porat 1981, 77.
163. Tsur and Yisra'eli 1985, 125.
164. Ibid., 127.
165. Z. Dor-Sinai, in Tsur, Zevulun, and Porat 1981, 190.
166. Ibid.
167. Y. Shviger, "'AL Asher Lo Medabrim," Mibifnim, Oct. 1933, 40; Sheffer and Fogiel-Bijaoui 1993.
168. Y. from Kibbutz Bet Alfa, H. from Kibbutz Negba, interviews with the author, Feb. 23, 2015; A.E.Z. related that Kibbutz Yagur forbade her parents to have more than two children, although they wanted more. Her mother had two or three abortions. By the time the kibbutz permitted larger families, her uterus was so damaged that she was unable to conceive. Interview with the author, Sept. 3, 2015.
169. Emphasis in original. Y. Shviger, "'Al Asher Lo Medabrim," Mibifnim, Oct. 1933, 40.
170. Dr. Y. Rivkai, "LaPsikhologiyah shel ha'Imahut Etzleinu," Ha'em Vehayeled, 1935, 48.
171. Gordon 1997, 147.
172. Moran Hajo 2012, 2.
173. Grossmann 1995, 68, 74.
174. Rene Varshaviak, "HaVikhu'ach shel haPe'ulah haTarbutit vahaSotzyialit," Davar, Feb. 19, 1932, 3.
175. Elisheva Kaplan, "Haganat haIsha ha'Ovedet," Davar, Mar. 3, 1932, 5.
176. Emphasis in original. H. H., "'Al Mah She'einam Medabrim," Devar Hapo'elet 7:5–6, Aug. 11, 1940, 103.
177. L. B., "Isha, Em Vayeled," Ha'em Vehayeled, 1933–1934, 178.
178. Lilia [Bassewitz], "Isha, Em Vayeled," Mibifnim, Apr. 1933, 16.
179. Lamdan 2004, 59.
180. Shechter 2011, 253, 256.

181. Lilia [Bassewitz], "Isha, Em Vayeled," *Mibifnim*, Apr. 1933, 17.

182. Meir Orlian, "HaTipul haMeshutaf," *'Alonim*, summer 1941, 10.

183. Roberto Bachi, "Be'ayat haYeludah BeYisra'el veHatza'ot leMediniyut haUkhlusiyah," undated, ISA 5588/2c; Committee on Birthrate Problems, "Tokhnit lePolitikah Demografit," Apr. 22, 1945, CZA J1/2383.

184. Committee on Birthrate Problems, "Tokhnit lePolitikah Demografit," Apr. 22, 1945, CZA J1/2383.

185. Roberto Bachi, "Be'ayat haYeludah BeYisra'el veHatza'ot leMediniyut haUkhlusiyah," undated, ISA 5588/2c.

186. Havah M., composition for a seminar for kibbutz movement emissaries at Kibbutz Givat Hashloshah, 1945, YTA 2-23/32/7.

187. L. Bein, "HaRibui haTiv'i veHishuvei he'Atid haKarov," *Hatzofeh*, June 8, 1945, 5.

188. Greenbaum 1999, 203–207.

189. Lavsky 2006, 9–10, 14–15.

190. Hazelton 1978, 56.

191. Schweid 2003, 253.

192. Tydor Baumel 1997, 102; Committee on Birthrate Problems, "Tokhnit lePolitikah Demografit," Apr. 22, 1945, CZA J1/2383; report from Bernstein (no first name), Jewish affairs adviser in the American headquarters in Germany, in Warhaftig 1984, 495; Shaul 2009, 82.

193. Dr. W [Walter] Falk, "Eikh Netapel beYaldei 'Olim?," *Eitanim* 1:3 (Aug. 1948), 10.

194. Lavsky 2006, 10.

195. Moshe Prager, "Kele haMahanot uMagefat haShmad," *Davar*, Feb. 24, 1947, 2.

196. "Agav" (no byline), *Hatzofeh*, Nov. 16, 1947, 2.

197. Lavsky 2006, 10.

198. M. [Meir] Dvorjetski, "HaYeludah bekerev Nizolei haSho'ah," *Eitanim* 14:4 (Spring 1961), 133.

199. Falk 1994, 48, 53, 75, 91.

200. A. P. Ston, "Igrot me'Eretz Nis'eret," *'Al Hamishmar*, Apr. 14, 1947, 2; "Agav" (no byline), *Hatzofeh*, Nov. 16, 1947, 2.

201. Moshe Prager, "Kele haMahanot uMagefat haShmad," *Davar*, Feb. 24, 1947, 2.

202. M. [Meir] Dvorjetski, "HaYeludah bekerev Nizolei haSho'ah," *Eitanim* 14:4 (Spring 1961), 133.

203. See, for example, Knei-Paz 2012; Even Hen 2006.

204. "Baderekh leShikum haUmah" (no byline), *Davar*, Oct. 2, 1949, 2.

205. DellaPergola 2009, 7–8.

206. Ofer and Weitzman 1999, 15.

207. "Imahut beTzel haSho'ah beRe'iy haOmanut haNashit," Exhibition Catalogue, Bar-Ilan University, 2014, 11.

208. Schweid 2003, 300.

209. M. [Meir] Dvorjetski, "HaYeludah bekerev Nizolei haSho'ah," *Eitanim* 14:4 (Spring 1961), 134.

210. Roberto Bachi, "Be'ayat haYeludah BeYisra'el veHatza'ot leMediniyut haUkhlusiyah," undated, ISA 5588/2c.

211. P. I., interview with the author, Apr. 10, 2012; H. F., discussion with the author, Oct. 1990.

212. Tova Berman, "Ha'Emtza'im haDerushim le'Idud haYeludah baYishuv," Feb. 1945, CZA J1/3717/3.

213. Report by Dr. Tova Berman, Feb. 16, 1945, CZA J1/3717/3; on the lack of family support in childcare in displaced persons camps, see Lavsky 2006, 15.

214. The birthrate among American Jewry grew from two children per family in the thirties to three children during the forties to the sixties. Exler 2000, 45.

215. Yocheved Bat-Rachel, "De'agat HaImahut," Merkaz Kupat Holim, Jan. 1945, YTA, 15-36/4/4, 6.

216. Report on the activities of the Committee on Birthrate Problems, during its two years of existence (May 1943–Apr. 1945), Apr. 29, 1945, CZA J1/1974.

217. Bachi 1943a, 15.

218. "Be'ayat haYeludah baYishuv" (no byline, apparently Bachi), Apr. 12, 1943, Ha'aretz (n.p.), CZA J1/3737/1.

219. Dr. Tova Berman, lecture on birthrate politics, June 17, probably early 1940s, CZA A516/165.

220. Ibid.

221. Roberto Bachi, "Sekirah Ketzarah 'al haYeludah vehaTemotah beE"Y beTekufat 1939–1941," CZA J1/1957/2.

222. Roberto Bachi, "Yeridat haYeludah: Sakanah Le'umit," Ha'aretz, 1940 (no specific day, n.p.).

223. Roberto Bachi, "Be'ayat haYeludah BeYisra'el veHatza'ot leMediniyut haUkhlusiyah," undated, ISA 5588/2c.

224. Bachi 1943a, 15.

Chapter Four

ABORTIONS IN PRACTICE

> I have suffered a psychic shock as a result of this needless infliction of pain. I suffered from insomnia the first week following the operation, and now I have terrible nightmares. I have become so nervous that I cannot carry on a normal home life.
>
> —Letter from Sarah L. to Tel Aviv Mayor
> Israel Rokach, Feb. 18, 1949[1]

IN A LETTER TO MAYOR ISRAEL ROKACH of Tel Aviv, a woman named Sarah described the harsh after-effects of the abortion she underwent in 1948 at the Ein Gedi private maternity hospital, a popular clinic among the women of Tel Aviv and its environs, for both giving and preventing birth.[2] She accused the doctor of not observing the minimal standards required of any modern hospital. Her letter offers much information about how abortions were carried out. In her case, it brought on long-term physical and mental anguish.

Even though modern contraceptive devices were available in Palestine in the 1930s and 1940s, abortions remained the most widespread way of avoiding the birth of a child.[3] As early as the 1920s, attempts were made in the Yishuv to encourage the use of birth control. For example, members of Hadassah's board, meeting in New York in 1925, resolved to obtain literature on contraception and send it to Haifa. They instructed the chief of the city's gynecological clinic to the "careful distribution" of the information.[4]

The women's health centers run cooperatively by Hadassah and Kupat Holim Clalit that operated in the Yishuv during the 1920s devoted some of their time to caring for pregnant women, but refrained from providing guidance and information on matters beyond the pregnancy itself. In the 1930s, these centers opened a small number of counseling stations, most of them run by Kupat Holim Clalit. They offered advice and assistance to women, and later to men and couples prior to and following marriage, on matters pertaining to married life and sexual relations. This included information on advanced contraceptive methods, both mechanical and chemical (such as diaphragms made of rubber and metal, creams and pills, cotton wool drenched in acid, and condoms).[5] Sometimes these were also dispensed at a reduced price.[6] Some doctors viewed birth control as essential given the circumstances in the Yishuv, necessary to keep women from choosing the more dangerous option of abortion.[7]

But despite the fact that contraceptive devices and methods were not unknown and sometimes could be obtained, most of the public chose to use the oldest but most dubious form of pregnancy prevention, coitus interruptus.[8] This was shown by a survey of 3,000 Israeli women in the 1950s. A full 62 percent of them testified that the "withdrawal method" was the one they and their partners used to prevent pregnancy.[9] Presumably this had been no less the case in the previous decade. Widespread reliance on it in the 1950s puzzled Roberto Bachi, who conducted the survey, both because of its inefficacy and because of the presence of contraceptives and the availability of medical services at the time in Israel in general and in Tel Aviv in particular.[10] But then, as during the Yishuv period, mechanical and chemical means of preventing pregnancy seem to have been little used, apparently because of the small number of counseling stations (only six of these operated throughout the Yishuv in 1935).[11] Other reasons were that even where such stations operated, they were open only for a few hours a week and offered their services only to special cases,[12] and to certain parts of the population. For example, the stations operated by Kupat Holim Clalit served only members of the Histadrut. The stations also handed out a limited number of devices.[13] Most important, many people were simply not aware that such means were available, and no widespread effort was made to promote their use.

At the end of 1933 doctors involved in the counseling stations held a series of conversations about their work. One of the participants was Dr. Max Marcuse, a sexologist with a global reputation, who had moved to Palestine that year.[14] They agreed that contraceptive devices should be available for a large range of medical, social, and subjective reasons. These included concerns about the health of the child about to be born, indigence, or the woman's general lack of interest in having a child. But, at the same time, they resolved to encourage motherhood and to seek to prevent long-term use of birth control.[15] In other words, the doctors favored permitting the use of contraception when needed, for a long list of reasons, but were not prepared to encourage their use. Part of the reason seems to have been the Mandate law against the publication of pornography, which included medical literature on sex and sex education.[16]

Writers in *Devar Hapo'elet*, a monthly published by the Council of Women Workers, called on women to use birth control. They also decried women's ignorance of the subject and the silence of doctors who refrained from encouraging the use of effective means of preventing pregnancy.[17] A Kupat Holim Clalit information booklet issued in 1935 declared, "We must wage a war . . . for open explanation about pregnancy prevention to the population."[18]

Lilia Bassewitz of the Council of Women Workers blamed the Yishuv's doctors. Elsewhere in the West, she charged, doctors promoted the use of birth control methods that rendered abortions unnecessary and which averted the suffering they caused women. Kupat Holim doctors, unlike their colleagues elsewhere, did not do so. Some, she explained, claimed to have no time to deal with it. Others think that women, especially those in the agricultural sector to which Bassewitz herself belonged, should have many children and thus opposes any regulation of pregnancy. Still others cast themselves in the role of guardians of public morals ("Who gave him that right?" she fumed) and thought that encouraging the use of contraceptive devices would lead to depravity. She presumed that there were also doctors who opposed birth control on religious grounds. But even those doctors who favored family planning and the use of contraceptive devices, she said, did nothing to disseminate their views among the public.[19] Public figures who sought to encourage larger families had national reasons for not wanting the use of birth control devices to spread.[20]

The result was that a large part of the public did not have access to modern contraceptive methods. These people sometimes turned to quacks who recommended methods that, at best, were merely ineffective and at worst could cause infertility in women.[21] Gynecologist Dr. Miriam Aharonova wrote that social and economic pressures forced women to find some way to regulate their pregnancies and births: "For this reason they sometimes seek advice from neighbors, swallow large quantities of harmful 'potions' and poison their bodies."[22] Recall that Henia Pekelman, the woman impregnated by her rapist, tried to end her pregnancy by bathing in what she called "potent drugs," but to no avail.[23]

The public, by and large realizing that these so-called experts could not really help them, but unable to obtain effective mechanical and chemical means of contraception, relied on other methods, most commonly coitus interruptus. Others used the rhythm method, which ostensibly computed the days on which a couple could engage in sex without fear of pregnancy. Still others simply remained celibate, a choice which the Kupat Holim information booklet of 1935 termed "damaging and destabilizing."[24] Given the doubtful efficacy of these methods, many simply gave up on preventing pregnancy "and abandoned [themselves] to the danger of abortion."[25] Obviously, once a woman became pregnant, abortion was the only way to prevent the birth of a child. Some traveled overseas for the procedure,[26] perhaps to conceal the operation from friends and family in the Yishuv or because they were acquainted with specialists in Europe.

The Praxis of Abortion

"A beautiful, pale Yemenite girl with huge eyes almost bulging out of their sockets, her head draped in a white kerchief and her dark arms yellowed . . . if she survives . . . God will see it as a great miracle." So testified a nun and nurse at the Jerusalem's French hospital about the condition of an unmarried young Jewish woman who underwent an abortion in 1936, her second.[27] The nurse said this at the trial of the doctor who performed the operation, and it shocked the audience. "This nurse handed [the prosecutor] a bottle of cologne," the press reported. "The judge, who also began to feel sick in the hospital atmosphere, also washed his hands and face with the same cologne. Everyone there felt sick."[28]

This abortion had been performed in a modern hospital, by a specialist. This was a common occurrence even though abortions were illegal, and helped women feel more secure about having them. In 1937, Dr. Abramovitz of Hadassah hospital in Tel Aviv asserted that abortions, the number of which grew by the years, were conducted, "under the conditions in our country," much better and more successfully than overseas, "because here they are performed by specialists."[29] The defendant in the mock trial of 1943 was asked, "When you had the abortion, was it clear to you that it put your life and health at risk?" She answered: "I was sure that everything would go well. All women do it and it always goes ok."[30] The doctor who participated in the mock trial, like Dr. Abramovitz himself, affirmed that abortions were risky even when performed by professionals. There were cases of death and complications, which could cause sterility, infection of the ovaries, and risks during subsequent pregnancies. But the public, the doctors said, was not cognizant of the bad outcomes and make no connection between women's difficulty conceiving and abortions they had previously undergone.[31]

Abortion opponents claimed that, while women often paid out of pocket for abortions in hospitals or private clinics, the cost was so low as to serve as an incentive.[32] Advocates, for their part, charged that the price was high and burdensome for women. Both in the Yishuv and overseas, Lilia Bassewitz complained, "abortions are performed by private physicians and often women have to use their last available resources to obtain the assistance of these doctors."[33]

It is hard to determine what an abortion cost in the period under discussion, that is, the 1930s and 1940s. It varied from doctor to doctor, by location, and over time. A young woman named Yonah who had had an abortion in a private clinic testified in 1936 that she paid the doctor P£6.[34] I noted in my discussion of the cost of hospital births that this was equivalent to the monthly income of many working-class families at the end of the 1930s.[35] At the beginning of that decade wages were even lower. The monthly income of a nonprofessional Jewish male day laborer ranged, in 1932, between P£3 and P£7.5 per month, but that assumed he found work every day, which was often not the case.[36] Women workers earned much less, even for equivalent work, both per hour and in the aggregate, sometimes as little as P£2 a month.[37] These figures support the claim of women's rights activists that the cost of an abortion was often beyond the means of many families.

The mother whom Shulamit Lapid tells about in her book sought a loan from an acquaintance so that she could have an abortion in a private clinic.[38] Moshav families sometimes sold livestock to pay for an abortion. Kibbutz women had to ask the commune to allocate money for an abortion, or made use of some private source of funding.[39] In the 1940s a kibbutz woman named Shenke testified that her community allocated her a sum of money to have an abortion in a private clinic.[40] At religious kibbutzim, which refused to fund abortions, women sometimes had them done with the help of family outside the kibbutz.[41]

When the cost of a professional abortion proved prohibitive for penniless women, they sometimes went to amateurs or used primitive means to try to abort their fetuses on their own. Sometimes poverty kept a woman from undergoing an abortion, as we have already seen in the case of Raful, later chief of staff of the Israel Defense Forces. He was born in 1929 because his parents did not have the P£2 to pay a doctor for the abortion they wanted to have. His father managed to scrape together P£1.20, Raful later related, but the doctor refused to perform the abortion if he did not receive full payment at the time of the operation.[42]

Lay or professional, home or clinic, little documentation exists to show how they were done. The cases that appear in the press were those that ended badly. Such news items tell of doctors who were tried for abortions that ended in death or injury, or for enticing women into having the operation. There are also news reports about self-inflicted attempts at abortion that were bungled, and about women who sought out "witch doctors and wonder workers" who ended up causing damage.[43] But even these reports are few and far between. Perhaps this is indirect evidence that most abortions were in fact successful and uncomplicated and that the procedure was, on the whole, a relatively safe one. Information about where the procedure could be done and the names of professional abortionists in hospitals and clinics apparently spread by word of mouth.[44]

Some newspaper articles from the 1940s describe women arriving one after another in recovery rooms after undergoing abortions.[45] "They brought in a patient after an operation. . . . The operation was so that she would not have a second child. . . . The next day they brought in another such woman . . . , and the day after that again and again," one newspaper reported, decrying the fact that Jewish hospitals in Palestine were performing abortions every day.[46] Such hospitals, the reporter protested, "do not only heal the sick but also wage vigorous war against what is called 'internal immigration.'" Who was allowing abortions in Jewish hospitals, the writer wondered.[47]

Abortions were in fact illegal and were allowed only under exceptional circumstances. The rule was that an abortion required the approval of two physicians.[48] But the law was seldom enforced except in cases when physical harm was done to the woman. "The law seems to be flawed and in any case is not properly applied," declared Abraham Fraenkel, a mathematician and former rector of the Hebrew University, condemning the lack of enforcement.[49] The British administration indeed looked the other way, perhaps because the Mandate allowed the Yishuv a large measure of internal self-government. But the British may also have seen abortion as a means of preserving the demographic balance between Jews and Arabs. That at least was the accusation made by Rabbi Yitzhak Una. Rabbi Una was the father of Moshe Una of the Religious Kibbutz Movement, who also sat on the National Council in the 1940s. In 1943 Rabbi Una spoke out against a Mandate law that provided for a salary supplement for each child, but only up to the third. "If the government makes such a law, perhaps it is not interested in Jewish natural increase," he charged.[50] Support for the claim can be found in Aviva Halamish's study of discrimination against women during the Mandate period. Halamish found that the Mandate administration deliberately sought to restrict the immigration of Jewish women so, among other things, as to keep the Jewish birthrate low and preserve the existing proportions of Jews and Arabs in the country.[51] It may well be that the lax enforcement of the abortion prohibition was motivated by the same consideration.

But it was not just the British who looked the other way. When it received complaints about doctors who had conducted abortions improperly in private hospitals in the city, the Tel Aviv municipality responded that it had no interest in or power to interfere with the operation of institutions not run by the city.[52] Department heads at Hadassah tried in some cases to keep doctors from performing abortions. With the backing of the Hadassah administration they took a strong stand, but with no result. The administration promised in the 1930s to take urgent measures in this regard.[53] But the documents show no concrete steps taken to battle the practice.

One of the few testimonies about how abortions were done in practice comes from 1936. The woman in question related she wished to have the abortion done secretly so that her family would not know about it. She told them she was having an operation of some sort. At the clinic she was given an injection that put her to sleep, "and when I woke up the doctor told me that she had cut the fetus and that tomorrow she would take it out. I slept that night at her clinic. On Saturday she operated on me again and took out the fetus." But when she got home she was in pain, fell ill, and was taken to the hospital. "Had I known that the operation would be so dangerous," the young woman declared, "I would have fled the country and given birth."[54] The mother in Lapid's novel "bled like a pig for two weeks and silently cursed the doctor" who performed the abortion. She did not know much about abortions, Lapid writes, "but even without being an expert, she was certain that the doctor in question was a butcher."[55]

Sarah, the Tel Aviv woman whose complaint to Mayor Rokach is quoted in the epigraph to this chapter, describes a horrendous procedure: "It was with a very unhappy heart that I took this measure. But, at the very least, if one did have to do such a terrible deed, I believed that these . . . abortions . . . would be conducted under sanitary and sterile conditions, and that anesthesia would be administered."[56]

But she was wrong. The personnel did not ensure a sterile environment:

> At the time I went for the operation, three other women were with me. In preparing us for the operation, the nurse used the same razor, cotton, and basin for all four of us, without changing or sterilizing the equipment. In the operating room, the assistant who handed the instruments to the doctor came straight from her task of washing the floors without changing her clothes or washing her hands.[57]

On top of that, there was no anesthesia. The doctor, she wrote,

> was abusive and inhuman in his treatment. He promised to administer anesthesia and then proceeded to operate without giving me any ether. When I mourned and begged him to give me ether, he still refused. . . . [There was] no reason for [such] absolutely needless suffering. I accuse this doctor of being a sadist who gloated upon the terrible torture he inflicted.[58]

Before World War I anesthesia was indeed not commonly available in Palestine and operations were conducted without it. For example, a woman from Merhavia who became pregnant began to bleed profusely. A doctor was called in and performed an abortion, using only ether as light anesthesia.[59]

But medical practice advanced thereafter and anesthesia became standard surgical practice.

Sarah, who had come to Palestine from the United States and knew about the use of anesthesia, was upset about it not being used in her case: "In America if dogs are used in experimental research, anesthesia is administered during operations. Is a human being considered less than a dog here?"[60]

Other sources also testify to abortions being carried out while patients were fully conscious and document the pain involved.[61] "He scraped me without putting me to sleep," Shenke later related regarding an abortion performed in the 1940s by a private physician in a clinic at his home. "I remember that I told him, 'Nu, maybe stop scraping already,' he did it all without anesthesia."[62]

The existing documentation does not explain why the procedure was done without anesthesia when that was available. The possibility that it was due to a lack of professional knowledge seems unlikely, given the relatively advanced state of medical practice in the Yishuv. Perhaps doctors were trying to save money, or preferred to save anesthetics for operations they considered more serious than abortions. It seems likely that doctors viewed abortion as an "easy" procedure and that women viewed it the same way. The very fact that abortions were conducted without anesthesia might have contributed to women seeing it as a minor medical procedure, "like pulling an infected tooth," as Dr. Miriam Aharonova, a gynecologist, said in describing how women viewed abortions.[63] "I put flowers on the table in the morning and went with our nurse for an abortion and then came home," a kibbutz woman related, making an abortion conducted without anesthesia sound like nothing much at all.[64]

Given the paucity of material, there is no way of determining whether abortion without anesthesia was common. Sarah, who suffered greatly, told the mayor that she knew that many doctors administered anesthesia for abortions, except in the cases of patients with heart problems. Nevertheless, it seems likely that no small number of women who had abortions had to endure all the pain it involved, and this was the case with women who had abortions done in hospitals or private clinics. Clearly women who performed abortions on themselves or had them done by nonprofessionals did not have the benefit of anesthesia.

Women also suffered psychological pain before and after an abortion. The procedure brought with it a jumble of shame, despair, and remorse. A Tirat Zvi woman went to the city to have an abortion dressed in "large sunglasses and a kerchief to conceal the shame of the sin."[65] For a religious woman, the mental distress of the procedure was augmented by a sense of committing a transgression against God. A kibbutz woman recounted in

1940 the bitter despair that came over a woman when she had to make a decision to end a pregnancy, and the mental devastation she suffered after the procedure.[66] Miriam Kimmelman was one: "I was weak and tired. I made inquiries and received the address of a good doctor. It all passed. But in my soul and on the surface a painful wound remained. Today, when I think about it, the operation without anesthesia, the pain, I know that most of the pain was not physical."[67] Sarah, the American immigrant, had hoped for compassion. "Abortion is terribly painful, psychologically as well as physically," she wrote. "There is no valid medical reason why it should not be done in the spirit of mercy."[68] Hers was certainly not.

But whatever pain the procedure involved did little to deter woman who did not want to bear the child they carried. True, a kibbutz woman described it as a "private tragedy." And *Hamashkif*, the Revisionist Zionist newspaper, referred to the tragedy of the woman prevented by "science" from "being a Jewish mother and multiplying the seed of Abraham the Patriarch in this land." But the newspaper went on to declare that "the private tragedy does not interest us in the least. What interests us is the public tragedy of the entire Jewish people."[69] In other words, whatever private suffering the procedure involved was irrelevant to the public issue. Every aspect of the low birthrate and abortions was discussed in that light, as the next chapter shows. It also explains in part the dearth of writing on the technical aspects of abortion and the suffering they caused.

NOTES

1. Letter from Sarah L. to Tel Aviv Mayor Israel Rokach, Feb. 18, 1949, TAA 4-4643.
2. Golz 2013, 100.
3. Bachi and Matras 1962, 224.
4. A report from Hadassah NY, Dec. 24, 1925, American Jewish Historical Society, Hadassah Collections, RG23/subjects/birth control/feminism.
5. Shvarts and Stoler-Liss 2011, 96–97.
6. Kozma 2010, 101–111.
7. For example, Dr. Miriam Aharonova, in Shvarts and Stoler-Liss 2011, 96.
8. Kozma 2010, 111.
9. Bachi and Matras 1962, 224–226.
10. Ibid.
11. Margalit-Stern 2011, 188; Shvarts and Stoler-Liss 2011, 96.
12. Shvarts and Stoler-Liss 2011, 96.
13. Kozma 2010, 111.
14. Levy and Levy 2008, 259.
15. Lilia Bassewitz, a meeting of women on women's hygiene issues, July 1933, YTA 15-28/14/1; Kaminski 2012, 71.
16. Kozma 2010, 101, 108.
17. Polia, "be'Ikvot Reshimah Ahat," *Devar Hapo'elet*, Aug. 25, 1935, 124.
18. P. SH., "HaBerihah mipnei haYeled," *Ha'em Vehayeled*, 1935, 52.

19. Lilia [Bassewitz], "Isha, Em Vayeled," *Mibifnim*, Apr. 1933, 16.

20. Roberto Bachi, "HaYeludah be Yisra'el uvaYishuv vehaDerakhim le'Idudah," apparently 1944, CZA J1/3717/3.

21. P. SH., "HaBerihah mipnei haYeled," *Ha'em Vehayeled*, 1935, 52.

22. M. A., "Tahanot ha'Eitza laNashim veTafkidan," *Ha'em Vehayeled*, 1933–1934, 6.

23. Pekelman 1935, 121.

24. P. SH., "HaBerihah mipnei haYeled," *Ha'em Vehayeled*, 1935, 52.

25. Ibid.

26. Frankel 2004, 96, 99.

27. "'Edutah haDramatit shel Yonah Tzadok," (no byline) *Do'ar Hayom*, Apr. 5, 1936, 4.

28. Ibid., 8.

29. Letter of Dr. A. Abramovitch, director of Hadassah municipal hospital, to A. Perlson, chairman of the board, May 28, 1937, TAA, Hadassah hospital, 4-4645.

30. Tova Berman, text for the mock trial on birthrate problems, 1943, CZA J1/3717/1.

31. Ibid.; letter of Dr. A. Abramovitch, director of Hadassah municipal hospital, to A. Perlson, chairman of the board, May 28, 1937, TAA, Hadassah hospital, 4-4645.

32. Dr. Shpruch-Pozner, "Yeludah Musderet," *Davar*, July 27, 1952, 2.

33. Lilia [Bassewitz], "Isha, Em Vayeled," *Mibifnim*, Apr. 1933, 17.

34. "Edutah haDramatit shel Yonah Tzadok," (no byline) *Do'ar Hayom*, Apr. 5, 1936, 8.

35. Tova Berman, minutes of a meeting of the Committee on Birthrate Problems, June 22, 1943, CZA J1/3717/1.

36. According to a government committee that in 1932 defined seven categories of unskilled workers according to the minimum daily wage of men (while neutralizing the lower wage levels of women and children), Bernstein 2003, 83–84.

37. Rene Varshaviak, "haVikhu'ah shel haPe'ulah haTarbutit vahaSotziyalit," *Davar*, Feb. 19, 1932, 3.

38. Lapid 2011, 83.

39. Lilia [Bassewitz], "Isha, Em Vayeled," *Mibifnim*, Apr. 1933, 17.

40. Lamdan 2004, 59.

41. Netzer 2012, 11.

42. Eitan 1985, 20.

43. [no byline, no title], *Davar*, Oct. 10, 1937, 6; [no byline, no title], *Davar*, Apr. 27, 1938, 3; [no byline, no title], *Davar*, Dec. 10, 1939, 6; [no byline, no title], *Do'ar Hayom*, Mar. 13, 1929, 4; [no byline, no title], *Do'ar Hayom*, June 13, 1935, 6; [no byline, no title], *Do'ar Hayom*, Mar. 26, 1936, 6; P. SH., "HaBerihah mipnei haYeled," *Davar*, Mar. 2, 1934, 8.

44. Dr. Haim Yassky, memorandum of discussion with Prof. Bernhard Zondek (from Dec. 18, 1935), Dec. 22, 1935, CZA J113/7487; letter of Dr. A. Abramovitch, director of Hadassah municipal hospital, to A. Perlson, chairman of the board, May 28, 1937, TAA, Hadassah hospital, 4-4645.

45. Kibbutz member, "Lo Zo haDerekh," *Devar Hapo'elet* 7:1, Mar. 31, 1940, 27.

46. Avishai, "She'elah Nikhbadah Me'od," *Hamashkif*, Apr. 15, 1940, 3.

47. Ibid.

48. Minutes of a meeting of the Committee on Birthrate Problems, Sept. 21, 1943, CZA J1/3717/2.

49. Fraenkel 1944, 32.

50. Una 1975, 367. I thank Dr. Zvi Zameret for this reference.

51. Halamish 2001, 53.

52. Letter from Yehudah Nedivi, City Secretary, to Dr. Roch, Feb. 21, 1949, TAA 4-4643.

53. Dr. Haim Yassky, memorandum of discussion with Prof. Bernhard Zondek (from Dec. 18, 1935) Dec. 22, 1935, CZA J113/7487.

54. "Edutah haDramatit shel Yonah Tzadok," (no byline) *Do'ar Hayom*, Apr. 5, 1936, 8.
55. Lapid 2011, 83–84.
56. Letter from Sarah L. to Tel Aviv Mayor Israel Rokach, Feb. 18, 1949, TAA 4-4643.
57. Ibid.
58. Ibid.
59. Auerbach 1997, 258.
60. Letter from Sarah L. to Tel Aviv Mayor Israel Rokach, Feb. 18, 1949, TAA 4-4643.
61. Kimelman 2003, 37.
62. Lamdan 2004, 58.
63. M. Aharonova, "MiProblemat haImahot," *Devar Hapo'elet* 1:4 (June 6, 1934), 81.
64. Lamdan 2004, 58.
65. Netzer 2012, 11.
66. Kibbutz member, "Lo Zo haDerekh," *Devar Hapo'elet* 7:1, Mar. 31, 1940, 27.
67. Kimelman 2003, 37.
68. Letter from Sarah L. to Tel Aviv Mayor Israel Rokach, Feb. 18, 1949, TAA 4-4643.
69. Avishai, "She'elah Nikhbadah Me'od," *Hamashkif*, Apr. 15, 1940, 3.

CHAPTER FIVE

LOW BIRTHRATE, HIGH ABORTION RATE
Responses

REGIMES THROUGHOUT HISTORY HAVE EVINCED AN interest in controlling fertility. The birthrate, after all, is key to any society's future. This was all the more true in the nineteenth century, as nationalism spread through Europe and population size was considered key to national might. In that period the ambition was to increase the birthrate. Paradoxically, however, nationalism developed within a Western culture that, as it passed (often violently, with regard to fertility) from tradition into modernity, tended to encourage smaller families.[1] The birthrate was thus a matter of public debate in many countries, some of which, aiming for population growth, prohibited the use of contraception and abortion.[2] The Yishuv, in the throes of a national struggle, also confronted the issue. Furthermore, one aspect of the Jewish national revival in Palestine under the Mandate was a new culture, with its own dress code, hygienic standards, educational principles, consumption practices, and leisure activities—in particular hiking, as a way of connecting with and knowing the homeland. These values and practices were instilled in society by mobilized national cultural agents.[3] The debate over the optimal size of the family, and the attempts to encourage larger ones, can be seen as part of these agents' efforts to build a new nation, to establish its normative practices, and to establish them as the entire nation's way of life. But the question of the birthrate took on unusual complexity, given the unique profile of Jewish society in Palestine.

The Public Debate over the Low Birthrate

The Yishuv's response to its low birthrate, and to abortions in particular, was thus not a simple one. On the one hand, a large proportion of the population actively limited childbirth, for any number of reasons. But they did not talk

113

about it publicly, whether because they considered it a private and intimate matter, because abortions were illegal, or because it was perceived as contrary to the national interest. Some did not limit the size of their families for ideological reasons they thought it necessary to fight for, but rather for practical considerations growing out of the conditions of their time and place. People who deliberately limited their family size were almost unheard of. As such, the public discourse over the issue was highly imbalanced—the proponents of a higher birthrate were vocal and salient while those who opposed them were largely silent and invisible. The latter eschewed public statements but made their position clear in their actions, by practicing birth control unannounced.

It is thus difficult to fathom what the average member of the Yishuv thought about contraception and abortion. Jews in Palestine apparently discussed them only in undocumented private conversations. But occasionally it is possible to detect the penumbras of such private speech. For example, in the summer of 1943, a newspaper reporter transcribed a conversation on the subject that he overheard while riding a bus in Jerusalem. "Sometimes you are able to capture a snapshot of public opinion [on a bus], as the passengers [come from] different classes and strata that represent entire worlds," the journalist wrote.[4] He stressed that he had eavesdropped on the conversation simply to allay the boredom of his trip.

The subject came up on the bus in response to a recent announcement of a public assembly on the birthrate issue. Some of the passengers categorically opposed deliberate limitation of family size. Others spoke of how difficult it was to raise healthy and strong children in Palestine, and argued that this was reason for family planning.[5] One woman, her face lined with suffering, protested the fact that the subject was only getting attention now. "Where were they before?" she cried, condemning those who only began taking action about the birthrate after learning of the annihilation of European Jewry. It was, she said, a fundamental issue that should have been addressed years before. "Had there not been a Holocaust would there have been no need to encourage births?" she wondered.[6] In the meantime, she claimed, limiting family size had become a habit difficult to break.

But only rarely were such exchanges jotted down. We can only presume that there were as many opinions as people. But the average person spoke with her actions. The fact is that limiting family size was a widespread phenomenon.

This chapter therefore focuses on the opponents of birth control and abortion. Whatever their motivations, they were far more vocal than the proponents and thus dominated the discussion of the subject. But they, too, pondered whether, fundamentally, such an intimate matter should be the subject of public debate.

Kibbutzim were the first societies to consider the birth of children as an issue that had implications beyond the individual or family. Even before World War I, the members of Degania, the first kibbutz, communally addressed the formation of couples, the establishment of families, and the birth of children. The fear was that all these would be detrimental to the collective, both in terms of its productive capacity and in terms of its very nature.[7] But it was an entirely internal discussion and did not extend beyond the kibbutz. In later years the issue continued to be considered one internal to the kibbutz movement, not part of a national debate.

In the 1930s the low Yishuv birthrate was flagged by the Hebrew press. The papers argued that the labor camp, which saw itself as leading the Yishuv as a whole in the creation of a new society, was obliged to consider family and birth issues, despite the fact that these were ostensibly intimate psychological matters. Whatever their private aspects, the papers said, the public implications were great. "A broad and open discussion" was a must, Lilia Bassewitz of the Council of Women Workers maintained in 1933. "The public should be educated to bring up these questions and grant them a public nature."[8]

The question of whether the issue should be discussed publicly continued to preoccupy the labor movement in the 1940s. "Should [having another child] be the concern of the family alone, of the individual, or is it a concern of the public as a whole, one that requires a public solution?" wondered Yocheved Bat-Rachel, also a leader of the Council of Women Workers and a figure in the Zionist Leadership, in 1945. As a member of a kibbutz and of the labor movement, she believed that in society the individual was subordinate to the needs of the collective, so her answer was unambiguous. "The working public in the Land of Israel has known how to organize and direct its way of life so that when principal questions of this sort come up, the public as a whole finds solutions. In our case, no social, settlement, or political problem is solved by individuals, but rather by the public as a whole." The same was true of the birthrate question, which "ought to be our primary concern, one that gives us no rest."[9] The birthrate was a public issue, both in theory and in practice, and it had to be discussed by the Yishuv as a whole and by the working public in particular, as part of a united and intense effort to find solutions.

The belief that the birthrate was a public issue spread from the labor camp to the rest of the public during the 1940s. When news of the Holocaust reached the Yishuv in 1943, the subject came to be perceived as acute and the legitimacy of a public discussion became widely recognized. "In the difficult times in which our people finds itself in," Tova Berman wrote in the 1940s, the Yishuv necessarily engaged in self-examination and self-criticism. "Yet, by consensus, we do not touch on one specific of life," she argued in relation to the birth issue, "which in fact determines the life of the nation. In fact, we disregard it entirely."[10]

It was an old claim that "society has no right to intervene in a matter as private as fertility and no leeway for doing so," remarked the Zionist demographer Roberto Bachi in 1943. It had, he said, been voiced a hundred years previously when society first began inserting itself into family life "to protect public hygiene." But he unambiguously took the opposite position. Society, he maintained, had not only the capacity to intervene in the birthrate issue but also the right to do so. It should keep, he said, the anarchic action of the individual from hindering the collective effort to build the land.[11]

That same year, Yitzhak Kanievsky, a leading Yishuv economist, argued that demographic issues should not be left to experts. Public institutions and leaders needed to be involved. In other countries, such as Britain, legislatures addressed the issue, and the same should be done in the Yishuv. The Jewish leadership should discuss the matter publicly and pursue demographically informed policies.[12]

A lively debate on the birthrate issue thus developed during the 1940s, involving large parts of the public and its leadership. But that did not keep the fundamental question of the legitimacy of such a debate from coming up at any number of opportunities. The Yishuv was, after all, to no small extent a traditional and conservative society. Many still thought it inappropriate for intimate matters involving women and families to be discussed openly.[13] For example, when a radio program addressed the birthrate issue in 1944, the announcer opened the discussion by asking whether the choice to have children was not solely a private matter that society should stay out of. But the potent nationalism of Yishuv society militated against that proposition. The national struggle was seen as paramount and all other issues subordinate to it. The nation and society, Berman declared on the program, frequently inserted themselves into private lives. Just as the Yishuv sent its young people to found and live in settlements and to fight in dangerous areas, so it could involve itself in the private lives of its members.[14] Indeed, this soon became a matter of general agreement, so long as it was conducted, as Bachi stipulated, not by force but "in a matter befitting a cultured society."[15]

Ideological Approaches to the Yishuv's Low Birthrate and Abortion

Thomas Malthus's *An Essay on the Principle of Population*, published in 1798, first prompted public deliberation over demographic issues in general and of the birthrate specifically.[16] The British clergyman and economist was the father of the Malthusian school that advocated public oversight of the birth-rate so as to serve economic ends. Leaders and thinkers around the world took the issue seriously and saw it as an essential national question.[17] The same was true in the Yishuv, in particular during the 1940s.

On the face of it, the Zionist ambition to create a Jewish majority should have predisposed the movement's leaders toward promoting large families.[18] But before the end of the 1930s the Yishuv grew mainly through immigration. The high immigration rate pushed the birthrate question aside. Warnings about the low birthrate were voiced sporadically in the 1930s, but were over-shadowed by the Arab Revolt that began in 1936.[19] When the British decided to limit Jewish immigration to Palestine in 1937, awareness of the importance of birthrate increased.[20] It increased further with the outbreak of World War II in 1939, given the peril in which the Jewish people found themselves and the threat to the Yishuv itself. More and more people began to speak out to condemn those who limited themselves to small families.

The first to do so were professionals and intellectuals with special sensi-tivity to the situation—demographers, physicians, and intellectuals who saw themselves as emissaries of the Zionist movement. While a number of orga-nizations aimed at fighting the low birthrate were established in the 1930s, they did not attract a great deal of attention from the public or leadership. But in May 1940 something changed. At the Hebrew University's graduation ceremony that year, Rector Abraham Fraenkel gave a speech that marked a turning point.

Fraenkel, a world-famous mathematician, had been born in Germany in 1891. An ardent Zionist and advocate of the Hebrew language, he immigrated to Palestine in 1929 and became politically active in the Zionist-religious Mizrahi movement. He served as a member of the National Council, the Yishuv's executive arm. A founder of the Hebrew University's mathematics department, he also worked to educate the public in his field. After serving as the first dean of the university's Faculty of Mathematics and Natural Sci-ences, he held the position of rector from 1938 to 1940.[21]

Fraenkel devoted his address to the Torah's first commandment, "Be fruitful and multiply."[22] He offered a grim forecast. Just a generation in the future, he declared, the number of Muslims in Palestine would double, while Jewish births would not make up for Jewish deaths.

The occasion and public nature of the speech, as well as Fraenkel's pub-lic standing, ensured its impact. He summed up all the principal arguments against the low birthrate. Later, in 1944, in a pamphlet devoted to the subject, Fraenkel, who had four children of his own, stressed the family's importance as the central component of the Jewish nation. Offering myriad quotes from Jewish sources in support of large families, he rejected the claim that women had the right to make decisions about their own bodies, including whether or not to have children and how many to have. "It is impossible to rule that way," he asserted, "not according to the law of our land and in all cultured countries . . . not according to Jewish tradition from ancient times to the present, and not from the national and Zionist point of view."[23] Fraenkel thus combined the religious obligation to have a large family and the family's traditional centrality in Jewish society, with the Zionist imperative. All three of these arguments were made by the opponents of birth control and, in particular, opponents of abortion.

ZIONIST DEMOGRAPHY

The Zionist demographic argument deserves to be considered first, as it was demographers and statisticians who first drew the Yishuv leadership's attention to the implications of the low birthrate.[24] They saw themselves not just as scientists but also as Zionists mobilized for the national cause.

The first to address the subject was David Gurevich. Born in Latvia, Gurevich first immigrated to the United States and then, in 1921, to Palestine. He headed the Jewish Agency's Statistics Department from its establishment in 1924 to his death in 1947. In 1929 he issued a statistical gazette of Palestine, which served as a model for later statistical works prepared by him and others and published by the Zionist Executive. They offer a wealth of valuable information about birth practices in the Yishuv.[25]

But it was Roberto Bachi who most visibly put his demographic knowledge and abilities at the disposal of his nation when it came to the birthrate. Born in Rome in 1909, Bachi earned a PhD in law and taught statistics and demographics at Italian universities. While still in Italy he was a well-known public figure and a member of the Advisory Committee for Students on the Population (Comitato di Consulenza per gli Studi sulla Popolazione, CCSP). Preaching against the low birthrate and high abortion rate, he worked to counter both trends and enlisted Zionist leaders in his campaign.

He had been an activist Zionist in Rome. In 1938, after the Fascist government promulgated a set of racial laws that led to his dismissal, he moved to Palestine. In 1941 he founded Hadassah's Central Bureau of Medical Statistics and founded the Hebrew University's department of statistics. After the establishment of the state, he served for many years as the scientific director of the country's Central Bureau of Statistics. His wife, Vera, referred to herself as "a housewife and mother."[26] They had four children, "a pretty large family compared to other professors," as one newspaper said.[27] According to Vera, he used all his time and energy to produce research studies. During the 1940s these focused on natural increase in the Yishuv.

The data that Bachi collected led him to a single conclusion. "The future existence of the Jewish people is at perhaps greater risk than ever in history," he proclaimed.[28] Birth control thus had dire implications for Zionism. "If we want the cherished enterprises that have come into being with such great effort over the last sixty years to remain in reliable hands," he wrote in 1943, it would be necessary "to ensure the Yishuv's future by means of sufficient births."[29] He also noted the importance of the quality of the Yishuv's future population, and warned that the low birthrate meant an aging populace in which, eventually, a large number of elderly people would become a burden on a small number of young people. The low birthrate of the Zionist element in the Yishuv meant that its proportion in the population would decline, he said. He also argued that the large number of only children would lead to severe educational problems.[30] For example, there was concern that only children would be spoiled, and thus improperly socialized and undisciplined.

Following the Holocaust, he was concerned about the Jewish people's demographic future. Founding a new generation of European Jews would be a miracle that would not happen on its own.[31] He worried about the future of the Jewish people as a whole—the annihilation of millions of Jews had followed years of persecution in which the Jewish birthrate had plunged drastically. As Jews fled from place to place, they also had fewer children. Before the war there had been about 16.5 million Jews in the world; after the war the number had dropped to 10 million. This led to two other problematic phenomena that, Bachi maintained, would cause a further decline in the Jewish population. The first was an imbalance between the two sexes, and the second a very small number of Jewish children in Europe.[32] Furthermore, in Western countries that had not been occupied by Germany, assimilation and intermarriage were causing a further decline, beyond that caused by a low birthrate and abortion.[33]

But Bachi's principal concern was the Yishuv itself. He did not see its future as assured. He presented his figures to the leadership and his findings were occasionally reported in the press. In 1944 he, Gurevich, and Aharon Gertz coauthored a book with the title *Immigration, the Yishuv, and the Natural Movement of the Population of Palestine*. It put Bachi's findings before the public.

THE ZIONIST POSITION

In the public discourse, the low birthrate was deplored principally for national reasons. Religious and medical arguments were themselves cast in a Zionist context.

The creation of a Jewish majority in Palestine in advance of the establishment of a Jewish state had been a principal Zionist goal from the start, and large families were considered essential to achieving it. The danger the low birthrate presented to the nation was trumpeted in the 1930s, although still not by many.[34] In the 1940s, following the Holocaust, the Yishuv leadership woke up to the danger presented by the low birthrate and high number of abortions.[35] These issues were now seen as matters of life and death for the Yishuv.[36] The danger that the low birthrate would lead to the physical debilitation of the Yishuv was a frequent subject of public discussion.

Soon after the war broke out, in 1940, even before the Final Solution had been put into practice, there were those who connected the desperate situation of Europe's Jews to the low rate of Jewish births and high rate of abortions. A kibbutz woman declared that the "killing," as she termed abortions, was the free choice of the Yishuv's citizens, "members of a nation whose lives are fair game throughout the Diaspora."[37] The physician and Revisionist polemicist Dr. Ze'ev (Wolfgang) von Weisl wrote in 1941 in *Hamashkif* with regard to the sharp drop in Jewish immigration to Palestine that "the future of the Land will be determined by the children born here, not those who have immigrated."[38] Many others spoke and wrote in the same spirit.

These claims were bolstered when news of the massive annihilation of European Jewry reached the Yishuv. Leaders, intellectuals, and the medical community had come to see the birthrate as no less important than immigration and settlement. As they saw it, if the Jews of the Yishuv could not be persuaded to have more children, Zionism would fail.[39] "Hitler will eradicate our nation on the one side, and on the other we will do it ourselves," said a character in a 1945 production of a play that addressed the issue.[40]

Von Weisl, born in Vienna in 1896 and religiously observant in practice, was considered a world authority on Islam. He immigrated to Palestine in 1922 and was one of the founders of the Revisionist Zionist Movement led by Ze'ev Jabotinsky. "A [Jewish] majority is created by mothers, not soldiers," he declared. The root of the evil was abortion, which he termed "the greatest of all crimes against the nation." If it were not for abortions, maintained von Weisl—a father of four who served as a combat officer from World War I through the War of Independence—the Yishuv would have tens of thousands more young soldiers available in the eventuality of war. "Our nation would not have had to fear Arab fertility," he stated bluntly, "had our Jewish mothers and fathers, as well as Jewish doctors, done their simple duty, had they not defied the command given to us on Mt. Sinai and by the laws of nature."[41] Having children, in his view, was a national, religious, and biological obligation, while abortion was a national, religious, and medical sin.

Another prominent voice against the low birthrate was David Ben-Gurion. Born in Plonsk in 1886, Ben-Gurion arrived in Palestine in 1906 and by the 1920s had become one of the leading figures in the labor movement and the Yishuv as a whole. He was one of the founders of the Histadrut labor federation, which he headed for fifteen years. In 1935 he was elected chairman of the Jewish Agency Executive, making him the leader of the Yishuv's autonomous government in Palestine. In 1948 he became Israel's first prime minister. In 1943 he stated his view as a Zionist on the low birthrate: The number of children per family is 1.2, Ben-Gurion emphasized in his speech before the Central Committee of Mapai, the largest political party in the Yishuv and early Israel, which later became the Labor Party. He then declared that this means the destruction of the entire Yishuv, cities and villages alike.

Ben-Gurion spoke on this issue with an acute historical consciousness. His view was not based on his personal worldview. Rather, he was a political leader concerned with the achievement of Zionism's goals—the establishment of a Jewish state, ensuring its security and stability, and shaping its society.[42] Ben-Gurion was a practical man of politics.[43] Increasing the birthrate was, as he saw it, inseparable from the Zionist effort.

In the 1930s, while immigration was at a high point, Ben-Gurion was not concerned with the low birthrate. The Zionist goal of creating a Jewish majority in Palestine seemed achievable. "We have fought for more immigration," he wrote to his son Amos in 1937, "which in and of itself will bring a Hebrew state into being."[44] In 1939, a few months before the outbreak of World War II, Ben-Gurion was still convinced that millions of Jews from the Diaspora would join the Yishuv: "Our entire young generation in Poland, Romania, America, and other countries will rush to us in the case of a conflict . . . the Jewish state will not depend only on the Jews living within it, but also on the Jewish people throughout the world, the many millions who wish and must settle the land. There are not millions of Arabs who need or want to settle Palestine."[45] The Yishuv's future thus depended not on the question of the relation between the number of Jews and Arabs in Palestine in February 1939 but rather on the one "between the size of the present Yishuv and the millions of Jews who can and want to come."[46] His optimism would be punctured just a few months later, when the new world war upended his axiomatic faith in the Diaspora.

By October of that year, a month after the war began, Ben-Gurion was already speaking of the birthrate as a means of realizing the Zionist goal. His mood was grim at a meeting of the Jewish Agency Executive convened to discuss the plunge in immigration caused by the onset of the war and Britain's refusal to allow more Jews into Palestine. "Who knows if not long from now our fate in this land will depend largely on the number of Jews in it," he said. "It is vital also to take into account the danger of *internal descent* that begins with us."[47] It was his first official remark on the Yishuv's low birthrate, but it was a one-off remark and he would return to the subject only in 1943. But the term Ben-Gurion used here, *yeridah penimit* in Hebrew, was significant.

In Zionist parlance, *aliyah*, literally "ascending," meant immigration to the Land of Israel; the opposite, Jewish emigration, was called *yeridah*, literally "descent." Others also used the term "internal ascent" to refer to the birth of Jewish children in the Yishuv and "internal descent" to refer to the low birthrate and attempts to prevent the birth of children.

Ben-Gurion became convinced that a high birthrate was critical to the Yishuv's future after seeing the numbers presented to him by Bachi.[48] He granted great credence to data and data analysis, and his diary is full of numbers and demographic statistics. He used them as a basis for practical politics and policy.[49] And the numbers were very worrying once the world war started. In April 1943 Ben-Gurion concluded that they painted a distressing picture of the Yishuv's chances of growing after the war. Increasing the Yishuv birthrate thus became a Zionist imperative.[50]

In November 1942 the Yishuv leadership issued its first official communication on the annihilation of Europe's Jews.[51] A few months later, in March 1943, Ben-Gurion made a speech before the Central Committee of Mapai, the largest political party in the Yishuv and early Israel, which later became the Labor Party. The future looked bleak. "This is a catastrophe that we did not expect, because it is not known how many Jews now remain for the Land of Israel."[52] His speech, a transcript of which was printed in newspapers, made a huge impression and brought in a wave of responses and letters.

In the speech, Ben-Gurion pointed to the Yishuv's low birthrate as a danger: "If it continues this way, without any supplement from outside, we are doomed to destruction in a few generations. The kibbutz is doomed to destruction, the village is doomed to destruction, the Yishuv is doomed to destruction, and the labor movement is doomed to destruction."[53] He directed his criticism specifically at the workers and the labor settlements, which he saw as the vanguard of the Zionist enterprise. Ben-Gurion's Zionist aspiration focused not only on the establishment of a Jewish majority in Palestine and a Jewish state but also on the need to fashion a new Jewish society. He thus wanted the birthrate to rise specifically among the kibbutz population, which he saw as the model for the new society he wanted to create, and an influence on urban workers.[54]

Ben-Gurion linked the low number of children born at the kibbutzim to the influence of what he called shoddy capitalism. People, he said, wanted to avoid the tribulations of raising children, and this was the product of "the moral degeneration of capitalist civilization in Western Europe." The most significant question facing the Yishuv as a whole and the labor movement in particular, he maintained, was "whether we, the remnant of the Jewish people, coming to renew our homeland, will be built on the substandard and defective foundation of the degenerate nations of Europe of recent years? Will each young woman and young comrade say that the entire world was built only for his personal enjoyment, and after us, the deluge?"[55] The low birthrate, he claimed, was inconsistent with the Yishuv's Jewish, human, socialist, and Zionist destiny. Ben-Gurion was right about Western Europe—Germany, for example, stood out with its small families and high abortion rate. But he was wrong to attribute it to the West alone. Abortions were widespread in Eastern Europe as well, and in the Soviet Union, unlike the countries of Western Europe, they had been legal for years. Ben-Gurion presumably knew this. But in speaking to the socialist working public, he preferred to point his finger at Western capitalism.

The kibbutzim, which issued a desperate cry during the war years for young people to come provide working hands to make up for the men who had enlisted in the British army, were a prime target for Ben-Gurion. "Do our farms produce young people?" he wondered:

> I mean the birthrate question . . . I ask what right a farm [kibbutz] has . . . to demand young people from outside? These young people they demand are composed of youngsters born of mothers. There is no boy there who has not born of a mother, and this mother did not have an easy time raising him, so there is a moral question: why should this mother send her son to another mother who did not want the trouble of raising children?[56]

"Children," he added, "do not come into being by being enlisted. You need to give birth to them, pure and simple."[57] Ben-Gurion even proposed a minimal number of children per couple (he would eventually demand four, even though he himself only had three children). Once Jews recognized the moral validity of the demand, they would act accordingly, he maintained.[58]

Despite the fact that the low birthrate implicated fathers as well as mothers, Ben-Gurion aimed most of his criticism at women. Motherhood, he maintained, was of key importance to the national enterprise. As such, he primarily blamed mothers for the low birthrate. "The question often comes to mind," he said, "whether our endeavor in this land would have begun had our mothers behaved as our daughters do? Most of us would not even be here."[59] He went so far as to acknowledge that he saw the issue as a "female" one and that as a man he had a hard time making a persuasive argument. "Right now I am sorry that I am not a woman," he said in his speech in 1943, "because it is perhaps easier for a man to talk about the importance of children, because he does not bear the burden of the trouble of bringing them up the way a woman does."[60]

Ben-Gurion's view of the birthrate issue was thus inextricably bound up with his views on women and their role in the Hebrew national revival. Ben-Gurion's private life exhibited a clear dichotomy in this regard. He married Paula, a nurse by profession, in 1917. He was a public figure who devoted all his time and energy to his work. Paula, in contrast, left her work and devoted herself to raising and caring for her children. All household matters were handled by her, sometimes under the most difficult conditions, in order to allow her husband to devote himself to public life.[61] Ben-Gurion was a labor leader who advocated social and gender equality.[62] Yet he wavered between advocating motherhood as the primary and essential role of women and promoting an egalitarian society that insisted on the full participation of women. Tellingly, he wrote to Paula in June 1933, "It would be good if you were to come to the [Zionist] Congress and I will make every effort to enable that. But what about the children?"[63] As he saw it, a family with multiple children needs the mother at home. Later the Ben-Gurions joined Kibbutz Sde Boker. Like other kibbutzim at the time, Sde Boker dismantled the traditional family and handed care of children over to the collective. But his own family was structured along traditional gender lines. While David Ben-Gurion advocated the idea of women's full participation in the national enterprise, he continued to see motherhood as their supreme mission and advocated confining women within bounds that cut them off from public involvement.

It is interesting to note that Roberto Bachi's family was, in this regard, much like Ben-Gurion's. Bachi had four children and devoted himself primarily to his work. He often locked his study from the inside so that his children would not be able to disturb him. His wife also took care not to bother him. "Her husband's scientific work is the Holy of Holies for Mrs. Bachi," a journalist wrote in a profile of her.[64] "First statistics, then me," Vera Bachi said, much along the same lines as Paula Ben-Gurion's relationship with her husband. "I wanted to immigrate to Palestine to do something," Vera Bachi later said. "My husband did, and I tried to help him by showing a happy face, by allowing him to pursue his path unhindered. I raised children—and I do not know if that is much or little."[65] Such a traditional division of gender roles in families that saw the low birthrate as problematic reflects the period they lived in. In fact, at this time most men were their family's principal earner and engaged in public activity while their wives were principally responsible for the home and children. Those who advocated larger families thus presumed that the burden of raising children would fall primarily on mothers. Given the lack at that time of social legislation and institutions to support and assist families, such as affordable childcare, maternity leave, and family-friendly workplaces, advocating larger families was tantamount to promoting stay-at-home mothers.

Fraenkel's speech was the first to broach the issue, but it was Ben-Gurion's speech in 1943 that kick-started public discussion of the low birthrate. Ben-Gurion soon became, in the eyes of the public, the most prominent advocate of large families. "I have followed your ideas and appearances," an inhabitant of Tel Aviv wrote to him in one of many letters that Ben-Gurion received in response, "and I have found that you are, unfortunately, the only person who . . . correctly perceives and understands our situation correctly, who wholeheartedly laments and hurts . . . the birthrate issue."[66]

The Yishuv leadership also raised the issue in the Assembly of Representatives, the Yishuv's legislature, briefly in 1942,[67] but then, in the wake of Ben-Gurion's speech, more extensively in March and September 1943.[68]

When Moshe Shertok (Sharett) gave the keynote address at a session of the Assembly of Representatives in December 1944, he stressed the birthrate issue. As head of the Jewish Agency's Political Department, meaning that he served as the Yishuv's unofficial foreign minister, Shertok might have been expected to address the war in Europe and its impact on the Yishuv and the goal of founding a Jewish state. But he put the birthrate first. "This is a matter on which, more than any other, the long-range political future of the Yishuv depends," he declared. "What is the basis of our political life in this land? Our presence here! That is, the primal political fact that we base ourselves on is the birth of Hebrew children in this country. . . . All our talk and demands for massive immigration and a regime of immigrant absorption stand glaringly opposed to the unending decline of the Yishuv birthrate."[69] Shertok, father of three, maintained that the peril and urgency of the issue had to be stated explicitly and placed at the top of the Yishuv's national agenda. He also maintained that the call for larger families could not be directed solely at the individual. The public was collectively responsible. The Yishuv had to create a "birth regime," under which it would devote time and resources to encouraging the birth of more children. He demanded that the Yishuv as a whole shoulder the burden of creating such a regime. If it did not, he warned, "this grave problem will not be solved."[70]

The members of the Assembly of Representatives agreed that the birthrate had to be put on the same level as immigration and settlement.[71] "Today a child is equal to ten settlements,"[72] especially given the death of so many children in the Holocaust, delegate Avraham Katznelson maintained. Following Shertok's speech, the Assembly resolved that the encouragement of the birthrate needs to be one of the fundamental tasks of Yishuv policy.[73] The Assembly charged the National Council's Executive Committee, its executive arm, with drawing up a policy to achieve this goal, in cooperation with the Jewish Agency Executive, and presenting an action plan to the Assembly's next session.

As the war came to an end, Ben-Gurion began to receive a huge stream of letters from members of the Yishuv. They viewed increasing the birthrate as a national priority that would determine the fate of the Jewish community in Palestine. "The essence of our present struggle is creating a Jewish majority in

Palestine," said one letter sent in November 1945. The Yishuv thus needed to adopt "the additional path . . . of internal immigration, which you previously declared. . . . The present need is to accelerate the birthrate."[74] Most of the letters called for economic support for large families in order to encourage the birth of more children. Others directed the leadership's attention to mothers "who are fulfilling their national mission" by having many children. Some wrote that they were doing so themselves, while facing difficult economic conditions.[75] They all linked large families to the Jewish national struggle.

Ben-Gurion did not need such letters to tell him what he already knew. He grew ever more concerned about the demographic threat. "There is one factor we do not talk about," he said when he appeared before the Anglo-American Committee of Inquiry on the future of Palestine in March 1946. "It is the Arab woman and our Jewish woman. We do not speak about the fact that the Arabs are multiplying . . . , and we are not entirely concerned with raising [our] birthrate."[76]

At a joint meeting of the Jewish Agency Executive and National Council in March 1947, he warned that "the situation is catastrophic and we must take up this problem in a serious way." The question on the table was the allocation of funds to establish a birth fund that would grant economic assistance to large families.[77] A few months later, even before this idea had been put into actual practice, events overtook the Zionist leadership and pushed the birthrate off to the margins of the national agenda. The War of Independence had begun. The birthrate would come up for discussion again only after the establishment of the state of Israel in May 1948, after the battles subsided and a certain tranquility came over the Yishuv. But that takes us into an era not covered by this book.

THE RELIGIOUS ZIONIST POSITION

In the discussion above I referred to religiously observant journalists and public figures. Fraenkel, von Weisl, and others were concerned about the low birthrate first and foremost for national reasons. But in making their arguments they also evoked the central place Jewish tradition assigned to the family and the religious obligation to have children. Fraenkel, active in the religious Zionist Mizrahi Party, viewed abortion as "the murder of the fetus in his mother's belly." He saw rabbis as playing an important role in the campaign against abortions and for large families. Like doctors, rabbis had opportunities to engage in intimate conversation with individuals and to influence large swathes of the population.[78] The important role he assigned to rabbis derived in part from the frequency of abortions in the religious Zionist public.

Procreation is an important and central precept in the Jewish religion. There is no general sanction to limit the number of children a couple has for reasons of economics, welfare, or education, and large families are encouraged. Likewise, Judaism, which sees all life as sacred, largely proscribes abortion. Most leading rabbinic authorities in the modern period have ruled that abortion is expressly forbidden by the Torah, with exceptions being made only if the mother's health is endangered by the pregnancy or birth, or if the fetus is seriously deformed.[79] While some rabbis of the Talmudic and medieval period argued that the ban on abortion was a rabbinic rather than an express prohibition of the written Torah (and could thus be more flexibly balanced against other precepts in certain cases), modern-day halakhic authorities issued strict rulings against it. Their stringent attitude may well have been a reaction to the prevalence of the practice at the time.[80]

One authority who took this unbending approach was Rabbi Yitzhak HaLevi Herzog, who held the post of Ashkenazi chief rabbi of Palestine during the latter part of the British Mandate administration and the early years of Israeli statehood, from 1936 to his death in 1959. Rabbi Herzog grew up in England, earned a PhD in literature from the University of London and served, from 1925 to 1936, as chief rabbi of Ireland. His wife, Sarah, was active in religious Zionist women's organizations; they had two children. Rabbi Herzog ruled that abortion was a serious crime under Jewish law. Aware that many men and women of the Yishuv engaged in sexual relations outside marriage even though this was prohibited by halakhah, he ruled that an unmarried woman who became pregnant was prohibited to have an abortion and had to give birth to the child.[81]

Toward the end of 1942, Rabbi Herzog spoke out vociferously against abortions, and likened the low Yishuv birthrate to the Holocaust, seeing the first as a crime and the second as its punishment:

> The news from the inferno in Europe has terrified the entire Jewish people from one end of the world to the other. . . . Our hearts quake and leap from their place over the horrifying slaughter committed against Jewish children . . . , and here an idea has started to beat in my heart and this idea gives me no rest . . . perhaps this is measure for measure! Under the influence of modern life, a great nation of high culture, a nation that has stood at the pinnacle of modern science and technology, has turned it into wolves of the night, creatures of the forest. This affliction of a low birthrate has spread among us also! It is a hideous sin, a double sin, against the laws of our holy Torah and against the future of our Jewish nation. It is a grave sin against the laws of our sacred Torah, which is a Torah of life, which desires life and the multiplication of life . . . , and a great sin against the Hebrew people. . . . Here we are assisting them by means of reducing our birthrate using forbidden means! And here divine justice has struck us, saying: You have learned the

ways of the modern nations, to shed the "burden" of large families, [and now] the evil people of the gentile nations are casting Jewish children into the water![82]

Here Rabbi Herzog mixed religious and national arguments and depicted the murder of Jewish children in the Holocaust as God's punishment for the Yishuv's use of abortion to prevent the birth of Jewish children. Herzog's position as chief rabbi accorded his pronouncement great weight, and its vehemence, coming from a man known for his level-headedness and sensitivity, lent it great force.[83] Directed at the entire Jewish community, not just the religiously observant, and published in the press, it reached a broad audience and produced many responses. One of them came from another leading religious Zionist figure, Rabbi Yehuda Leib Maimon.

Rabbi Maimon, born in Bessarabia in 1875, settled in Palestine in 1913. He served as a member of the Jewish Agency Executive and was one of the founders of the religious Zionist Mizrahi Party and one of its important leaders in the Yishuv. He minced no words in his reply to Rabbi Herzog's pronouncement:

In such a hellish hour, as our nation convulses in agony, drowning in a sea of blood and tears, as divine judgment is being imposed on all of us, the duty of every true and upright rabbi and great man of Israel . . . is to come to the defense of every Jewish person, to look at his good qualities and not his faults and defects, to tip the balance toward mercy and not toward guilt. At this time of wrath we require defenders and advocates and we must not allow the accuser to testify against us; "he who enumerates [his own] sins is insolent," whether in the case of the individual or a collective of Israel at a time of wrath and rage and tribulation. Those who make a pretense of being zealots of the Jewish faith, be they great men of Torah and rabbis of Israel . . . seek out sins in the tents of others and sound a public alarm over every lapse and publicly declare every transgression and crime of the individual or the public, in these days, at this time—they will in the future be called to task and their sin is unbearable.[84]

Both these public pronouncements by prominent rabbis familiar to the entire Yishuv were exceptional in their passion. Both should be read as primal emotional responses to the initial news of the systematic annihilation of Europe's Jews. That news could not but put the deliberate prevention of the birth of Jewish children in a new light. For that reason, neither rabbi restricted himself to the strictly halakhic aspects of the issue.

Many in the religious Zionist camp drew a line between the Holocaust and the Yishuv birthrate. For them, encouraging larger families in the Yishuv was both a comfort and a way of avenging the slaughter of Europe's Jews, as well as a way of ensuring the Jewish people's future. But, unlike Rabbi

Herzog, they did not see it in the framework of sin and divine retribution. Abraham Fraenkel believed that, in the face of the Holocaust, the Yishuv had a responsibility to maintain the entire nation, and thus had to produce many children and fight limitations on their numbers.[85] *Hatzofeh*, the daily newspaper of the religious Zionist movement, often protested the low birthrate of the Yishuv as a whole and of the kibbutzim in particular.[86] In 1944 it declared that the low birthrate was a "national crime in light of the loss of a large part of our people." It stressed that for the religious public "it is also a serious religious transgression."[87] Again, the national and religious aspects of the issue were intertwined. The same connection was made by the Religious Kibbutz Movement.

"The Yishuv has been shocked to its very foundations," proclaimed a speaker at a convention of the movement's members in December 1942. The way to recover from the heavy blow dealt by the Holocaust was to fill the vacuum produced by the annihilation of "the dense ranks of rooted and popular Judaism." That would be accomplished by natural increase. Jews should not surrender to economic and psychological barriers to having children, the movement said: "We will establish a healthy and huge generation. This is the most natural response, which will realize the nation's healthy desire. This will be our revenge."[88]

The enemy sought to destroy the Jewish people, the Religious Kibbutz Movement proclaimed. The proper response was thus maximum procreation, as the Israelites in Egypt had done: "The more they were oppressed, the more they increased" (Exodus 1:12). "All the surviving House of Israel should raise up other seed in place of the seed that was cut down," the movement declared.[89] A national convention of religious women's organizations in 1944 issued a similar call for a higher birthrate as a response to the killing in Europe: "Here, the cry of the daughter of our people comes from the distance, millions of Jews, our brothers and sisters, were annihilated and killed mercilessly by the enemy and nemesis. . . . Let us fill this great void by fulfilling the sturdy foundation of the Torah of Israel . . . to produce a fit and pure generation in our holy land."[90]

As I have already noted, religious Zionist families in the Yishuv also practiced birth control and abortion. The halakhic strictures regarding these issues were only one consideration they took into account. Now, in the face of the Holocaust, the movement's leaders and thinkers also seriously weighed the national aspect of the issue. "The individual needs to take an internal religious-national attitude toward the problem of [natural] increase," a writer in *Hatzofeh* declared.[91] Each religious Zionist, in other words, should evaluate these issues through the prism of his or her religious and national obligations.

Like the rest of the Yishuv, physicians stood on both sides of the issue of the low birthrate. On the one hand, as shown in the previous chapters, no few doctors performed abortions in private clinics and in private and public hospitals. Women of all ethnic groups and ages flocked to Hadassah's hospitals in Tel Aviv and Jerusalem, seeking to end their pregnancies.[92] The doctors performed abortions for a variety of reasons, some economic and some ideological.

In contrast, not a few doctors were concerned about the low birthrate and particularly so about abortions, which were against the law. Physicians of both opinions worked side by side, and sometimes arguments over the issue broke out among them. Dr. Samuel Zondek, chief of the Department of Internal Medicine at Hadassah Hospital in Tel Aviv, opposed the performance of abortions for social reasons in his hospital, while his colleague, Dr. Arieh Sadowski, performed the procedure in Zondek's ward, in keeping with his liberal ideas.[93]

Doctors of a variety of specializations voiced their disapproval of the low birthrate and widespread practice of abortion in the Yishuv. The opponents included psychiatrists, among them Prof. Yehoshua Fishel Schneerson, who diagnosed an "only-child melancholy" syndrome that, he maintained, was a product of the inclination of many families not to have more than one child. He warned that only children growing up in a home environment devoid of other children were susceptible to neurosis.[94] Gynecologists, pediatricians like Dr. Bilhah Puliastor and Dr. Rosa Meyer, and several general practitioners opposed birth control and abortion on national grounds.[95] Some doctors were also active politically. For example, Dr. Avraham Katznelson was a member of the Zionist Executive and director of the National Council's Health Department, charged with enforcing the authority of the Yishuv's autonomous governing bodies over the medical profession.[96]

Doctors were also concerned with the purely medical side of abortion and the dangerous consequences it could have for women. The risk was especially high when abortions were performed covertly. "The abortion done in secret endangers women's health and even their lives. Many women have experienced it on their own bodies," Dr. Miriam Aharonova, a gynecologist, warned in an information booklet put out by Kupat Holim.[97] Born in 1889 in Mogilev, Belarus, she studied medicine and specialized in St. Petersburg, and arrived in Palestine in 1929. As part of her work in Ein Harod hospital and later in Kupat Holim Clalit in Tel Aviv, she counseled pregnant women."[98]

Dr. Aharonova spoke openly about contraceptive devices and encouraged their use. Rather than seeing them as a means of liberating women, she viewed them as a way of spacing births so as to create better conditions for each family's children. She adamantly opposed abortions, however. "The rough hand of man comes and subverts nature's delicate wisdom of accommodation. It tears out and destroys the fetus," she wrote in 1934 in her book *The Hygiene of Women's Lives Stage by Stage*.[99] She hoped that she could prevent them by explaining how the procedure endangered women's physical and mental health. It takes a long time for the body to return to its former state after an abortion, Aharonova claimed. Even when the procedure is successful, it can bring on weakness, tension, and depression. If it fails, the outcome can be life threatening.[100]

But it was not only the health risks that made Aharonova oppose abortions; she also viewed abortion as murder and thus as immoral. To her mind, women who did not want to have a child for social reasons were pathological. Like other doctors, she also had eugenic reasons for opposing the procedure. Abortions were most common among the educated urban public, those whom she and others saw as the desirable breeders.[101]

Eugenics was a biological and social theory that sought to improve the human species by overseeing reproduction and determining who should have children with whom. It first spread through the West at the end of the nineteenth century and gained widespread acceptance in the interwar period. Many scientists sought to spur people "of high genetic-hereditary value to produce many offspring." This view, termed "positive eugenics," had no connection to the doctrine of a superior race.[102] The Nazi regime, which transformed eugenics into racism, discredited eugenics among scientists and the general public.

In the Yishuv the eugenic discourse began in the 1920s, when many teachers, political leaders and, in particular, doctors took it up during their studies in Europe and brought it to Palestine.[103] Proclaiming that the Yishuv should forge a healthy nation made up of a new kind of Jew, they advocated eugenic ideas to ensure the creation of a strong and fit younger generation who would serve as the core of the new society.[104]

Dr. Joseph Mayer, Kupat Holim Clalit's medical director, held eugenist views.[105] "Our nation has returned to live, to a life of nature in the land of its fathers," he wrote. "Is it not our duty to see to it that it will have healthy children, whole in body and soul? . . . For us, eugenics as a whole and, specifically, being on guard against the transmission of inheritable diseases, has much greater value than it does for other nations."[106] He maintained that children should be born to the nation the Yishuv was building only if it was certain that they would be healthy in body and mind. He thus advocated abortion for eugenic purposes—to prevent the transmission of genetic diseases. Parents should be freed of the obligation to be chained their whole lives to the care of a defective child. Doctors had an obligation to perform abortions when there was a risk of the transmission of diseases from parents to children.[107]

The corollary to the eugenic views held by many physicians was a complicated attitude toward contraception and abortion. On the one hand, they favored a high birthrate and opposed abortion in order to achieve the goal of producing a Jewish majority in Palestine. On top of this they pointed to medical and moral reasons for this position. Yet, on the other hand, they did not want just any children to be born. They wanted to breed not Diaspora Jews but rather new Jews of an entirely different physical and mental type.[108] This dictated the judicious and systematic use of contraception and abortion to prevent the birth of undesirables.

In short, they sought to encourage a higher birthrate among certain populations only, specifically that of the largely Ashkenazi New Yishuv, composed of middle-class city dwellers, the Zionist labor movement, and urban and rural pioneers. Many members of the Yishuv saw these groups as the foundation of the new Jewish society. A high birthrate among them was thus desirable in the extreme. Perversely, as they saw it, these groups were characterized by a low birthrate. The Jewish populations with high birthrates were precisely those that the eugenicists saw as detrimental to the national project—the Haredi Old Yishuv and the Mizrahim. These groups needed to be taught to use contraception and abortion to reduce their family size.

Ironically, by the 1930s the Yishuv had gained more than a few members, among them demographers and physicians, who had arrived from fascist countries like Germany and Italy. These people had personal experience of how eugenic policies could lead to prejudice and gross discrimination against Jews. They nevertheless continued to aspire to its implementation in Palestine. Bachi, for example, had advocated eugenics in Italy, yet the very policies he advocated served as the basis for the racial laws that ended up destroying his career there and prompting him to move to Palestine. Yet in Palestine he continued to advocate the encouragement of a higher birthrate only among certain populations, and the reduction of births in others. This paradox reflected the complexity of the Yishuv itself, characterized as it was by rival conceptions of what Jewish society should be and by great social, ethnic, and religious fissures.

Perceptions of the Mizrahi Community's Birthrate

The Jews who came to Palestine from Asia and Africa had large families, but this was not viewed favorably by many other parts of the Yishuv. The press regularly described the overcrowded conditions in which the Mizrahim lived as a result of their many children. Their neighborhoods were said to be derelict and many of them lived in dire poverty.[109] While many Ashkenazim also suffered privation during this period, they, unlike the Mizrahim, did not generally have large families. The press often asked whether, under these circumstances, the Mizrahim should be encouraged to maintain their high birthrate or, alternatively, taught and encouraged to reduce it.[110]

One Zionist goal was to fashion a new modern—that is, European—society. Modern European families were small. Many in the Yishuv thus viewed large families as both economically and culturally feeble, as well as foreign to their vision of the Jewish nation.[111] Dr. Mayer of Kupat Holim maintained that the huge Yemenite families living on Tel Aviv's margins were not really part of modern Zionist society. "They have really just exchanged one Exile for another Exile, and today, in the Land of Israel, they remain in Exile," he wrote.[112]

Prof. Yehoshua Fishel Schneersohn, a psychiatrist and educator who headed the Childhood Psycho-Hygienic Station in Tel Aviv, maintained in 1937 that there was a correlation between Mizrahi ethnicity and "pedagogical retardation." His claim, widely accepted by professionals and teachers, was that the difficulties experienced by Mizrahi children were a result of growing up in a culturally primitive environment, and that their cognitive inferiority was caused by the backward culture of the Mizrahim.[113] The large number of children in Mizrahi families was, in his view, an element of this cultural benightedness.

Bachi remarked that those sectors of the Yishuv in which large numbers of children were the norm—meaning primarily the Mizrahim—families had trouble managing. Multiple children led to negative social phenomena such as neglect, delinquency, and nonproductivity, all of which were evident among Mizrahi youth.[114] Bachi's and Mayer's views were typical of large portions of the Yishuv—the Mizrahim were seen as a menace to the new Hebrew society being built in Palestine.[115]

The Mizrahim were a minority in the Yishuv, but their high fertility meant that was only temporary, it was feared. "In a few years these communities are liable to become a majority," a writer in 'Al Hamishmar, the newspaper of the revolutionary Marxist-Zionist HaShomer HaTza'ir movement, wrote in 1948. "It needs to be stated clearly: if we do not give our attention to this, this backward part of our nation may well leave its impression on the economic and sociological level of the Yishuv as a whole."[116] The writer stressed that he did not see all Mizrahim as a problem. Many of them were well-off and even intellectuals, he maintained, but these were a minority. He was speaking, he said, of the vast majority of the community that lived in poverty, the "large strata encumbered by children."

This paradox, in which Yishuv leaders sought to encourage a higher birthrate, but only selectively among those they saw as members of the "right" population, was not unique. A research paper regarding the birth patterns in Britain, submitted to the Royal Commission on Population in 1947 by Cyril Burt, a British educational psychologist, claimed to show a negative correlation between the education of parents and the number of children, while families lacking intellectual abilities had more children. He concluded that if this trend continued, the number of feebleminded children would double by the end of the century, whereas the number of young people fit for higher education would halve.[117] Britain was thus also wondering how families of developed mental and intellectual capacities could be encouraged to have more children and less fit ones to have fewer. Mayer asked, regarding the Mizrahim, and in particular the Yemenites, whether "we will teach them Malthus's theory immediately upon their arrival in Palestine—one child per family?"[118]

But this was not the focus of public discussion of the birthrate issue prior to the founding of the state. Only afterward, when huge numbers of immigrants from the Islamic world arrived in Israel, did such sentiments take center stage. Nevertheless, the sentiments were certainly there during the Yishuv period, displaying the ambiguity of the attitude toward the birthrate, which was seen as something to be increased in certain parts of the population but not in others. They are evidence of the ethnic divides that already split the Jewish community in Palestine.

NOTES

1. Clark and Kaiser 2003.
2. Offen 1991; Tomlinson 1985; Reggiani 1996.
3. For example, Helman 2012; Hirsch 2014; Shoham 2013.
4. Avraham Bar-Orian, "'Ad shelo Notzarti," *Hatzofeh*, July 13, 1943, 4.
5. Ibid.
6. Ibid.
7. Dayan 1959, 95–101.
8. Lilia [Bassewitz], "Isha, Em Vayeled," *Mibifnim*, Apr. 1933, 18.
9. Yocheved Bat-Rachel, "De'agat haImahut," Merkaz Kupat Holim, Jan. 1945, YTA, 15-36/4/4, 8.
10. Tova Berman, "'Al Be'ayot haYeludah," apparently 1943, CZA A516/100.
11. Bachi 1943a, 19.
12. Kanievsky 1944, 195.
13. Shechter 2011, 252.
14. Program for a radio talk for a week devoted to birthrate issues, July 1944, CZA J1/3717/2.
15. Bachi 1943a, 19.
16. Ir-Shai 2006, 28.
17. Usborne 2011; Brewer 2000.
18. Winckler 2007; Portugese 1998.

19. Report on the activities of the Committee on Birthrate Problems, during its two years of existence (May 1943–Apr. 1945), Apr. 29, 1945, CZA J1/1974.

20. Letter of Dr. A. Abramovitch, director of Hadassah municipal hospital, to A. Perlson, chairman of the board, May 28, 1937, TAA, Hadassah hospital, 4-4645.

21. Fraenkel 1967.

22. "Ne'um Rektor ha'Universitah, Professor A. H. Fraenkel baTekes haSiyum," *Hatzofeh*, May 5, 1940, 3; report on the activities of the Committee on Birthrate Problems, during its two years of existence (May 1943–Apr. 1945), Apr. 29, 1945, CZA J1/1974.

23. Fraenkel 1944, 28–29.

24. Alroey 2010, 87.

25. Ibid., 89–90.

26. Tikva Weinstock, "Seder Nashim: Vera Bachi," *Maariv*, Nov. 22, 1957 (n.p.).

27. Ibid.

28. Committee on Birthrate Problems, "Tokhnit lePolitikah Demografit," Apr. 22, 1945, CZA J1/2383.

29. Bachi 1943b, 6.

30. Roberto Bachi, "HaYeludah be Yisra'el uvaYishuv vehaDerakhim le'Idudah," apparently 1944, CZA J1/3717/3.

31. Roberto Bachi, "Be'ayat haYeludah BeYisra'el veHatza'ot leMediniyut haUkhlusiyah," undated, ISA 5588/2c.

32. Ibid.

33. Committee on Birthrate Problems, "Tokhnit lePolitikah Demografit," Apr. 22, 1945, CZA J1/2383.

34. Report on the activities of the Committee on Birthrate Problems, during its two years of existence (May 1943–Apr. 1945), Apr. 29, 1945, CZA J1/1974.

35. Program for a radio talk for a week devoted to birthrate issues, July 1944, CZA J1/3717/2; "Be'ayat haYeludah baYishuv" (no byline, apparently Bachi), Apr. 12, 1943, *Ha'aretz* (n.p.), CZA J1/3737/1.

36. Tova Berman, "Ha'Emtza'im haDerushim le'Idud haYeludah baYishuv," Feb. 1945, CZA J1/3717/3.

37. Kibbutz member, "Lo Zo haDerekh," *Devar Hapo'elet* 7:1, Mar. 31, 1940, 27.

38. Dr. Ze'ev von Weisl, "HaYeludah bein haYehudim Haitah vaNemukhah beYoter," *Hamashkif*, July 18, 1941, 3; "Mispar haYehudim ba'Aretz" (no byline), *Hamashkif*, Dec. 17, 1939, 3; Ba'al Heshbon, "Mah Garam leHafhatat Ahuz haUkhlusiah haYehudit," *Hamashkif*, Aug. 3, 1942, 2.

39. Kanievsky 1944, 23.

40. Play transcript, Hava'ad leHaganah 'Al Kvod Bat Yisrael, 1945, TAA 8-1109.

41. Ze'ev (Wolfgang) von Weisl, "Me'et ha'Elef She'avdu Lanu LaNetsah," *Hamashkif*, Oct. 10, 1947, 3.

42. Bareli 1986, 10; Sheffer 1997.

43. Tzahor 1996, 136.

44. Letter from David Ben-Gurion to Amos, his son, July 27, 1937, in Ben-Gurion 1968, 179, 182.

45. Letter from David Ben-Gurion to Amos, Oct. 5, 1937, in ibid., 213.

46. Letter from David Ben-Gurion to Paula, Feb. 10, 1939, in ibid., 292.

47. My emphasis; Jewish Agency Executive meeting, Oct. 30, 1939, in Ben-Gurion 1997, 219. I thank Dr. Zvi Zameret for this reference.

48. Letter from D. Gurevich to David Ben-Gurion, May 6, 1936, CZA S44/203.

49. Barell 2012, 92, 99–100, 105.

50. BGA/Correspondence/210542.

51. Porat and Weitz 2002, 112.
52. Ben-Gurion speech, Mar. 3, 1943, BGA/Shabtai Teveth Collection/concepts/12-100.
53. David Ben-Gurion, "Shalosh He'arot," *Hapo'el Hatza'ir* 27, Mar. 18, 1947, 2.
54. A meeting in Jerusalem, May 2, 1944, BGA/Diaries/225700.
55. David Ben-Gurion, "Shalosh He'arot," *Hapo'el Hatza'ir* 27, Mar. 18, 1947, 2.
56. Ben-Gurion speech, Mar. 3, 1943, BGA/Shabtai Teveth Collection/concepts/12-100.
57. David Ben-Gurion, "Shalosh He'arot," *Hapo'el Hatza'ir* 27, Mar. 18, 1947, 2.
58. Ibid., 3.
59. Ibid.
60. Ibid.
61. Bar-Zohar 1975, 158–159; Ben-Ami 2010, 33.
62. Berkovitz 1999, 283, 290–291; Tzahor 1986.
63. Letter from David Ben-Gurion to Paula, June 13, 1933, in Ben-Gurion 1968, 85.
64. Tikva Weinstock, "Seder Nashim: Vera Bachi," *Maariv*, Nov. 22, 1957 (n.p.).
65. Ibid.
66. Letter from Mr. Hefetz to Ben-Gurion, Nov. 25, 1943, BGA/Correspondence/209609.
67. Letter from Dr. Ephraim Waschitz to Bachi, Apr. 18, 1943, CZA J1/3717/1.
68. For example, Dr. Ephraim Waschitz, Assembly of Representatives, Mar. 3, 1943; Dr. Avraham Katzenelson and Jacob Cohen, Assembly of Representatives, Sept. 29, 1943, CZA J1/7220.
69. Moshe Shertok, Assembly of Representatives, Dec. 4, 1944, CZA J1/7192.
70. Ibid.; Moshe Shertok speech (no byline), *Davar*, Dec. 5, 1944, 1.
71. Uri, Assembly of Representatives, Dec. 5, 1944; Rachel Kagan, Elazar and Tabib, Assembly of Representatives, Dec. 6, 1944, CZA J1/7222.
72. Dr. A. Katznelson, Assembly of Representatives, Dec. 8, 1944, CZA J1/7222.
73. A summary of discussions of the Assembly of Representatives meetings on Dec. 1944 (no byline, undated), CZA J1/1974.
74. Letter from Meir Gurevich to Ben-Gurion, Nov. 23, 1945, BGA /correspondence/183876.
75. Letter from Shlomo Yatom to Ben-Gurion and Moshe Shertok, Jan. 18, 1945; letter from Zila Tishbi, Jan. 14, 1945; letter from A. Shrem, Jan. 14, 1945, CZA S44/719.
76. Minutes of meeting of the Jewish Agency Executive, Mar. 24, 1946, BGA/Shabtai Teveth/collection/concepts/12-100.
77. Minutes of meeting of the Jewish Agency Executive, Mar. 20, 1947, BGA/Protocols/227529.
78. Fraenkel 1944, 42.
79. Ir-Shai 2008, 437–439.
80. Ibid., 428–436. I am grateful to Ronit Ir-Shai for this insight.
81. Memorandum from a meeting with Rabbi Yitzhak Herzog, Prof. Avraham Fraenkel, and Prof. Roberto Bachi, 1943 (no specific date), CZA J1/3717/2.
82. Yitzhak Halevi Herzog, "Daber el ha'Am," *Hatzofeh*, Dec. 7, 1942, 1.
83. Eshkoli-Wagman 2012, 288.
84. Rabbi Y[ehuda] L[eib] Hacohen Maimon, "Tokhakhat Megulah—laMokhikhim," *Bamishor*, Dec. 8, 1942, 2–3.
85. Fraenkel 1944, 5–8.
86. Ben Bracha, "BeAspaklariyah," *Hatzofeh*, June 18, 1941, 2.
87. "Le'Inyanei haSha'ah" (no byline), *Hatzofeh*, Oct. 5, 1944, 2.
88. *'Alonim* (no title, no byline) 12, Dec. 20, 1942 (n.p.).
89. Ibid.
90. HaMerkaz leTaharat haMishpakhah ba'Aretz (no author), Sept. 1944, TAA 8-1110.
91. L. Bein, "HaRibui haTiv'i veHishuvei he'Atid haKarov," *Hatzofeh*, June 8, 1945, 5.
92. Letter of Dr. A. Abramovitch, director of Hadassah municipal hospital, to A. Perlson, chairman of the board, May 28, 1937, TAA, Hadassah hospital, 4–4645.

93. Dr. Haim Yassky, memorandum of discussion with Prof. Bernhard Zondek (from Dec. 18, 1935), Dec. 22, 1935, CZA J113/7487.

94. Razi 2009, 166–167.

95. Dr. Bilhah Puliastor, "HaHapalah ha Mela'akhutit," *Davar*, July 29, 1931, 3; letter from Dr. Shoshana Meyer to the Health Department of the National Council, May 20, 1940, CZA J1/3717/1; "Be'ayat haYeludah baYishuv" (no byline, apparently Bachi), Apr. 12, 1943, *Ha'aretz* (n.p.), CZA J1/3737/1.

96. Levy 1998, 238; Dr. Avraham Katznelson, Assembly of Representatives, Dec. 8, 1944, CZA J1/7222.

97. M. A., "Tahanot ha'Eitza laNashim veTafkidan," *Ha'em Vehayeled*, 1933–1934, 6.

98. On Dr. Aharonova, see Shvarts and Stoler-Liss 2011.

99. In ibid., 97.

100. Ibid., 98.

101. Ibid.

102. Zalashik 2008, 92.

103. Falk 2006, 139–161.

104. Zalashik 2008, 94.

105. Shvarts and Stoler-Liss 2011, 89.

106. J[oseph]. M[ayer]., "Mi Rashai Leholid Banim," *Ha'em Vehayeled*, 1933–1934, 3.

107. Ibid., 4.

108. Biale 1992, 231–267.

109. "LeGoral ha'Aliyah me'Artzot haMizrah" (no byline), *Davar*, Dec. 10, 1947, 2.

110. A. Abas, "Keitzad Napil et haMekhitzot bein ha'Edot baYishuv," *'Al Hamishmar*, Mar. 25, 1948, 2; J[oseph]. M[ayer]., "Mi Rashai Leholid Banim," *Ha'em Vehayeled*, 1933–1934, 4; Dr. Joseph Mayer, "Hagbarat haYeludah o Ribui haYeladim," *Eitanim* 5:3–4 (Spring 1952), 76.

111. Letter from Dr. A. Abramovitch, director of Hadassah municipal hospital, to A. Perlson, chairman of the board, May 28, 1937, TAA, Hadassah hospital, 4-4645; see also Melamed 2004, 69–73.

112. Dr. J[oseph] Mayer, "Havah veNa'aleh Otam leEretz Yisra'el," *Davar*, Apr. 10, 1946, 2.

113. Razi 2009, 104.

114. Roberto Bachi, "Maskanot Politiyot metokh Hakirotay 'al haHitpathut haDemografit shel haYehudim veha'Aravim beE"Y," Oct. 1944, CZA J1/3717/2, 1.

115. Schenkolewski 2009.

116. A. Abas, "Keitzad Napil et haMekhitzot bein ha'Edot baYishuv," *'Al Hamishmar*, Mar. 25, 1948, 2.

117. Eliezer Levinstein, "Be'ayot Sotziyaliot Hadashot," *Davar*, Feb. 25, 1947, 2.

118. Dr. J[oseph] Mayer, "Havah veNa'aleh Otam leEretz Yisra'el," *Davar*, Apr. 10, 1946, 2.

Chapter Six

MAKING MORE BABIES

The Yishuv, like many other countries, recognized the need for a systematic policy to raise the birthrate. As such, it sought to fashion a policy for itself while taking into account what other Western countries were doing in the same area.[1]

European nations concerned about their low birthrates, Roberto Bachi remarked in 1943, "long ago woke up to the danger that awaited them." From democratic France to fascist Italy, from peace-loving Sweden to war-like Germany, countries had crafted a "demographic politics" to address the issue, Bachi wrote.[2] Before taking measures to encourage a higher birthrate, the Yishuv wished to take stock of the means used by other nations, "which also face the danger of ongoing population decline."[3] The policies pursued by Western nations to encourage larger families were examined in lectures,[4] research literature,[5] and at professional and public meetings, placing the Yishuv's situation in a larger context. A variety of solutions and the possibility of adapting them to local conditions were discussed.[6]

Encouraging Larger Families in the West

The management of fertility and the birthrate is closely connected to nationalism. The nation sees fertility as an important part of its survival and development strategy,[7] and it mobilizes the family to serve the nation's needs in this regard.[8] The national discourse stresses in particular the important role of the woman as mother of the nation. She is responsible for its physical, cultural, and social development, and is the guarantor of the nation's future.[9] As such, when the birthrate declines, women's intimate, private, and individual decisions about whether and when to bring children into the world come under the public spotlight.

Fertility policies were implemented in Europe as early as the seventeenth century.[10] But it was during the nineteenth century, with the awakening of nationalism in the West, that societies ratcheted up their treatment of fertility. It became more and more acceptable for the nation to intervene in the family so as to guarantee its survival and strength. In light of the decline in the birthrate, many Western countries began to adopt policies to encourage a higher birthrate; many made abortion illegal.[11] Turning abortion into a serious crime marked the transition of fertility from a personal to a social issue, and became a model for social and government intervention in the lives of individuals.[12]

Demographic panic at the plummeting birthrate was evident in many European countries, especially in the period between the world wars, most notably in Germany, Britain, Russia, and France.[13] In both democracies and dictatorships individual reproductive rights were subordinated to national demographic needs.[14] This was especially evident in nationalist and fascist regimes such as Nazi Germany, Mussolini's Italy, and Franco's Spain.[15] But other countries also placed national control of the birthrate at the center of public discourse, implementing anti-abortion measures with the express intent of encouraging the birth of more babies.[16]

Forbidding abortions was, however, just one of a three-pronged effort to raise the birthrate. The other two means pursued were education and economic incentives.[17] Different countries weighted these approaches in their own and sometimes opposite ways. Some countries liberalized abortion laws while others enforced them strictly. Such differences arose from different views about fertility, conception, and contraception, and from the special circumstances of each nation.[18]

Some countries took different approaches to the birthrate at different times. The prime example is Germany, which, as I have noted, had three different kinds of regime between 1871 and 1945: it was a monarchy until 1918, a republic between that year and 1933, and then a dictatorship until 1945. The birthrate declined during each of these eras.[19] In 1871 abortion was made a criminal offense with severe penalties.[20] But after the World War I, during the Weimar Republic, especially during the depression years of the 1920s, the public climate was relatively liberal. Attempts were made then to rethink the birthrate issue and craft policies in tune with the socioeconomic situation and real life. An eugenic approach to the issue came into currency: "fewer but better children." The government sought to balance individual rights with the national interest, family and personal welfare with larger eugenic considerations. This was the background to the liberalization of the anti-abortion law in 1926–1927. But the issue remained a live one, with proponents and opponents of abortion contending with each other.[21]

Government intervention in fertility and the birthrate reached its climax when the Nazis came to power. They viewed abortion as a crime against life and against the German people. The new regime also began fashioning a selective fertility policy based on racial factors. Individual rights were no longer recognized. Material and ideological support for increased fertility were lent to so-called Aryans, in order to restrict family planning among them. At the same time, repressive measures were instituted to suppress fertility among the Jews, who were considered an inferior race, as well as among the unhealthy and other undesirables. State oversight of fertility was tightened and punishments for abortions were toughened dramatically. But in 1935 the regime ruled that abortions were permitted if needed to preserve the purity of the Aryan master race. At the same time, Nazi Germany adopted other measures aimed at encouraging Aryan fertility.[22] One example was the Lebensborn program, headed by Heinrich Himmler, which included drastic actions such as the kidnapping of children who were identified as belonging to the "master race" and placing them in special reeducation camps.[23] During World War II the treatment of women who had abortions became more severe, and the death penalty was imposed on abortionists. After the war, both East and West Germany voided these provisions as part of their effort to separate themselves from the Nazi past. Abortions were permitted in cases of rape and for health reasons.[24]

During the 1920s the Soviet Union sent out contradictory messages regarding women and the birthrate. While the regime was committed to the liberation of women, women were nevertheless told that they had to have children for the sake of the nation and to renew the working class and Soviet society after the loss of millions of lives in World War I and the Revolution. Nevertheless, in 1920 the Soviet Union became the first country in the world to explicitly permit abortions by law, not because it saw them as desirable but out of concern for women's health. It wanted to ensure that women who had abortions did so in a proper professional setting. But the Soviet regime was also concerned about the birthrate and sought to increase its population in keeping with the needs of industry and modern warfare. To strengthen families the regime restored the prohibition on abortions in 1936, excepting only cases in which the pregnancy put the woman's health at risk.[25]

Another country that attracted the Yishuv's attention in this regard was France. Laws passed there in the 1920s prohibited both contraception and abortion,[26] and the birthrate was much debated by politicians, professionals, and feminists. France offered a variety of solutions to the problem, some of which the Yishuv sought to adopt.[27]

Legal measures, such as those that banned abortion or guaranteed working mothers assistance and labor rights, were one way countries sought to raise the birthrate.[28] Many laws aimed to provide families with greater social and financial security. Some, like labor laws and social programs, were meant to guarantee a decent standard of living and a livelihood for working people during periods of unemployment or incapacity. The state also took it upon itself to provide housing and proper nourishment. Some countries paid a stipend for each child, subsidized housing for families, and granted large families tax benefits. Some awarded prizes for having a baby or for nursing or mandated several weeks of vacation for the mother before and after a baby's birth.

A large variety of financial incentives were tried. France and Belgium were the first to take this tack, offering family salary supplements and tax breaks, as well as establishing, at large industrial concerns, provident funds that collected dues from workers and used the money to provide salary supplements for the heads of families. France imposed a tax on single adults and families that had not produced a child within two years of marriage. Some American states offered women prizes for having a child within two years of marriage. A proposal raised in Germany before Hitler's rise to power sought to modify inheritance laws so that only children would receive just half of their parents' estate, with the state taking the other half. That money would then be used to provide support for large families. Both Germany and Italy offered loans to enable newlyweds to purchase vital household goods and to finance projects and business initiatives that would enable the family to advance economically. A part of the loan was forgiven when a child was born. In Russia, pregnant women were given four months of leave, and when abortions were banned, assistance to mothers was increased. Belgium offered fathers the right to cast votes in the names of their children, on the grounds that "he who has more children has done more for the nation."[29]

In considering such matters, the Yishuv took into account local circumstances and the cultural environment, as well as its unique characteristics. "Many nations . . . have taken political measures to encourage the birthrate, of which there are many, but only some of them are appropriate for our situation and our land," Bachi maintained.[30] Tova Berman noted that what made the Yishuv unique was that, in its case, the birthrate question was a matter of life or death.[31]

The Yishuv also differed from other polities in its nature and structure, and in its limited ability to enforce any decisions its leadership made. Rather than a state, the Yishuv was a voluntary public association that aspired to found a state, but which was in the meantime subject to British rule. The Yishuv saw itself as a state-in-the-making and tried to conduct itself according to the same standards that applied to well-run countries. It thus ran its elected and public institutions democratically, and these institutions provided a wide range of social and national services. But it had little in the way of enforcement mechanisms and its resources were limited. "We do not have the resources of a state," Berman said in the early 1940s. Nevertheless, she said, "We can do much with the poor resources we have."[32] The greatest of these resources was the consensus around the national goal, to which many individual aspirations and needs were subordinated. This goal became the basis of the local campaign for a higher birthrate. In fact, the Yishuv's grappling with the birthrate issue and its attempts to shape a systematic policy with regard to it was mortar in the construction of the future state.

The Beginning: Local and Private Initiatives

The Yishuv followed two paths to encourage larger families. First, it offered positive support for the birth of more children; second, it fought abortions. These were ostensibly two different aspects that required separate channels of activity, but they were in fact two sides of the same coin. To encourage more births, one had to fight the means of limiting them. In most of the available sources these two aspects are interwoven, sometimes to the extent that it is difficult to separate them out, and in keeping with those sources I take the same approach. However, when a clear distinction is made in the sources, I reflect that here.

From the beginning of the 1930s voices were raised warning of the danger that the low birthrate presented to the Yishuv.[33] The press warned that the phenomenon of limiting families to one son and one daughter had become standard in the Yishuv.[34] Concerned citizens began writing to the press, to public citizens, public figures who had spoken out on the subject (such as Bachi), physicians, and health organizations with proposals for increasing the birthrate.[35]

Health professionals like Dr. Shoshana Meyer, a pioneer in her early days in Palestine, and Dr. Fritz Noak, deputy director of the National Council's Health Department, opposed abortions and the low birthrate on national grounds and believed that the most important way to counter it was to deal with the doctors who were performing abortions.[36] Even they accepted, however, that the only way to influence doctors who were operating independently was a top-down change beginning with the responsible institutions. Lilia Bassewitz argued at the beginning of the 1930s that well-off women could do as they wished. But working women, or the wives of working men, most of who struggled to make a livelihood, were dependent on the institutional doctors in her place of residence. This dependence, Bassewitz said, "raises the demand that the entire institution, not just each individual doctor, fix a policy on these intimate-public matters."[37]

In keeping with this approach, private individuals demanded that the responsible institutions, such as Hadassah and the National Council, take action. Hadassah was seen as a national institution, duty-bound to contribute to the building of the nation rather than to limit itself to purely medical issues. Accordingly, Dr. Phillip Rivlin of Petah Tikva argued that "it is the duty of the Hadassah medical centers to place this problem on a national-political level." Hadassah should investigate the dimensions of the low birthrate problem and campaign against it in cooperation with municipal and other institutions.[38] Hadassah's Statistics Department indeed looked into and confirmed that the Yishuv birthrate was declining,[39] but it took no real counteraction.

Assigning Hadassah this mission also had a local and municipal character. In 1932, for example, the board of the Hadassah hospital in Tel Aviv warned that a decline in births should be of concern to medical institutions and that "energetic measures should be taken, in particular against abortions, which have taken on huge dimensions."[40] Nothing was done directly to prevent abortions, but in the years that followed an attempt was made to improve conditions for new mothers so as to encourage them to have babies. As I have already noted, having a baby in Palestine was not an easy matter. Hospital maternity words could not provide adequate care for the Yishuv's growing population, and many women had to go to private clinics at considerable cost, or to give birth at home with all the risks that involved. In 1935 the Tel Aviv City Council directed the board of the Hadassah hospital to immediately expand its maternity ward and to equip it to meet the needs of the growing city.[41] Two years later, Dr. Leon (Arieh) Abramovitz, the hospital's director and the head of its maternity ward, asked the board to expand his department so that it could take in more women and to institute other measures that would make births easier on women. Abramovitz was concerned by the rise in abortions, but also realized that hospital conditions were not the only factor encouraging them and that hospital improvements were not in and of themselves a solution. He thus also called for consultations among the directors of medical institutions and medical experts on the best way to pursue what he termed the war against abortion.[42]

Municipal and public organizations also demanded that other local governments and the Mandate administration expand the services they offered to new mothers, and to establish public maternity hospitals.[43] Private physicians also responded to the need, whether out of public-minded awareness of the need or merely out of economic situations, establishing the many private clinics that sprouted up around the country during the 1930s.[44] But the birthrate, instead of growing, continued to plunge throughout the 1930s.

The Adloyada, a carnival pageant in Tel Aviv each year on the Purim holiday, was used by the city in the 1920s and 1930s to encourage larger families. The event attracted participants and spectators from all over the Yishuv. More than just fun, the parade proudly displayed the Yishuv's achievements

and the fruits of its labors. Floats displayed manufactured goods and produce—and children as well. Parents paraded buggies full of infants and large
families marched. Prizes were awarded to the prettiest and most developed
baby and for the best-decorated baby carriage. Floats were emblazoned with
relevant slogans, such as a biblical verse extolling the rapid reproduction of
the Children of Israel in Egypt: "But the more they were oppressed, the more
they increased" (Exodus 1:12).[45]

Citizens and professionals pleaded with the National Council to encourage births and fight abortions. Pediatrician Rosa Meyer maintained that
women should not be able to make this choice for themselves. Writing to the
National Council's Health Department in 1940, she argued that "only a board
of physicians acting together with social assistance, [that is] a public hygiene
committee, can decide in each individual case if a woman is permitted or forbidden to have an abortion."[46] Such a board, she stressed, had to be established
in each city, such that "it is forbidden for a doctor to perform an abortion
without [its] sanction."[47] The fact that she herself was a woman did not help
her understand the women's view of the procedure and their demand to maintain control of their own bodies. As Dr. Meyer saw it, women's right to control
their fertility had to be subordinated to the pressing needs of the nation.

The labor movement, argued Yocheved Bat-Rachel of the Council of
Women Workers, ought to be leading the campaign to encourage births,
both in terms of explaining the importance of large families and helping out
with funding. "As in all other areas of Yishuv national activity, in which the
working public is the initiator and the pioneer," she proclaimed, "we must
also [on this issue] take the lead in actual concern and in action."[48] In other
words, the movement that saw itself as the Yishuv's vanguard and conscience
had to take up the birthrate as well.

Others argued that religious figures should be enlisted in the campaign,
because "they have great influence in pious circles," as well as Jewish municipal authorities, who could implement decisions such as oversight of abortions and awards to large families. Still others claimed that, to succeed, the
crusade had to rope in people far from politics,[49] or that Yishuv-wide institutions needed to pursue pronatalist policies.[50]

At the beginning of 1943, just after the Yishuv leadership confirmed that
the Nazis were systematically exterminating the Jews of Europe, a new wave
of proposals to encourage large families appeared.[51] "The published numbers
on our low birthrate have shocked a part of the public," Bachi said on a radio
program that year.[52]

The shock prompted local initiatives. The Jerusalem lodge of B'nai
B'rith, for example, constituted a special committee to address the birthrate
problem. "In our view the time has come for *immediate* action," the lodge

declared.[53] That same year saw the establishment of an organization called Yarbeh Ha'Am—The People Will Multiply—an organization to promote Jewish fertility and "foster in our nation in this land and overseas the need and obligation to increase the birthrate."[54] Various proposals were floated by private individuals. One such initiative was to establish a roving exhibition titled "The child is a blessing to the family and the nation," which would convey the message that a child was not an "economic disaster," while clarifying "what the dangers of abortion are for women and for the public." Other proposals were to found a "Mother and Child Day," and to hand out prizes to families with large numbers of children, for the most developed child, or for families that cared for their children the best.[55]

Most of these initiatives never got off the ground. In some cases, initial organizational steps were taken, but nothing was accomplished. One project that was implemented, however, was a prize for mothers with large numbers of children. It was first awarded in 1944, after an anonymous dentist donated P£30 to encourage "internal ascent."[56] He gave the money to Hadassah, the most important organization involved in the birthrate issue, out of a commitment to national values. Hadassah formed a prize committee headed by Bachi and instructed it that the prize should be awarded to a woman who had had multiple births, had raised many children, or who had undergone difficult births but had not been deterred from having further children.[57] In other words, the prize was meant to express appreciation and esteem for women who had made an effort to have children, not necessarily for the one who had had the most. In that it differed from the prize that David Ben-Gurion instituted after the establishment of the state, which was granted to women whose contribution to the demographic effort had been proven—that is, to mothers of ten living children, all of them living in Israel.

News of such initiatives, alongside articles, lectures, and speeches on the birthrate, appeared nearly daily in the press. Bachi called on the public to remain alert to the issue "and not to allow it to come to an end." At the same time, he understood that private initiatives were liable to create a situation in which there was no organization or unified message, and where resources were divided so that no single project could have more than a limited impact. This at a time, he thought, when the issue required coordinated action on the economic, political, social, religious, educational, and moral levels, organized by the Yishuv's highest body, the National Council.[58] Only such concerted action, he believed, could truly encourage a higher birthrate and ensure the Jewish people's future.[59] His insistence led to the establishment of the National Council's Committee on Birthrate Problems.

The calls for action and individual initiatives did not have much of an effect. Yet they constituted an important stage in encouraging people to have more children by bringing the issue into public awareness and creating a fairly broad base for action. Once this watershed had been crossed, the Yishuv leadership had no choice but to take up the issue by establishing the committee. Its guiding principle was that "without children, we have no future in our land."[60]

The Next Stage in Encouraging Larger Families: The Committee on Birthrate Problems

Much like France, where the National Alliance for the Growth of the French Population was founded in 1896, the Yishuv resolved that circumstances required that birth be removed from the private into the national realm and that a nationwide committee was needed to coordinate all efforts to battle the low birthrate.

The decision to found the Committee on Birthrate Problems emerged from consultations held in the National Council's offices in Jerusalem in May 1943, with the participation of doctors, demographers, and intellectuals. The committee, which would operate under the National Council's auspices, would draft "a systematic action plan against the distressing decline in the birthrate."[61] It was composed of twenty members with long involvement of one sort or another in the issue, representing the fields of medicine, social work, economics, and demography. The chairman was the demographer Prof. Roberto Bachi. Four physicians were among the original members: Dr. Tova Berman, Dr. Helena Kagan, Dr. Fritz Noak, and an obstetrician, Dr. Arieh Sadowski. The membership also included four women—Drs. Berman and Kagan and two social workers, Sidi Wronsky and H. Zaslevsky. Other members were mathematician Prof. Abraham Fraenkel of the Hebrew University and the economist Yitzhak Kanievsky.[62] The committee's fundamental view was that every Jew in Palestine, and first of all their leaders, had to be made to realize that the low birthrate was a dangerous nemesis that threatened the Hebrew nation and the project of reestablishing it in its ancestral land.[63]

The committee was led by an executive of three members, Bachi, Berman, and Kagan.[64] Berman, who had been born in Ukraine in 1898, had been accepted into the University of Kiev's medical school at the age of seventeen, at a time when there was a strict quota on Jewish admissions. There she joined the Zionist movement and in 1923 immigrated to Palestine, where she worked at occasional jobs until being hired by Kupat Holim Clalit to serve in the Jezreel Valley settlements. She remained employed there until 1928. In 1929 she married Mordechai Yeshurun and the couple had two children. They settled in Tel Aviv. Berman was very active in Kupat Holim; from 1928 to 1932 she served as chair of Kupat Holim's doctors' organization, and in 1932 she was appointed head of the central office's Preventive Medicine Department. In that capacity she worked to disseminate proper hygienic standards and increase public awareness of health issues and practices, with a special emphasis on fostering pediatrics.[65] Exceptionally, she was a public health activist who had worked both as a physician caring for individual patients and as an administrator with a broad view of public health. She held a number of leadership positions in Kupat Holim Clalit, the Yishuv's largest health organization (and after the establishment of the state served as its medical director). That naturally led her to become one of the Yishuv's leading figures in the field of family planning and, specifically, the campaign to increase the birthrate.

Kagan, the Yishuv's first woman pediatrician, was born in Russia in 1889 and studied medicine in Bern. She immigrated to Palestine in 1914, where she settled in Jerusalem and made a living working as a nurse at the Turkish municipal hospital. She was gradually assigned a variety of medical responsibilities, until, at the height of World War I, she became the hospital's director. Kagan was the first woman certified by the Turkish regime to practice medicine. During World War I Jerusalem's population suffered acutely, and Kagan worked assiduously to help all those in need. After the war, when Hadassah's hospital in the city reopened, she was appointed head of its pediatric department. In 1936 she founded the pediatric department of Bikur Holim hospital in Jerusalem and headed it for several decades. That same year she married a world-famous violinist, Emil Hauser, and their home became a meeting place for the Zionist leadership. Among other projects, she founded a day-care center for working mothers and Beit Tinokot, a home for orphans and abandoned children. She attended international conferences around the world.[66] Children and their health, both physical and social, were the prime concern of the childless Kagan. She was active in promoting public health and initiating health and welfare projects. She was a leading member of the Women's Zionist Organization (WIZO) and a member of the National Council.

In other words, two out of the three members of the executive were Zionist woman doctors whose activity reached far beyond the treatment room. For both, the birthrate issue was a central concern. This may have reflected the public perception that the birthrate was an issue with special relevance to women. Women were seen as both bearing primary responsibility for creating the problem and as the key players in its solution.

The committee was a temporary body, preliminary to the establishment of a permanent department of the National Council devoted to the issue. But its mandate was extended from time to time and it became for all intents and purposes the only Yishuv body that formally addressed the subject.[67] It pursued its assignment intensively for two years, until May 1945, when it submitted its proposals for addressing the birthrate issue to the National Council Executive.[68]

Its starting point was the principle that "the dimensions and importance of the problem determine the dimensions of the means that need to be used."[69] But the committee's budget was insufficient for that mission. Its expenses were covered on a monthly basis, but the National Council did not allocate funds to implement its programs.[70] Its outlays always exceeded its budgets; at the beginning of 1945 it had built up a deficit of more than P£4,000.[71]

While many in the Yishuv welcomed the committee's establishment, some objected. A member of the Mizrahi community was furious, alleging that "a committee has been founded for children not yet born, while hundreds and thousands of Mizrahi Jews of all lands are wandering around without treatment and without education in holy Jerusalem, and no one cares."[72] The same argument would later be made by others, not against the establishment of the committee but rather in opposition to its activities.

THE COMMITTEE INVESTIGATES

"The birthrate question is multifaceted in the extreme," the committee declared. "It is affected by a variety of factors—medical and demographic, social and economic, moral and religious," it continued.[73] That being the case, solutions should not be proposed prior to obtaining broad and precise knowledge of the subject.[74] The committee thus first investigated in-depth how a higher birthrate might be encouraged. It also established a demographic library that would gather together local literature on the birthrate and translations of literature from other countries. In parallel, the committee prepared and issued a series of pamphlets addressing the Yishuv's birthrate and demography.[75]

The committee also collected data on the Yishuv birthrate and possible explanations for it. These data were organized into tables displaying the birthrate of different societal sectors.[76] Yitzhak Kanievsky studied the links between social and economic security and the population problem; Berman and Bachi gathered information on women's maternity hospitalization.[77] Berman studied abortions;[78] Fraenkel issued a booklet presenting information on the Yishuv's birthrate patterns and problems.[79] The committee printed these research findings and presented them to the Yishuv leadership.[80] It also drafted political recommendations, based on its demographic findings, and conveyed them to the political leadership. These recommendations were kept confidential, apparently because of fears of how they might affect Jewish-Arab relations in Palestine.[81]

The data and other findings produced by the committee led it to the unhappy conclusion that the Yishuv's future did not depend on the number of immigrants but rather on its own natural increase.[82] The problem was that there was barely any natural increase—the opposite, in fact. Their research reinforced the view of the committee's members that small-scale and specific interventions were insufficient, and that the birthrate issue had to be placed on a par with immigration and settlement.[83] They began to draft a demographic politics program that would create the same kind of birthrate regime instituted in other countries facing demographic crises.[84]

But instituting a birthrate regime presented a dilemma. The question was what measures would be effective in producing more children. There were two main avenues. One was to invest most efforts in increasing public awareness and knowledge of the issue while leaving to each individual the ultimate decision about whether or not to have more children. The other was to devote all resources to creating economic incentives for larger families.

Education or Economics

In Western countries, education, economic incentives, and legislation were all used to combat abortions and battle the declining birthrate. As there was no need for new legislation in Palestine—abortions were already forbidden by law—the Yishuv's efforts focused on the first two areas.[85] The committee's initial assumption was that an integration of the two approaches would be the most effective. Each individual member of the Yishuv, from the pioneer standing guard on the land to the laborer establishing new industries, from professionals bringing the Yishuv the fruits of scientific advancement to the businessmen weaving the Yishuv's commercial relations with the rest of the world, had to be instilled with the knowledge that "the entire future of all that we build and our standing [in the world] depend on our capacity for bringing forth the generations to come, and that every family in Zion is charged with the sacred duty to ensure the nation's future."[86] But this effort to win over the hearts and minds of the Jews of Palestine had to be augmented by concerted action by the Yishuv's governing institutions to provide financial assistance to large families doing their duty to the nation, so as to help them cope with the task of raising their children.

The problem was that the Yishuv leadership did not have an effective way of enforcing its policies, and had little money to allocate for incentives and assistance. It had to decide where to allocate the limited resources it had available to apply to the birthrate issue. Should most of them go to a public relations campaign to create public awareness and urge families to fulfill their obligation to have more children? Would that not be the most appropriate approach for the Yishuv, which was, after all, a voluntary society in which individuals acted in concert out of identification with the Zionist project? Or, given the economic plight faced by much of the Yishuv population, were economic incentives the best way of bringing about the desired social changes?

Tova Berman maintained that educating the public was the best way to raise the birthrate. "All our efforts will be useless if we do not know how to awaken the desire for a child," she declared.[87] Bachi also thought that the will of the individual was the critical factor. "Wanting to shed the yoke [of child rearing]," he declared, "the individual has ceased to have children; out of its desire to maintain its existence in the generations to come, the nation can raise back the level of its birthrate."[88] If the will of the individual was the critical factor, then the effort had to be focused on persuading individuals that they should have larger families.

In Europe, they argued, financial benefits had not been particularly effective. Furthermore, there was no correlation between income and family size in the Yishuv. On the contrary, better-off families were the smallest.[89] While supplementary income certainly provided relief for large families with low incomes, it did not necessarily encourage families to have more children. To increase the birthrate, the Yishuv had to undergo "a far-reaching spiritual revolution," one newspaper maintained.[90]

Those who advocated public education also argued that it was the approach most in tune with modern life. When "we were healthy in body and soul, when the nation lived in accordance with the laws of the Torah, its Torah of life, there was no need for propaganda," declared *Hatzofeh*, the religious Zionist newspaper. Neither a physically and spiritually healthy person nor nation needed to be told to want to live and maintain itself. They intuitively wanted to be fruitful and multiply. In the past, the Jewish people had done so naturally, "by force of their inner life and desire to survive." But over the years, "when we ceased to live our autonomous lives and began to follow the laws of the gentiles . . . our spiritual health was shaken to the extent that our life instincts do not work as they should—we need to be berated and educated to repair the situation."[91]

Opponents of educating the public cited two objections. First, action was better than words, as representatives of the Yishuv's women's organizations said when the Committee on Birthrate Problems asked to consult with them on the issue.[92] "A nation cannot be built by preaching at it," wrote Yehudit from Kfar Yehoshua in the workers' journal *Hapo'el Hatza'ir* in response to Ben-Gurion's speech on the birthrate in the spring of 1943.[93] Yocheved Bat-Rachel wondered whether "on an issue as fateful as the birthrate issue we will make do with no more than *declarations*?"[94]

The second objection was that public education campaigns were ineffective. "Children do not get born because we have changed the way we look at our lives," said a member of the committee.[95] Furthermore, Kupat Holim

Clalit's medical director, Joseph Mayer, thought that "the Jewish woman has no need of propaganda, because every Jewish woman wants a child."[96] A public campaign would not bring about any decisive changes. "At most, there will be a regime of two children [per family] rather than one," one newspaper asserted.[97] Furthermore, those sectors of the population that already enjoyed a high birthrate, such as the Mizrahi community, needed not propaganda but economic benefits.[98] Mayer cautioned that "preaching," as he called encouraging families to have more children, could have dire consequences if by some chance it succeeded. Increasing the birthrate without first putting into place an economic safety net that would enable families to raise their children properly could lead to neglect and delinquency. He offered the example of a young couple who remained childless after seven years of marriage because of the hardships they had endured. They wanted a child but found it difficult to decide to bring one into the world when they had to use half the husband's income to pay for the rent on a room and half a kitchen. Such a couple hardly needed propaganda broadcasts on the radio: "They don't have a radio at home and are prepared to give up on having a radio if they can just have a child."[99] They needed economic assistance, not a massage of their parental instincts. The way to increase the birthrate, in his view, was to provide each family with economic and social security so as to dispel fears about not having the resources to raise children. Resources had to be focused, then, on providing economic incentives for larger families.

Mayer sarcastically suggested to Berman that they divide the job between them: "You can preach to the well-off and I will do my best to improve economic conditions for those who are motivated [to have a child] but lack the economic capacity to do so. Thirty years on we'll look at the results."[100]

The opponents of a public education campaign also cited European precedents, and, in fact, the birthrate issue and the attempts to solve it were complex enough there to provide grist for both sides. Even before the establishment of the Committee on Birthrate Problems, data from some European countries showed that propaganda had been useless, while in some countries economic assistance had changed the picture.[101]

Unsurprisingly, the economist among the committee members also advocated assistance to families over public education. Born in Russian in 1896, Kanievsky immigrated to Palestine in 1919 after completing advanced studies in London and Vienna. He took part in the Histadrut's founding convention and took a senior position in Kupat Holim Clalit. Married in 1923 to Rachel, the couple had two children. Kanievsky devoted much of his research to an analysis of social security and social services programs. His findings led him to conclude that the key to increasing the birthrate was raising the standard of living for the masses. Heads of families had to be able to earn enough such that "an additional child will not be frightening but rather a welcome guest in the home."[102]

Kanievsky found pronatalist propaganda discomfiting because it was so typical of fascist countries. Such campaigns were detrimental to individual rights, he maintained. The very nature of the Yishuv was at stake. Was it to become a totalitarian or fascist society in which the individual was merely a tool in the hands of society, or would it remain a free and modern society that respected individual autonomy? For him, the answer was clear: "The only way open to us is that of a free society that has no desire to turn back the wheel of culture and development."[103]

It was not that Berman opposed economic assistance as a means of encouraging larger families. A survey she conducted proved that many women chose abortion for economic reasons.[104] But she maintained that economic incentives could not be fully effective at achieving their goal if local conditions were not ripe for instituting them. Both the public and Yishuv institutions had to fully internalize the fact that boosting the Yishuv's population was a matter of life and death for the entire Jewish people, she said.[105] Only then would the Yishuv's leadership and public institutions provide all possible assistance and prepare the ground for its acceptance by the public. Public education was thus a precondition for an economic approach to the problem. Mayer, for his part, did not deny the need to change public attitudes toward the issue, but maintained that the leadership would have to pay for it.[106] Public institutions should help families overcome financial obstacles. This in turn would change attitudes toward having children. Economic assistance thus had to precede persuasion.

Bachi, the committee's chairman, tipped the balance. With his long experience in the field, his views had signal influence on his colleagues. He maintained that both policies were important. The birthrate was certainly dependent on economic factors, he asserted, but it was also influenced by "mental, religious, national, and moral orientation, and a people's social and political organization.[107] Propaganda alone, he said, would not produce "a miracle that would suddenly reverse the birthrate curve." But, given the Yishuv's unique characteristics, public education was likely to offer many advantages. "It seems to me that in a land built on the foundation of the pioneering efforts of those who have sacrificed themselves for the rebirth of the people in its land," he said, "we cannot begin from the skeptical point of view that society cannot affect the individual."[108] In other words, the Zionist project was to no small extent the product of the internalization of an idea and the willingness of many to labor and engage in self-sacrifice to achieve it. Many members of the Yishuv, and not just those of the pioneering labor movement and those who had immigrated for ideological reasons, were prepared to forego personal comfort for the achievement of national goals and subordinate their individual desires to the needs of the collective. They voluntarily accepted a communal leadership and carried out its decisions. Bachi took all this as proof that an idea could lead to action. A Yishuv inured to hardship for the sake of national goals would also devote itself to producing more children if it accepted that this was of vital national importance.

When Bachi looked to Europe, he saw that nations could not increase their birthrates by compulsion. The Yishuv, under British rule, certainly could not do so as it was not a state and its leadership lacked means of enforcement. As such, public education had to be the priority. It was necessary, he maintained, "to create an atmosphere amenable and conditions appropriate to more children."[109] An amenable atmosphere could be created by a public relations campaign and appropriate conditions via economic assistance. In other words, he saw the two approaches as interdependent, but with education as the first step. First, a systematic effort had to be directed at the Yishuv as a whole and at each of its sectors, fashioned with the help of professionals and intellectuals—physicians, nurses, social workers, journalists, writers, teachers, and counselors—with influence over the public. The second stage would be a broad economic program to encourage motherhood. Without that, "all propaganda will fail," he said.[110] In short, the ground for a higher birthrate had to be prepared via public education, but for the propaganda to produce results in the field it had to be followed by an economic program.

STAGE 1: PUBLIC EDUCATION FOR A HIGHER BIRTHRATE

After the huge loss of life suffered in World War I, the French government launched a campaign to imbue its citizens with the idea that the state and society could legitimately intervene in family life. Specifically, the state sought to spur couples to do their patriotic duty to reproduce.[111] The French approach had considerable influence on the Yishuv.[112]

The Committee on Birthrate Problems believed that its first and foremost task was to inform the public at large, the Yishuv's institutions, and professionals like doctors and teachers that the low rate of natural increase was a cause for alarm. They had to be persuaded that the birthrate was no less urgent a problem than the classic Zionist pillars of immigration, settlement, and the promotion of the Hebrew language.[113]

The campaign took place on two levels. The first message, aimed at the public, was that the Yishuv could not survive with its current low birthrate. The second, aimed at the individual, was that only children, or those with only one sibling, were liable to suffer psychological damage and educational disadvantage.[114] Another message related to women and their vocation as mothers. "The café and cinema woman" who pursued her own pleasures was blamed for the low birthrate.[115] Such propaganda was designed to morally pressure the Yishuv's women to have more children. It is important to stress, however, that such criticism, directed largely at middle-class women in the West, was not only spurred by concern about the plunge in the rate of natural increase. It was sometimes also a response to changes in the status of women and their struggle for equal rights. The enhancement of women's rights was seen as putting their roles as mothers at risk, and the fear this aroused had many of the characteristics of a moral panic.[116] Presumably the hedonistic woman of the Yishuv was condemned for more than just not having enough children.

From the start, a top priority for the committee was organizing a large public meeting to encourage a higher birthrate. The event was considered the high point of its public relations campaign. It would be the climax of an intensive weeklong media campaign and focus on the national, social, and medial aspects of the birthrate.[117] But the plan turned out to be controversial and was approved only after much debate over points of principle. The committee's members divided over whether such an event would have any practical effect on the birthrate. Some saw it as a trivial and pointless act that distracted the committee from delving into the subject and finding real solutions.[118] Others saw it as a useful public relations tool, especially since the participating institutions and organizations had the ability to take real action on the subject. In the end, the public meeting never took place, apparently because of the argument over its efficacy.[119]

The members also disagreed about whether abortion should be addressed at the public meeting. On the one hand, the subject was a very sensitive one, too private to be brought up before a heterogeneous audience accustomed to leaving intimate matters out of the public realm. Furthermore, abortion was illegal. On the other hand, abortion was one of the principal factors in the low birthrate. It could hardly be disregarded at a large meeting called to encourage a higher birthrate.[120] Perhaps because of these disagreements, the public meeting was never held.

While it failed to organize a mass national convocation on the subject, the main way the committee spread its message was via smaller meetings at which members of the committee lectured. Such events were held in the cities and on kibbutzim. Some were open to all comers and others designated for professionals. Meetings were held for parents "feeling the pain of the issue"; for nurses and social workers, who were seen as direct influences on parents; for educators, who were seen as agents of socialization who imbued the younger generation with the Yishuv's values.[121] "The desire for a child can be instilled through education, just as other values are," Tova Berman declared, and her colleagues agreed. They called for the demographic problem to be included in the high school curriculum.[122] For the same reason, the committee believed that youth movement counselors had to be involved. They shaped the Yishuv's young people and instilled values in them. As such, they had to present their charges with "the question of our people's rebirth along with the question of our survival in the future," and teach them about demographic trends and their significance for the Yishuv's survival.[123]

The committee also devoted a special campaign to "gaining friends for our activity among the Yishuv leadership and in circles with influence and facility."[124] To this end the committee met with political leaders, among them David Ben-Gurion; Moshe Shertok, head of the Jewish Agency's Political Department; and David Remez, a leading figure in the Histadrut. It also met with industrialists such as Aryeh Shankar, one of the pioneers of the Yishuv's textile industry; Leo Cohen, a jurist; representatives of the national fundraising bodies; and the leaders of political parties.[125] The committee believed that these people could put the birthrate issue on the national agenda and allocate resources to relatively large-scale and effective activities to promote larger families.

The committee devoted particular attention to groups directly involved with the issue—women's organizations, religious leaders, journalists, and physicians. Women were seen as directly responsible for the low birthrate and the necessary starting point for any solution. They had to be enlisted in the effort because their primary national duty was motherhood. Women's organizations were thus seen as essential players. From time to time the committee's members met with women active in organizations from different sectors of the population to explain and discuss the issue.[126] In August 1943 the committee called in representatives of major Yishuv women's organizations with the object of organizing a large meeting on the birthrate— Hadassah, WIZO, the Council of Women Workers, the Union of Hebrew Women for Equal Rights, and the religious Zionist Mizrahi Women. The committee viewed all these women—socialists, bourgeois, feminists, religious, and secular—as a single group united by gender identity. They were all meant to be mothers first and foremost, and this dwarfed all differences. But that is not how the women themselves saw it. While they were all women, they pointedly informed the committee, they had vastly different ideologies and lives. Each organization had its own view of female identity and women's roles in the family and society, and as such their views about how many children women should have and whether that was a national or individual issue were quite varied.

Bat-Sheva Margalit-Stern distinguishes between three major approaches to motherhood taken by women of the Yishuv. The traditional view, held mostly by religious and Mizrahi women, saw motherhood and having children as a woman's principal task in life. The progressive view, subscribed to by educated and modern women of both the middle and working classes, used the centrality of motherhood for women as a means of bringing women onto the public stage and enhancing their status there. The revolutionary view was promoted mostly by labor-movement women who "stressed the woman's right to decide for herself whether to be a mother."[127]

In a general sense, the major women's organizations can be classified in the same way. Religious women's organizations, both those representing the middle and working classes, favored encouraging a higher birthrate and fighting abortion, for both traditional and nationalist reasons. They saw motherhood as women's principal religious and national mission in the Yishuv.[128] Members of the Union of Hebrew Women for Equal Rights viewed childbirth and motherhood as central roles for women, of national importance, but demanded that Yishuv society provide women with support and protection.[129] The socialist women's workers organizations voiced revolutionary ideas about the birthrate. In the West in the twentieth century, as already noted, socialist movements condemned the double burden born by women who had to both work outside the home and be mothers. They demanded that women be given access to effective and inexpensive means of contraception and viewed this as a precondition for emancipation. Furthermore, they viewed abortions as a means of fighting social inequality. Feminist movements legitimized abortions as part of their struggle to fight patriarchy.[130] This was the view taken by the Yishuv's Socialist women workers, both in kibbutzim and the city. They called for legal, safe, and affordable abortion both in keeping with women's fundamental right to decide for themselves about their bodies, and to put an end to class distinctions in the practice and consequences of abortion.

In the 1930s, women workers demanded an end to laws that imposed penalties on women who terminated their pregnancies and called for the legalization of abortion. The Council of Women Workers worked to educate women about the "rationalization of [women's] sex lives." But socialist working-class women were not of one mind on these issues. Alongside the position of women such as Rachel Yana'it Ben-Zvi, who viewed motherhood as a restriction on women,[131] there were other leaders of the group who maintained that the national project should not advance at the expense of the birthrate. Rachel Katznelson-Shazar declared that women should act on their aspirations to have a child, if necessary outside marriage.[132] Yoheved Bat-Rachel believed that the labor movement needed to be in the vanguard of promoting motherhood, just as it was in all areas of life.[133] Hadassah also took a complex position. As already noted, the organization's New York office had, in the 1920s, investigated the possibility of sending literature on contraception to Palestine.[134] In conjunction with Kupat Holim Clalit, it operated counseling stations for pregnant women that also provided information on contraception. On the other hand, during the 1930s Hadassah fought abortion and tried, unsuccessfully, to deter physicians from carrying out the procedure in hospitals. It was thus decided that, initially, the representatives of each organization would meet with the committee separately, with a central women's event being held only at a later stage. Even so, questions arose about the proposed public meeting. Should it be a large one attended by members of all the different organizations? If so, its purpose would be largely informative and educational. Or should it be a smaller one at which representatives of the different bodies would focus on seeking practical solutions? In the end a compromise was reached—the National Council would invite representatives of the organizations, some fifty or sixty in number, to discuss the issue, but their other members could attend as observers. The goal was to raise consciousness of the issue by presenting demographic information. The birthrate would be presented and the reasons for its decline presented, and the participants would present proposals for encouraging larger families and providing assistance to working mothers.[135] While the plans for the meeting were quite detailed, no documentation of the event itself survives. It may well not have even taken place in the end. The planning demonstrates the committee's commitment to operating on different planes, but also shows how difficult it was to move from ideas to practical action.

The committee also sought to enlist rabbis in its efforts. These religious leaders believed that having children was a religious imperative that should not be put off. They wielded influence over their congregations and communities, but also over a broader swathe of the public. As such, it was only natural for the committee to seek their help in its campaign. Yet some members were opposed. "We should not get tangled up in religious matters," argued Dr. Avraham Katznelson at a committee meeting in September 1943. "The question should be framed socially," not religiously, he maintained.[136] But his was a minority opinion. Bachi and Fraenkel met with Ashkenazi chief rabbi Yitzhak Herzog to discuss ways of encouraging families to have more children. Rabbi Herzog strenuously opposed abortions (even, as we have seen, in the case of pregnancies outside marriage) and promised to help in the public education campaign. He wanted especially to speak out against abortion.[137] Following the meeting, even Katznelson agreed that Herzog's positions and his support for the committee should be widely disseminated.[138]

Efforts in this direction were successful. Rabbis mobilized to speak out on the issue. The verse "I will look with favor upon you, and make you fertile and multiply you; and I will maintain My covenant with you" (Leviticus 26:9) appeared prominently on a poster issued by the chief rabbis in 1944, prior to a Sabbath on which rabbis spoke in synagogues and study halls on the issue of the Yishuv's declining birthrate.[139]

The press was also assigned an important role. Journalists, the committee believed, shaped public opinion and thus needed to be informed about the demographic problem and to bring it before the public. They had proven influence. Just as they "raised the banner of all the actors in the rebirth of the nation, they have also known to do so with the birthrate problem," Tova Berman declared.[140] Soon after it was founded, the committee established contacts with journalists and maintained contact with and provided regular updates to a correspondent from each newspaper.[141]

The committee also held press conferences in 1943 and 1944 at which it stressed the damage done to the nation by the low birthrate and high level of abortions.[142] Dozens of articles and items on the subject appeared in every newspaper, journal, and periodical, of all political affiliations. Almost all supported an active policy of encouraging a higher birthrate.[143]

The committee placed special emphasis on educating the Yishuv's doctors. These professionals advised couples on their family lives, and treated women before and during pregnancy, at birth, and thereafter. They thus were informed about and could discuss the most intimate aspects of women's and couple's lives.[144] "They must be acquainted with the demographic problem and must be aware of it when they advise families on the birth of children," the committee determined. To hone physicians' awareness of the issue, members of the committee met with representatives of the Hebrew Medical Association. Unlike that organization's European counterparts, which largely pursued professional and scientific goals, the Yishuv doctors' organization stressed the national aspect of its profession.[145] It thus had to be made aware of the national aspects of the birthrate problem.

The committee also saw doctors as bearing no little responsibility for the low birthrate because of their practice of abortion. The war against abortion came up at committee meetings from the moment it commenced its work.[146] Some members believed that this had to be the top priority. One of these was Fraenkel, who maintained that "there is proof that all the achievements of Hitler's Germany were achieved as a result of the war on abortion."[147] Fighting abortion had to be the center point of the campaign to raise the birthrate for two reasons. First, it was a matter of principle. Abortion was seen as the Yishuv's weakest point, a practice that sullied it nationally, religiously, humanly, and morally. Second, practically, reducing the abortion rate was the easiest and quickest way of raising the number of births.[148]

But there were other positions as well. Dr. Theodor Grushka, a social medicine expert who also served as director of Hadassah hospital in Tel Aviv, believed that abortions should be permitted in some hardship cases. He also argued that unrestricted fertility should not be the aim. "We do not want women to give birth to children throughout their fertile periods. We want three to four children," he said.[149] As such, he said, battling abortion should not be the top priority. While his was a minority opinion on the committee, it gave voice to the complex positions of some of the people involved—they wanted to encourage larger families, but not too large. As I will show, this complexity hampered the campaign for a higher birthrate. Most of the committee's members maintained, in any case, that abortion needed to be fought.

The committee appointed a medical subcommittee to focus on the abortion issue. It was composed of three of the full committee's physicians—Dr. Arieh Sadowski, Dr. Tova Berman, and Dr. Helena Kagan. They met with officials of the Hebrew Medical Association and asked them to lead the campaign. It was vital, they said, to create a public atmosphere hostile to abortions.[150] The subcommittee also contacted gynecologists in order to pressure them to stop performing abortions that were not medically justified.[151] The Medical Association was sympathetic to the committee's position and proposed the establishment of a medical board that would have the sole jurisdiction to issue permits for abortions. Gynecologists, it suggested, should sign commitments to refrain from performing abortions not sanctioned by the medical board.[152] But members of the committee opposed the approach. Such a board would have little effect, argued Dr. Fritz Noak. Most cases would not come before it, and many induced abortions would be camouflaged as miscarriages.[153] Even worse, Grushka argued, the board would have the perverse incentive of encouraging "abortions by bad doctors or by despairing women themselves."[154] Another reason raised against a medical board was that some of its members might not place the national interest at the fore. "We want national oversight of abortions," Noak insisted.[155] Most members of the Committee on Birthrate Problems advocated a central board to approve abortions, one that would include not only physicians but also representatives of the National Council, jurists, and representatives of other institutions. The board would function under the supervision of the committee itself. The issue could not, they believed, be left to individual physicians.[156]

But the Yishuv had its hands tied when dealing with doctors who performed abortions. "We do not have the capacity to organize a detective service" to track the actions of doctors, Katznelson admitted, and the British authorities were making no effort to enforce the law against abortions. Under the circumstances, the principal weapon available to fight abortions was also public education.[157] In fact, the only way to gain the cooperation of physicians, the committee believed, was through a public relations campaign against abortion.

Another dilemma was whether contraception should be promoted as part of the anti-abortion campaign. Lilia Bassewitz broached this idea publicly in 1933,[158] and physicians who opposed abortions out of concern for women's health indeed encouraged contraception as an alternative. While Dr. Miriam Aharonova opposed contraception in principle, arguing in 1934 that it was a violation of nature,[159] she encouraged it and even instructed women in the use of contraceptive devices as a way of preventing them from seeking abortions. But the committee's goal was to encourage the birth of more babies for national reasons, not just to lower the abortion rate for medical or moral reasons, so it did not encourage contraception.[160] This approach was the opposite of that taken in the United States, where information about contraception was publicly disseminated with the clear message that it was better to prevent a pregnancy than to have an abortion.[161]

AT THE FOREFRONT

The committee's public relations work was felt more at some times than at others. This happened in particular when it turned to the media and theater to disseminate its ideas. In April 1944 the committee initiated a week-long campaign that highlighted the low birthrate and the need to counter it. Among the elements of the campaign were special radio broadcasts, newspaper articles, and public lectures.[162]

The committee worked hard on the radio talks. It discussed a number of possibilities for their format—should they be in the form of interviews or panel discussions? Should they have a personal cast or address the issue directly? The question, as always, was what would attract the most listeners. In the end the panel format was chosen, with a moderator who summed up the issue at the end.[163]

There were also different ideas about what the nature of the radio programs should be and whether they should be addressed directly to women. Berman, for example, proposed a format in which a broadcaster would pose questions to a woman who had one or two children, after which he would turn to experts from a variety of fields and then sum up the ways a higher birthrate could be encouraged. In other words, as Berman saw it, while both fathers and mothers were responsible for the birthrate, the primary responsibility and duty fell on women. To the extent that she deliberately had fewer children, she was at fault. Katznelson took the opposite view. He agreed that women were the key players and did not suggest that a father be included in the radio program. But the mother interviewed should not be cast as the guilty party. "The woman who appears must represent the position of freedom of choice," he said. In his view, women could legitimately make their own decisions about the size of their families.[164]

Another event organized by the committee was a mock trial that would "present the problem of the low birthrate among the Jewish people and in the Yishuv."[165] It would be a theater piece open to the public. Such performances were a common type of cultural event during the Mandate period, an inseparable part of cultural life at the time. They were staged on a variety of subjects and served as a framework for conducting social discussion and for shaping society and culture.[166]

Few objected to the idea of conducting a mock trial on the issue of the birthrate. Katznelson suggested that it would "have sensational propaganda value" but, given that not that many people would be able to see it, it might be a waste of the committee's limited budget. Berman countered, however, that similar mock trials staged by Kupat Holim Clalit had been on a high level and had attracted good audiences. Fraenkel agreed that, presented in a city, a mock trial would draw the desired audience, those whose birthrate needed to be raised. Others pointed out that a mock trial, unlike a radio program, spoke to the public directly, giving them a chance to express their feelings by applauding, laughing, or booing.[167]

Berman assumed the task of writing the script and casting the roles, subject to the committee's approval. She structured it as a courtroom drama. The defendant was the imaginary Yahalomi family, but the case was based on Berman's experience working with patients. The family was accused of raising but a single child and thus endangering the future of the Jewish nation as a whole and the Yishuv in particular. Mr. and Mrs. Yahalomi were also accused of seriously violating their only child's rights by imposing loneliness on him, along with all the adverse developmental and educational consequences this had. The script lays out the indictment and the plea:

> The Yahalomi family—husband thirty-eight years old, wife thirty-six years old—immigrated twelve years ago from Poland. The husband began to work as a construction worker. The woman, a preschool teacher by profession, did not work at first because she did not know the language. Five years after their immigration their first child was born. Seven years have passed since. Three years ago an abortion was performed because of an unsatisfactory economic situation. The family does not want more children. Their income, they say, is not even enough to provide for a single child. The wife is also irritable and thinks that she should not be caring for babies at her age. She is also afraid of losing her job if she becomes pregnant. Counsel for the national institutions has filed charges against the family for its paucity of children, which endangers the nation's future existence. The presiding judge asked the family for their plea. Their reply: "not guilty."[168]

The defendants were the first to testify, after which the defense called a plethora of witnesses. These included the principal of a boarding school who described the plight of the children enrolled there and a Jewish Agency economic expert who spoke to the issue of wages and employer's preference for single rather than married workers. Also testifying for the defense were an expert on housing and a lawyer who spoke of the need for legislation to provide for maternity leave and to forbid the dismissal of pregnant women. The prosecution witnesses included experts in political demography who presented data on the current and desirable birthrate, as well as a physician and educator who warned of the detrimental national, educational, and health consequences of the present situation. Presenting the entire range of reasons for the low birthrate, the witnesses demonstrated that the issue touched on every area of life—health, education, economics, law, women's rights, and views on what kind of life children ought to be guaranteed.

The trial presented the Yishuv's dilemma in all its complexity. The prosecution presented the low birthrate as a tragedy for the Jewish people in the wake of the Holocaust, and as a danger to the Yishuv's future. It also argued that women suffered from anxiety and thus refrained from having another child. The defense attorney, for his part (played at most performances by Dr. Joseph Mayer)[169] presented the difficult economic circumstances in which the family lived and the lack of decent conditions for raising children. He stressed that if children were considered national assets, the nation had to lend its shoulder and provide economic assistance.

But the verdict required the family to make significant changes in its attitudes.[170] It reflected the position of the Committee on Birthrate Problems in supporting larger families and opposing deliberate limitation of the number of children by families.

Central figures in the birthrate debate were invited to take part, as were leading theater professionals. The committee originally wanted to cast as the mother the first lady of the Yishuv theater, Hannah Rovina. Rovina broke with convention in 1934 when, at the age of forty-one, she had a child outside of marriage. She certainly would have roused public debate and interest had she taken part, but for some unknown reason she did not in the end appear in the role. Nevertheless, the very fact that the committee sought her out for the role testifies to the importance they attached to the mock trial. For most of the shows the presiding judge was played by the well-known Judge Tzidkiyahu Harkabi, who in 1937 became the first Jew to be appointed as clerk of the Tel Aviv District Court.[171]

When the mock trial was first presented in Tel Aviv in September 1943, the hall was packed. "The audience listened attentively and with great interest for the three hours in which the trial was conducted," Fraenkel reported to the committee. This was taken as a success in two ways. First, the trial served as a barometer that showed a high level of public interest in the birthrate issue. Second, the trial proved that there was no reason "to fear the cheapening of discourse by putting such intimate questions on stage."[172] Nevertheless, some of the members had reservations about the relative humor with which the subject was presented. They feared that such a presentation would encourage audiences to see it as a fictional entertainment rather than as the presentation of a real public issue. Public education had to be pursued in a more scholarly and serious way.[173]

But despite this criticism, the mock trial was a huge success in Tel Aviv and not long thereafter in Jerusalem.[174] It presented the rather ponderous subject of the birthrate to the general public in an accessible way and paved the way for further activity. It became a popular attraction, with the public eagerly buying up tickets to see it as it was staged throughout the country in 1943–1944.[175] The press criticized the commercial aspect of the mock trials,[176] but selling tickets seems to have been necessary to cover the costs of staging them, given the constant shortage of funds. When not enough tickets were sold, events were canceled.[177]

In these mock trials, the mother was the central figure. She was the number one defendant—she, and not the family itself composed of both mother and father. She stood accused and was charged with having more babies, with society called on to assist her in doing her duty. The prosecutor asked her about the abortion she had after having her first child: "Is it permissible, in your opinion, to demand of a young person to enlist? . . . Is it permissible to send young people to take possession of new points [of settlement] despite the danger of disease and malaria?" The mother responded yes to both questions. If that is the case, the prosecutor wondered, why can a woman not be required to make her contribution to the nation by means of having babies? The defendant responded: "You can demand that the woman give birth to the child, but if she can't feed and educate him then, if the child is an asset to the nation, the nation should do so."[178]

But when the press reported the mock trial, it also interpreted it. Instead of finding the individual—that is, the woman—responsible, some newspapers took the Yishuv's institutions to task, demanding that they act to change the situation. The call was taken up in particular by Revisionist periodicals, which formed the leading opposition to the Yishuv leadership and had obvious political reasons for criticizing current policy. These journals saw the trial as an indictment of the Yishuv's governing bodies for not pursuing a demographic political program, and for not assisting large families in the areas of housing, education, medicine, and welfare.[179]

The success of the mock trial led to imitations that were not supervised by the committee, staged by other organizations such as the Council of

Women Workers[180] and municipal authorities. The committee feared independent ventures of this sort, perhaps out of fear that the data would be misrepresented or perhaps out of concern that the verdict would not accord with the committee's policy. Presumably it also simply did not want competition for its own events. Whatever the case, the committee decided in 1944 that too many mock trials were being held. It would approve new ones, it declared, only if sponsored by a public institution and if the committee approved the cast and content.[181]

The mock trial's popularity perfectly served the committee's purpose of bringing the birthrate issue and its national implications to the forefront of public discussion. But it was not a formative event that brought about change. Neither did sporadic lectures and radio talks bring about significant change at that time. The members of the committee understood that, while the public campaign itself was raising awareness of the problem, it could not bring about a real change in the short run. Clearly it was but a first stage, to be followed by further steps. On the basis of the change in awareness, the committee sought to introduce economic solutions. As Bachi stressed, it was not right to demand that families have more children and then abandon them in the difficult circumstances they faced.[182]

Stage 2: Economic Incentives

In his book of 1944, Yitzhak Kanievsky asserted that a public campaign to encourage larger families could succeed only if it was accompanied by concrete measures that would create proper conditions for raising children and guaranteeing families financial security. Without knowing that they could afford to feed, clothe, and educate their children properly, the prospect of a second and third child would seem to most Yishuv families a perilous rather than a joyous prospect.[183] He called for higher wages and better working conditions, as well as social and economic guarantees that would dispel people's fears about raising children. The term the Committee on Birthrate Problems used for these was "economic incentives."

The committee had two major economic goals: covering some of the direct costs of raising a child, and offering a subsidy to make up for some of the income a family lost when a mother stayed home to care for her children. To this end, it worked on crafting a demographic economic policy that would achieve the following goals: augmentation of family incomes; reduction of family expenses; preferential treatment and discounts in receiving essential services, such as housing, medical care, and education; and reduction of the burden on mothers.[184] It proposed economic incentives in each of these areas that had implications for the birthrate.

First, the committee sought legislation that would provide protections for working women. At the time it was difficult to combine motherhood with work outside the home, given the lack of legal rights and guarantees. To enable women to meet their obligations both in the home and in the workplace,[185] the committee advocated laws to guarantee maternity leave, prohibit the dismissal of pregnant and new mothers, and provide nursing breaks at workplaces,[186] as well as wage benefits such as a minimum wage, especially important for women given that their wages had long been lower than those of men doing comparable work.[187] The committee also proposed a stipend or wage supplement for families with stay-at-home mothers,[188] and the creation of part-time positions appropriate for mothers.[189] None of these proposals were in fact implemented during the Yishuv period, but in 1954 the state of Israel enacted a women's labor law that offered similar protections.

Second, it also sought tax and salary benefits for men with families. It proposed tax breaks in accordance with the size of the family, as well as discounts for large families for educational, health, and social services. One idea was to eliminate tuition fees at all the Yishuv's schools, at least from a family's third child onward.[190]

One particular goal was a salary supplement for families with children to be paid out of a workplace fund that all employees would pay into, perhaps supplemented by additional monies from employers and the government. The supplement would be proportional to the number of children in the family.[191] Another proposed incentive was that fathers would receive a larger bonus if they had a child within a certain period after their marriage.[192] In addition to encouraging couples to have more children, these benefits were also seen as a matter of social justice,[193] an important consideration in the Yishuv, which aspired to create an egalitarian and just socialist society.

Roberto Bachi proposed that the program should first be instituted in the labor sector, "because only among them is there a common national aspiration and the required readiness for mutual assistance that the establishment of such a fund requires." Furthermore, since the salary supplements would be paid for largely out of workers' contributions, Bachi reasoned that it might be best to structure them in the form of a personal savings plan in which each worker would deposit money while he was single or married but childless, and receive it back when he became a father. As such, he suggested that workers pay in to the fund only up to a given age, "above which it is reasonable to believe that they will not have families and thus they will have no interest, individually, in paying money into the fund."[194]

The idea of a salary supplement to encourage families to have more children was controversial. Bachi thought that the most effective supplement would be a progressive one—in other words, that each additional child would bring a higher supplement than the previous one. But he was also concerned that such a system would "give an inflated prize to families that had children without any consideration of their responsibilities toward them."[195] In other words, he did not think that quantity was the only goal. Families should have children only responsibly, in accordance with their capacity for raising them well. Because most of the Yishuv's large families lived in indigence, he realized that the progressive method was problematic and that it would be better to provide an equal supplement for each child, no matter what number it was.[196]

A third form of incentive addressed the housing problem. The high cost and low supply of housing was a significant factor in persuading many couples to have only one or two children. To raise the birthrate it was thus necessary to find a way to provide young couples with adequate housing.[197] The committee thus proposed that heads of large families be given priority in receiving and discounts on the cost of housing built on land owned by the Jewish national organizations, or in homes to be built by public and municipal authorities.[198]

European governments and city administrations, noted Leo Kaufmann (Kadman), a Yishuv economist involved in the establishment of working-class housing projects in Palestine and an advisor to the committee, provided housing to large families as a means of encouraging the birthrate. They were given larger homes and very generous discounts on rent, in direct proportion to the number of children they had. The committee thus demanded that the Yishuv institutions establish a fund to provide housing for large families.[199]

Fourth, the committee supported the establishment of a birth fund with a fixed annual income.[200] It would provide assistance to new mothers in the purchase of baby equipment, for home caregivers during the first two weeks after birth, and rest cures for new mothers. The fund would also help defray the costs of hospitalization in a maternity ward and assist in the establishment of maternity hospitals, day-care facilities, and preschools.[201] Some demanded that this category of assistance be given first priority. It was supported in particular by women, such as Tova Berman and Yocheved Bat-Rachel, who were especially concerned about improving conditions in maternity wards and helping women who could not afford to have hospital births.[202]

The committee indeed took action to increase the number of beds in the maternity wards of public hospitals, which required budgets that it did not have. It enlisted Kupat Holim Clalit, Hadassah, and municipal authorities in this initiative,[203] as well as an organization sponsored by the National Council of Jewish Women called the HaEzra Association: Maternity Aid for Palestine.[204] HaEzra was founded in Jerusalem in 1908 with the purpose of supporting poor new mothers of all ethnic communities. It had granted assistance to tens of thousands of needy mothers of all political and religious camps and all classes. The aid package included cash and food, undergarments and clothing for both mother and child, home visits by specialist physicians when needed, and subsidies of hospital fees. HaEzra transferred funds to Hadassah hospital in Tel Aviv so that it could provide free treatment for poor women in its maternity ward.[205] The organization raised money from donors in the United States and the Yishuv.[206] Mayor Israel Rokach of Tel Aviv said that HaEzra had enabled hundreds of mothers to bring their children into the world under medical supervision and was essential in providing for a generation of healthy babies.[207]

As already noted, in the absence of help from their own mothers or other women from an extended family, new mothers returning home from their hospital stays often faced an overwhelming burden that deterred them from having another child. The committee thus viewed assistance to new mothers during these early weeks as essential.[208] Hence the effort to establish rest homes that would provide assistance and respite for new mothers for two weeks following their release from the hospital. Mothers could then resume their homemaking and child-rearing responsibilities in much better health. In addition, the committee proposed that mothers who could not be accommodated in these facilities because of lack of space, or because they could not be absent from home and their other children for so long, should receive a home aide who would help with the baby and housework for the first two weeks at home.[209] Yocheved Bat-Rachel maintained that rest homes for new mothers were especially vital for women who lived far away from health providers during the period prior to birth, as well as for difficult pathological and social cases in which women required rest before giving birth. She also believed that such institutions should take in new immigrant mothers, who could be provided with elementary knowledge regarding the care of babies in Palestine.[210] The rest houses would thus provide a double national benefit.

Kupat Holim Clalit resolved in 1943 to establish a birth fund, to be financed by a raise in the dues workers paid to the Histadrut labor union, of which the health fund was an arm.[211] In practice, however, nothing happened. One reason was the claim that the issue was one for the entire Yishuv to address, not just the working public. Furthermore, it required resources that were beyond the capacities of Kupat Holim and the Histadrut.[212]

The Committee on Birthrate Problems viewed economic incentives through a moral rather than an economic prism. Beyond their direct effect on increasing the birthrate, the committee saw them as ethical in nature, showing the public that the issue was a national one, and that the Yishuv accepted collective responsibility for all its children.[213] Yet, while the committee's public education campaign was put into operation, its economic plans remained on paper. It could not fund the economic benefits it proposed out of its own budget, so it could only demand that other Yishuv institutions provide the necessary funds. Those institutions also lacked money and were not inclined to take on a new and costly obligation.

In practice, the committee saw its principle role as setting the stage for future change. In May 1945, after two years of work, it concluded that the public education campaign had achieved its goal of raising consciousness and that it was time for policy measures to be instituted by a body with broad authority and an appropriate budget. It was up to Yishuv national institutions to create such an authority.[214] It would be charged with carrying out the economic aspects of a demographic political program. But no such body was established until the state of Israel came into being. The Yishuv leadership had to allocate limited funds to a wide range of areas, all of them important to the Zionist enterprise. During the second half of the 1940s, when the establishment of a Jewish state seemed imminent, tensions increased between the Jewish and Arab communities and between the Yishuv and the British authorities. The Yishuv's physical security became the leadership's top priority. Some of the economic incentives proposed by the committee would be instituted after the state was founded—a social security system was established by law in 1953, and legal protections for working women the following year.

Results

Just a few months after the Committee on Birthrate Problems was founded, its public education program was in full swing and it was able to report that "the question has been placed in the center of the Yishuv's issues and is making an impression."[215] Hardly a day went by, the report stated, that the major newspapers did not address the issue at length. An examination of the period's leading newspapers shows this to be the case. Nevertheless, not all the newsprint devoted to the public discussion can be credited to the committee. After all, it had itself been born out of a debate that was already taking place in the press. It seems likely, however, that the committee helped intensify that discussion and thus encouraged the press to give it even more space. At the same time, the press became a channel of communication between citizens and the committee. In letters to the editor, men and women of the Yishuv urged the committee to take real measures to raise the birthrate. "For the attention of the committee to encourage births," said a letter to *Hatzofeh* in the summer of 1943. "Mrs. Y.N. gave birth yesterday . . . to triplets, two boys and a girl . . . , and with these triplets the family now numbers ten. The father . . . is an indigent worker, a day laborer. . . . It would be fitting for the committee to encourage births and officials who have issued calls to increase the birthrate to grant the N. family concrete encouragement!"[216]

Large families applied also directly to the committee for assistance. "In keeping with your decisions about encouraging the birth of more children," a father from Afula wrote to the committee in Jerusalem, "I hereby notify you that I have ten living children and request that you award us a prize."[217] "I permit myself to ask your honors," wrote another father, from Tel Aviv, "upon the birth in May 1944 of my tenth child, may the evil eye not be upon him, I have heard that there is a fund for families with many children. I hereby ask if you have any information about this."[218] The writers were generally disappointed. "I must notify you," a typical response went, "that we do not have a fund to provide prizes to families with children. But we have brought your letter to the committee's attention."[219] The public was certainly informed about the committee's work, but it is not at all clear what contribution this made to the birthrate.

In 1944 the committee continued to raise public consciousness. It noted with satisfaction evidence for a major change in the attitudes of doctors, the middle class, the labor movement, and the Yishuv leadership.[220] The latter of these was of particular importance. It took credit for Moshe Shertok's attention to the subject in his speech for the Assembly of Representatives on December 4, 1944, along with other speeches on the subject at the same session. Even David Ben-Gurion had responded to the challenge made by the committee. "Clearly this is a most serious problem that we must attend to," he wrote to Berman in May 1944, stressing that "we must find ways to make society a partner in the care of children, which is sometimes beyond the strength of parents alone."[221] The committee believed that it had turned around the attitude, previously prevalent in most parts of the Yishuv, that families should not have more than one or two children. It prided itself for having sponsored demographic research and for the practical work it had done.[222] When the birthrate indeed rose slightly during 1943–1946, Bachi attributed it to the committee's encouragement of larger families.[223] *Hatzofeh* also credited the rise in part to the committee's "energetic public relations campaign in this direction," while noting that the economy's upswing had also been a factor.[224] But, as I have already noted, that improvement was short lived and attributable to any number of factors.

In fact, bringing the issue into public consciousness did not bring about any real change over time. "Ask new mothers themselves," *Hamashkif* acerbically asked in the summer of 1944, if the Yishuv "birthrate regime" made any difference in their doubts about having another child, or "in their search for a hospital bed, a rest home, or daycare for their baby?"[225] Fraenkel admitted at a meeting of the Committee for Birthrate Problems that "to a certain extent we are making fools of ourselves; everyone is always telling me that we are talking and not doing."[226]

The incompatibility of the desire to encourage a higher birthrate, the complexity of how to do so, and the practical inability to implement what seemed to be the necessary measures was the committee's fundamental dilemma from the start. It was the reason its members put so much effort into public education, into preparing the ground for a more comprehensive program. It was seen as the starting point for future steps, since employers, economic entities, and Yishuv governing bodies would not put out the necessary resources or make the necessary effort if they did not accept the pressing nature of the issue. Unsurprisingly, the committee often used language such as "X must be induced to . . ." Seeking the cooperation of the entire Yishuv—workers, employers, and organizations—in carrying out its plans for a "birthrate regime," it wanted to obligate all public and national institutions to make the encouragement and care of large families a top priority.[227] But its call was not answered, for two main reasons.

The first was the context of the era. The late 1940s were a tumultuous time for the Yishuv. The campaign for independence, free Jewish immigration, and settlement, along with increasing internecine violence with the Arabs, pushed all other issues into the margins. These pressing issues monopolized the emotional, economic, and security resources of the Jewish community in Palestine. Ironically, the struggle for independence actually made the need for a higher birthrate even more pressing, but it was a long-range issue, not an immediate solution to the Yishuv's pressing needs. On the contrary, the uncertainty regarding the Yishuv's future probably induced many people to put off having children.

The second factor was the limited enforcement power possessed by the Yishuv's governing institutions. Bachi's starting point was that what he called "cultural means" had to be used to encourage families to have more children, primarily by means of public education and maximum assistance to the individuals who would bear the brunt of child rearing. "Demographic politics cannot be based on compulsion," he argued.[228] His view was consistent with the unusual nature of the Yishuv, which was addressing the issue as if it were an independent state when in fact it had little executive power or financial resources.

Both these factors were evident in Ben-Gurion's responses to the committee's requests. When members of the committee met with him in 1944, he posed them a number of questions. Was Kupat Holim abetting the low birthrate, he asked, referring to doctors who performed abortions? Would requiring that employers offer economic benefits to mothers not discourage them from hiring women and thus make it even harder for women to find jobs? Furthermore, "there's something even worse—there are many women workers who do not get married."[229] He may have meant that all these other problems were also connected to the birthrate and that perhaps they should be dealt with first. When Bachi and Berman proposed establishing a department of the Jewish Agency and National Council responsible for crafting a pronatalist policy, Ben-Gurion replied that the birthrate did not fall under the scope of his responsibility. He argued that the only Yishuv body that had the organizational and financial wherewithal to carry out such a policy was the Histadrut, which in addition to being a labor union initiated and ran projects ranging from housing construction to providing medical care and running a school system.[230] Ben-Gurion really was disturbed by the low birthrate and had alerted the public to its implications, but he did not feel empowered to do anything about it. It may well be that the pressing needs of the time, in particular the establishment of a Jewish state under his leadership, were one part of his reasoning. But that was not the whole story. He also told Bachi and Berman that the solution had to come from the people, not from the leadership.[231] Given that the issue touched on the private lives of individuals, it seems that Ben-Gurion felt that no top-down solution was appropriate, perhaps because he believed that individuals and families would not want and would not allow the nation to intrude in their most private affairs.

Ben-Gurion was above all a pragmatic leader. He was well aware that the birthrate policies pursued by European countries had produced only limited results,[232] and that the recovery of the European birthrate in the 1940s had been a product not only of the campaign to encourage it but also of a wide variety of other factors.[233] Ben-Gurion was willing to devote public resources to realistic goals that would produce significant results. The inefficiency of allocating already limited public resources to encouraging larger families made it a nonstarter for him. Given that he was apparently unwilling to use compulsion to encourage the birth of more children, whether in principle or because he thought it would not work in the Yishuv, he thought that the major effort had to be made in the area of increasing public awareness and knowledge of the issue.

The Committee on Birthrate Problems thus succeeded only partially. It indeed managed to persuade the public and leadership that the low birthrate was a threat to the Yishuv. How to reverse it became a matter of lively public debate. But the bottom line was that Jews did not have more children.

Conclusion: The Paradox of Raising the Birthrate

The efforts to encourage families to have more children and to fight against deliberate restriction of family size demonstrate how unique the Yishuv was.

During the British Mandate, the Yishuv sought to create a Jewish majority in Palestine as the basis for the establishment of a Jewish state, at the same time that it sought to create a democratic and egalitarian Jewish society. The birthrate was a factor in both those efforts, but in contradictory ways. Creating a Jewish majority required natural increase. Democracy and modern society required individual autonomy, including in the area of how large a family to have, and equality required that women be able to fulfill themselves as full members of society as they saw fit. There were no simple answers to this contradiction.

The Zionist movement, and especially the labor movement that was its vanguard, sought to fashion a modern European society in Palestine. Even the keenest advocates of a higher birthrate thus did not think that women should have children one after the other. On the other hand, it was also clear that the European ideal of a family with one or two children was not appropriate given the Yishuv's national imperative.[234] As such, the advocates of a higher birthrate did not believe in turning the wheel back to a state of what Bachi called "unrestricted fertility."[235] There was something of a contradiction in the desire to encourage families to have more children without giving up on family planning. Presumably, because this conflict made action difficult, the effort did not succeed during the Yishuv period.

In addition to this were the complexities of the Yishuv's ethnic and religious fault lines and the eugenic principles prevalent at the time. The advocates of a higher birthrate in fact sought a higher Ashkenazi birthrate and a lower Mizrahi one. The Mizrahim were perceived as backward and alien to the European social and cultural ideal that the Zionist movement wished to create in Palestine. This required broadcasting different messages to each community. Bachi, for example, opposed social, economic, and educational activity to encourage a higher birthrate across the board, among all communities. To do so, he believed, would be to ignore the true needs of the Mizrahim, or "putting Mizrahi communities on paths that are not appropriate to their real nature."[236] In other words, in Bachi's view, not only did each ethnic community need to be addressed differently; different communities had different inherent qualities.

The Yishuv's view of gender added another layer of complexity. It was traditional in its gender perceptions, for the most part seeing motherhood as women's most important responsibility. This became even more important in the context of the national struggle, seeing the emergence of a proud new generation of young Jews committed to the principles of Zionism as essential to creating a Jewish state. In contrast, the Yishuv aspired to be an egalitarian state in accord with socialist principles, and this included gender equality under which women would not be confined to the home and would be full partners in the construction of the new country. To put it another way, the Yishuv raised the banner of traditional motherhood in the spirit of nationalism, while at the same time extolling the women pioneers who worked side by side with men.

Women's identity also metamorphosed, in keeping with the spirit of modernity and democracy. Many of them no longer saw motherhood as their only or even their central purpose in life, and sought to be active in the Zionist public sphere. "Contemporary mothers," Yehudit from Kfar Yehoshua wrote in 1943, "can no longer accept the role of homemaker and mother alone, a role the value of which has declined . . . women have sought and found other spiritual values."[237] Paradoxically, the Yishuv was not ready to accept the ideal it extolled. As a prestate society, it lacked laws to protect working women. Without the rights and benefits that such legislation provided in other countries, it was nearly impossible to combine motherhood with pioneering Zionism or even with a job. (Even today, when such rights and benefits are standard, it is not easy.) "The demands made [of women] exceed their capacity," Yehudit said. "Building the country, producing children, educating them, keeping home and tending the farm, are all difficult and exhausting work."[238] Women were expected to be both modern women with interests and responsibilities outside the home and at the same time continue to bear the principal burden for keeping house and raising educated and cultured offspring. It is hardly surprising that so many chose to have only one or at most two children. Yehudit noted that the rabbinic tradition had exempted women from many ritual practices to allow them to devote their time to motherhood. The Zionist enterprise in Palestine needed to find a solution of its own, as women could not be expected to do two jobs at once.

The effort to boost the Yishuv's birthrate was thus a reflection of the complicated profile of this society, which sought to establish a Jewish state at the same time as it founded a new and modern society, one that sought to integrate tradition with innovation. One outcome was the exacerbation of gender disparities and ethnic fissures. These conflicts thwarted the committee's efforts to achieve its goals.

The birthrate campaign's preference for propaganda over practical measures reflects, in part, the society's ideological nature. But, while the Yishuv is often portrayed as a society in which personal aspirations and needs were subordinate to national ideology, the real picture is more complex. The Committee on Birthrate Problems indeed declared that the birthrate was of such urgent national importance that it could not be left to individuals. The nation's need for larger families should, its members maintained, determine how many children couples would have, even if that meant that they would be expected to have more children than they themselves wanted. But the difficulties the committee encountered in pursuing its goals shows that national needs were not paramount for the members of the Yishuv. The limited results of the public education campaign showed that the leadership could not do much to indoctrinate the masses. The Yishuv's shaky economy meant that there was no money to fund economic benefits for families that had more children, and its basically conservative nature evidenced itself in a reluctance to make as intimate and private an issue as abortions the subject of public debate.

Yet the campaign was an important step in shaping the future Jewish state. The attempts to grapple with the low birthrate included study of birthrate patterns in the Yishuv and the factors causing smaller families in different sectors of Yishuv society, with attention to both the public and the leadership. It also addressed dilemmas and conflicts that grew out of the birthrate question and the attempt to encourage larger families, but which were also fundamental questions touching on the character of the society in formation. As such, the attempts to fashion a birthrate policy, along with the committee's efforts to encourage people to have more children, can be seen as part of a practice carried out by cultural agents who sought to shape Yishuv society in a variety of areas, among them health, hygiene, dress, and culture. The attempts to encourage a higher birthrate had only limited success, but they were an important factor in shaping Yishuv society. By including all parts of the Yishuv, it empowered the Hebrew collective and reinforced the sense of mutual responsibility that was essential for the realization of Zionist, political, and social objectives. On top of that, it raised the question of to what extent society could use legal powers to impose its family planning views on the public. This question, which has been a subject of debate for years,[239] might seem irrelevant to the Yishuv period, in which Jewish society organized itself on a voluntary basis under British rule and its organizations lacked any real executive power. Nevertheless, the subject came up for discussion and the Yishuv sought solutions that were appropriate for its circumstances. It sought to address the birthrate issue in the same way that well-run states did, even before the Jewish state came into being. This is yet one more important step by which the Yishuv prepared itself to become a state. In practice, the proposals fashioned by the Committee on Birthrate Problems were ahead of their time; they would be implemented only years later, by the government of the state of Israel.[240]

Notes

1. "Be'ayat haYeludah baYishuv" (no byline, apparently Bachi), Apr. 12, 1943, *Ha'aretz* (n.p.), CZA J1/3737/1; letter from Roberto Bachi to Avraham Katznelson, Nov. 19, 1942, CZA J1/3717/2; report of the Committee on Birthrate Problems, Oct. 15, 1944, CZA J1/3717/3.

2. Roberto Bachi, radio talk, 1943, CZA J1/3717/1.

3. Tova Berman, "Ha'Emtza'im haDerushim le'Idud haYeludah baYishuv," Feb. 1945, CZA J1/3717/3.

4. Roberto Bachi, radio talk, 1943, CZA J1/3717/1.

5. Report of the Committee on Birthrate Problems, Oct. 15, 1944, CZA J1/3717/3.

6. Tova Berman, script for the mock trial on birthrate problems, 1943, CZA J1/3717/1.

7. Anson and Meir 1996; Drezgic 2010.

8. Razi 2010; Mosse 2008.

9. Yuval-Davis 1997; Rosenberg-Friedman 2008.

10. Maynes and Waltner 2012, 95–96.

11. Hoffer and Hull 2010, 11; Abrams 2002, 123; Zahra 2009; Blom 2008.

12. Hoffer and Hull 2010, 11.

13. Reggiani 1996; Van de Kaa 1999, 18–19; Abrams 2002, 306; Taylor Allen 2008, 17; Alpern Engel 2004, 161; Bridenthal, Grossmann, and Kaplan 1984.

14. Abrams 2002, 123; Hoffmann 2000.

15. Saraceno 1991; Nash 1991; Kuklien 1990.

16. Maloy and Patterson 1992.

17. Reggiani 1996.

18. Linders 1998.

19. Grossmann 1995, 3.

20. Frevert 1997, 111, 186.

21. Grossmann 1995, 4; Mouton 2007, 108.

22. Frevert 1997, 111, 186–187, 236; Grossmann 1995, 4.

23. The national program to encourage the Aryan birthrate took children identified as racially Aryan from their family and placed them with "racially pure" foster families or in special facilities, with the goal of educating them and preparing them for life as members of the master race. The program was funded by contributions from German citizens, and families of SS personnel were required to allot part of their salaries to the program, in accordance with the number of children they had.

24. Bridenthal, Grossmann, and Kaplan 1984, 16, 25; Usborne 2007, 3–5, 19; Usborne 2011; Kaplan 1998, 82; Frevert 1997, 187, 236.

25. Alpern Engel 2004, 161–162, 177–180; Hoffmann 2000.

26. Tomlinson 1985; Offen 1991.

27. Pedersen 1996; Hunter 1962.

28. Kanievsky 1944, 21–22; Tova Berman, "'Al Be'ayot haYeludah," apparently 1943, CZA A516/100.

29. H. Sh. Halevy, "'Al Medukhat haYeludah haYerudah," *Hamashkif*, July 16, 1943, 4; Dr. Tova Berman, Lecture on the Politics of Births, June 17, probably early 1940s, CZA A516/165; letter from Y. Kanievsky to the Committee on Birthrate Problems, Feb. 20, 1945, CZA J1/3717/3; Tova Berman, "Ha'Emtza'im haDerushim le'Idud haYeludah baYishuv," Feb. 1945, CZA J1/3717/3.

30. Roberto Bachi, "HaYeludah be Yisra'el uvaYishuv vehaDerakhim le'Idudah," apparently 1944, CZA J1/3717/3.

31. Tova Berman, "Ha'Emtza'im haDerushim le'Idud haYeludah baYishuv," Feb. 1945, CZA J1/3717/3.

32. Tova Berman, lecture on the politics of births, June 17, probably early 1940s, CZA A516/165.

33. Report on the activities of the Committee on Birthrate Problems, during its two years of existence (May 1943–Apr. 1945), Apr. 29, 1945, CZA J1/1974.

34. Ya'akov Halperin, "Ben Yehidut," *Ha'em Vehayeled*, 1933–1934, 261.

35. Letter from Dr. Rivlin to Bachi, Apr. 16, 1943, CZA J1/3717/1; Yisrael Tunis, "Ha'Aliyah HaPnimit," *Davar*, Apr. 5, 4; kibbutz member, "Lo Zo haDerekh," *Devar Hapo'elet* 7:1, Mar. 31, 1940, 27.

36. Letter from Dr. Fritz Noak to the Central Committee of the Hebrew Medical Association, July 16, 1940, CZA J1/3717/1; letter from Dr. Shoshana Meyer to the Health Department of the National Council, May 20, 1940, CZA J1/3717/1.

37. Lilia [Bassewitz], "Isha, Em Vayeled," *Mibifnim*, Apr. 1933, 16.

38. Letter from Dr. P. Rivlin to Hadassah management, Jan. 19, 1939, CZA J113/2312.

39. Letter from Dr. Haim Yassky to Dr. P. Rivlin, Jan. 30, 1939, CZA J113/2312; memorandum from Hadassah's Statistics Department with regard to Dr. Rivlin's letter (from Jan. 1, 1939) Mar. 1939 (precise date not given), CZA J113/2312.

40. Chairman of the board of Hadassah city hospital in a letter to the municipal administration of Tel Aviv, May 2, 1932, TAA 4-4643a.

41. Letter from the deputy mayor of Tel Aviv, in the name of the municipality council, to the commissioner of Negev district, Jaffa, Mar. 28, 1935, TAA 4-4644.

42. Letter of Dr. A. Abramovitch, director of Hadassah municipal hospital, to A. Perlson, chairman of the board, May 28, 1937, TAA, Hadassah hospital, 4-4645.

43. Letter from the deputy mayor of Tel Aviv, in the name of the municipality council, to the commissioner of Negev district, Jaffa, Mar. 28, 1935, TAA 4-4644.

44. Golz 2013.

45. Shoham 2013, 283.

46. Letter from Dr. Shoshana Meyer to the Health Department of the National Council, May 20, 1940, CZA J1/3717/1.

47. Ibid.

48. Yocheved Bat-Rachel, "De'agat HaImahut," Merkaz Kupat Holim, Jan. 1945, YTA, 15-36/4/4, 16.

49. Letter from Dr. Ephraim Waschitz to Bachi, Apr. 18, 1943, CZA J1/3717/1.

50. *'Alonim* (no title, no byline) 12, Dec. 20, 1942 (n.p.).

51. Letter from Roberto Bachi to Hadassah Medical Organization, Apr. 27, 1943, CZA J1/3717/1.

52. Roberto Bachi, radio talk, 1943, CZA J1/3717/1.

53. Emphasis in original. Letter from Prof. Abraham Fraenkel to Dr. Avraham Katznelson, May 16, 1943, CZA J1/3717/1; letter from Roberto Bachi to Hadassah Medical Organization, Apr. 27, 1943, CZA J1/3717/1.

54. The organization's regulations (no date), CZA J1/3717/1; letter from Dr. A. Polak to the National Council, May 21, 1943, CZA J1/3717/1.

55. Letter from Dr. Rivlin to Hadassah management, Jan. 19, 1939, CZA J113/2312.

56. Letter from M. Krupnik-Hadassah management to Dr. Yardeni, Nov. 15, 1944, CZA J113/1930.

57. Letters from M. Krupnik-Hadassah management to Dr. Z. Polishuk and Prof. Roberto Bachi, Nov. 13, 1944, CZA J113/1930; letter from Prof. Bachi to Hadassah management, Jan. 16, 1945, CZA J113/1930; letter from M. Krupnik to Hadassah women Council in Jerusalem, Jan. 22, 1945, CZA J113/1930; letter from M. Krupnik-Hadassah management to Dr. Yardeni, Feb. 9, 1945, CZA J113/1930.

58. Letter from Roberto Bachi to Hadassah Medical Organization, Apr. 27, 1943, CZA J1/3717/1.

59. Roberto Bachi, radio talk, 1943, CZA J1/3717/1.

60. Committee on Birthrate Problems, "Tokhnit lePolitikah Demografit," Apr. 22, 1945, CZA J1/2383.

61. Committee on Birthrate Problems in a press release, May 28, 1943, CZA J1/3717/1.

62. Ibid.

63. "HaYiten haYishuv leMi'ut haYeludah Livloa' et Hesegeinu be'Aliyah?" (no byline), *Davar*, Jan. 26, 1944, 4.

64. Report on the activities of the Committee on Birthrate Problems, during its two years of existence (May 1943–Apr. 1945), Apr. 29, 1945, CZA J1/1974.

65. Shehori-Rubin 2013; Levy and Levy 2008, 113.

66. Levy and Levy 2008, 212.

67. Letter from the Committee on Birthrate Problems to Dr. A. Katznelson, Dec. 19, 1943, CZA J1/3717/2.

68. Letter from Dr. A. Katznelson to the management members, May 2, 1945, CZA J1/1974.

69. Tova Berman, "Ha'Emtza'im haDerushim le'Idud haYeludah baYishuv," Feb. 1945, CZA J1/3717/3.

70. The committee's monthly budget was initially P£15. During the next two years, the amount rose to P£25. The budget was used for current expenses. Committee expense report, June 1944–Feb. 1945, CZA J1/3717/3.

71. Minutes of meetings of the Committee on Birthrate Problems, June 22, 1943, Dec. 14, 1943, CZA J1/3717/1; letter from Dr. A. Katznelson to the National Council Treasury, Jan. 9, 1944, CZA J1/3717/2; letter from Bachi to the National Council Treasury, Mar. 2, 1945, CZA J1/3717/3; committee expense report, June 1944–Feb. 1945, CZA J1/3717/3.

72. Avraham Bar-Orian, "'Ad Shelo Notzarti," *Hatzofeh*, July 13, 1943, 4.

73. Report on the activities of the Committee on Birthrate Problems, during its two years of existence (May 1943–Apr. 1945), Apr. 29, 1945, CZA J1/1974.

74. Letter from the Committee on Birthrate Problems to Dr. A. Katznelson, Dec. 19, 1943, CZA J1/3717/2.

75. Minutes of a meeting of the Committee on Birthrate Problems, Sept. 21, 1943, CZA J1/3717/2.

76. Letter from Roberto Bachi to David Ben-Gurion, Oct. 27, 1944, CZA J1/3717/2; Roberto Bachi, "Maskanot Politiyot metokh Hakirotay 'al haHitpathut haDemografit shel haYehudim veha'Aravim beE"Y," Oct. 1944, CZA J1/3717/2.

77. Letter from Kanievsky to Mr. Gordon, Jewish Agency, Dec. 10, 1943, CZA J1/34358; letter from Roberto Bachi to Avraham Katznelson, July 19, 1944, CZA J1/3717/3; report of the Committee on Birthrate Problems, Oct. 15, 1944, CZA J1/3717/3; letter from the Committee on Birthrate Problems to Dr. A. Katznelson, Dec. 19, 1943, CZA J1/3717/2.

78. Report on the activities of the Committee on Birthrate Problems, during its two years of existence (May 1943–Apr. 1945), Apr. 29, 1945, CZA J1/1974.

79. Fraenkel 1944.

80. Letter from Dr. Mayer to David Remez, Dec. 10, 1944, CZA J1/1974.

81. Letter from Roberto Bachi to David Ben-Gurion, Oct. 27, 1944, CZA J1/3717/2.

82. Roberto Bachi, "Maskanot Politiyot metokh Hakirotay 'al haHitpathut haDemografit shel haYehudim veha'Aravim beE"Y," Oct. 1944, CZA J1/3717/2, 4.

83. Tova Berman, "Ha'Emtza'im haDerushim le'Idud haYeludah baYishuv," Feb. 1945, CZA J1/3717/3.

84. Committee on Birthrate Problems, "Tokhnit lePolitikah Demografit," Apr. 22, 1945, CZA J1/2383.

85. Minutes of a meeting of the Committee on Birthrate Problems Executive, May 27, 1943, CZA J1/3717/1.

86. Roberto Bachi, radio talk, 1943, CZA J1/3717/1.

87. Tova Berman, "Ha'Emtza'im haDerushim le'Idud haYeludah baYishuv," Feb. 1945, CZA J1/3717/3.

88. Bachi 1943a, 20.

89. Bachi, minutes of a meeting of the Committee on Birthrate Problems, June 22, 1943, CZA J1/3717/1.

90. Eliezer Levinstein, "Be'ayot Sotziyaliot Hadashot," *Davar*, Feb. 25, 1947, 2.

91. B., "Limnoa' Ason," *Hatzofeh*, May 19, 1944, 2.

92. Minutes of a meeting of the Committee on Birthrate Problems, Dec. 14, 1943, CZA J1/3717/2.

93. Yehudit, "LeShalosh He'arot shel Ben-Gurion," *Hapo'el Hatza'ir* 47, Aug. 12, 1943, 25.

94. Emphasis in original. Yocheved Bat-Rachel, "De'agat HaImahut," Merkaz Kupat Holim, Jan. 1945, YTA, 15-36/4/4, 7.

95. Dr. Leibowicz, minutes of a meeting of the Committee on Birthrate Problems, Apr. 6, 1944, CZA J1/3717/2.

96. Program for a radio talk for a week devoted to birthrate issues, July 1944, CZA J1/3717/2.

97. L. Bein, "HaRibui haTiv'i veHishuvei he'Atid haKarov," *Hatzofeh*, June 8, 1945, 5.

98. A. Abas, "Keitzad Napil et haMehitzot bein ha'Edot baYishuv," *'Al Hamishmar*, Mar. 25, 1948, 2.

99. Program for a radio talk for a week devoted to birthrate issues, July 1944, CZA J1/3717/2.

100. Ibid.

101. Memorandum from Hadassah's Statistics Department with regard to Dr. Rivlin's letter (from Jan. 1, 1939) Mar. 1939 (precise date not given), CZA J113/2312. See also Blom 2008.

102. Kanievsky 1944, 83.

103. Ibid., 21.

104. Tova Berman, "Ha'Emtza'im haDerushim le'Idud haYeludah baYishuv," Feb. 1945, CZA J1/3717/3.

105. Program for a radio talk for a week devoted to birthrate issues, July 1944, CZA J1/3717/2.

106. Ibid.

107. Bachi 1943b, 6.

108. Ibid.

109. Roberto Bachi, "Maskanot Politiyot metokh Hakirotay 'al haHitpathut haDemografit shel haYehudim veha'Aravim beE"Y," Oct. 1944, CZA J1/3717/2, 5.

110. Committee on Birthrate Problems, "Tokhnit lePolitikah Demografit," Apr. 22, 1945, CZA J1/2383.

111. The National Alliance for the Growth of the French Population was a leading program of this sort. Reggiani 1996.

112. "HaYiten ha Yishuv leMi'ut haYeludah Livloa' et Hesegeinu be'Aliyah?" (no byline), *Davar*, Jan. 26, 1944, 4.

113. Minutes of a meeting of the Committee on Birthrate Problems, Dec. 14, 1943, CZA J1/3717/2; letter from Dr. A. Katznelson to the National Council Treasury, Jan. 9, 1944, CZA J1/3717/2.

114. "HaYiten ha Yishuv leMi'ut haYeludah Livloa' et Hesegeinu be'Aliyah?" (no byline), *Davar*, Jan. 26, 1944, 4.

115. "Be'ayat haYeludah baYishuv" (no byline), *Hatzofeh*, June 29, 1943, 5.

116. The concept of "moral panic" was developed by the South African–British criminologist Stanley Cohen, who used it to refer to a widespread sense of panic that pervades a society facing what it sees as a problem liable to harm or destroy that society's collective moral standards.

117. Minutes of meetings of the Committee on Birthrate Problems, Sept. 21, 1943, Feb. 15, 1944, CZA J1/3717/2.

118. Dr. Sadowsky, minutes of a meeting of the Committee on Birthrate Problems, Feb. 15, 1944, CZA J1/3717/2.

119. Dr. Katznelson, minutes of a meeting of the Committee on Birthrate Problems, Feb. 15, 1944, CZA J1/3717/2.

120. Dr. Noak, minutes of a meeting of the Committee on Birthrate Problems, Apr. 6, 1944, CZA J1/3717/2.

121. Memorandum of a meeting of the Committee on Birthrate Problems, June 1, 1944, CZA J1/3717/3; minutes of a meeting of the Committee on Birthrate Problems Executive, May 27, 1943, CZA J1/3717/1; report on the activities of the Committee on Birthrate Problems, during its two years of existence (May 1943–Apr. 1945), Apr. 29, 1945, CZA J1/1974; minutes of a meeting of the Committee on Birthrate Problems Executive, Feb. 15, 1944, CZA J1/3717/2.

122. Tova Berman, "Ha'Emtza'im haDerushim le'Idud haYeludah baYishuv," Feb. 1945, CZA J1/3717/3.

123. Ibid.

124. Memorandum of a meeting of the Committee on Birthrate Problems, June 1, 1944, CZA J1/3717/3.

125. Report on the activities of the Committee on Birthrate Problems, during its two years of existence (May 1943–Apr. 1945), Apr. 29, 1945, CZA J1/1974.

126. Minutes of a meeting of the Committee on Birthrate Problems Executive, May 27, 1943, CZA J1/3717/1; report of the Committee on Birthrate Problems, Sept. 5, 1943, CZA J1/3717/2; report on the activities of the Committee on Birthrate Problems, during its two years of existence (May 1943–Apr. 1945), Apr. 29, 1945, CZA J1/1974; minutes of a meeting of the Committee on Birthrate Problems Executive, Feb. 15, 1944, CZA J1/3717/2.

127. Margalit-Stern 2011, 178–179.

128. Rosenberg-Friedman 2005, 42, 122.

129. Ajzenstadt 2010, 84.

130. Gordon 1997, 147; Grossmann 1995, 68, 74.

131. Shilo 2007, 270–271.

132. Shechter 2011, 240.

133. Yocheved Bat-Rachel, "De'agat HaImahut," Merkaz Kupat Holim, Jan. 1945, YTA, 15-36/4/4, 11.

134. A report from Hadassah NY, 24.12.1925, American Jewish Historical Society, Hadassah Collections, RG23/subjects/birth control/feminism.

135. Minutes of a meeting of the Committee on Birthrate Problems Executive with representatives of women's organizations, Aug. 10, 1943, CZA J1/3717/2.

136. Minutes of a meeting of the Committee on Birthrate Problems, Sept. 21, 1943, CZA J1/3717/2.

137. Memorandum from a meeting with Rabbi Yitzhak Herzog, Prof. Abraham Fraenkel, and Prof. Roberto Bachi, 1943 (no specific date), CZA J1/3717/2; minutes of a meeting of the Committee on Birthrate Problems Executive, June 1943 (no specific date), CZA J1/3717/1.

138. Minutes of a meeting of the Committee on Birthrate Problems, Sept. 21, 1943, CZA J1/3717/2.

139. B., "Limnoa' Ason," Hatzofeh, May 19, 1944, 2.

140. Tova Berman, "Ha'Emtza'im haDerushim le'Idud haYeludah baYishuv," Feb. 1945, CZA J1/3717/3.

141. Minutes of a meeting of the Committee on Birthrate Problems Executive, May 27, 1943, CZA J1/3717/1.

142. "HaYiten ha Yishuv leMi'ut haYeludah Livloa' et Hesegeinu be'Aliyah?" (no byline), Davar, Jan. 26, 1944, 4.

143. Report on the activities of the Committee on Birthrate Problems, during its two years of existence (May 1943–Apr. 1945), Apr. 29, 1945, CZA J1/1974.

144. Report of the Committee on Birthrate Problems, 1945 (no specific date), CZA A516/100.
145. Levy 1998, 152.
146. Minutes of a meeting of the Committee on Birthrate Problems, June 22, 1943, CZA J1/3717/1.
147. Ibid.
148. Fraenkel 1944, 31.
149. Minutes of a meeting of the Committee on Birthrate Problems Executive, Feb. 15, 1944, CZA J1/3717/2.
150. Memorandum of a meeting of the Committee on Birthrate Problems, June 1, 1944, CZA J1/3717/3; minutes of meetings of the Committee on Birthrate Problems, Dec. 14, 1943, Feb. 2, 1944, CZA J1/3717/2.
151. Minutes of a meeting of the Committee on Birthrate Problems Executive, Aug. 10, 1943, CZA J1/3717/2.
152. Minutes of a meeting of the Committee on Birthrate Problems Executive, Sept. 2, 1943, CZA J1/3717/2; minutes of a meeting of the Committee on Birthrate Problems, Sept. 21, 1943, CZA J1/3717/2
153. Letter from Dr. Noak to the Committee on Birthrate Problems Secretariat, Feb. 4, 1944, CZA J1/3717/2.
154. Minutes of a meeting of the Committee on Birthrate Problems Executive, Feb. 15, 1944, CZA J1/3717/2.
155. Minutes of a meeting of the Committee on Birthrate Problems, Sept. 21, 1943, CZA J1/3717/2
156. "Be'ayat haYeludah baYishuv" (no byline), *Hatzofeh*, June 29, 1943, 5.
157. Minutes of a meeting of the Committee on Birthrate Problems Executive, May 27, 1943, CZA J1/3717/1.
158. Lilia [Bassewitz], "Isha, Em Vayeled," *Mibifnim*, Apr. 1933, 16.
159. Kozma 2010, 115.
160. Minutes of a meeting of the Committee on Birthrate Problems, Sept. 21, 1943, CZA J1/3717/2; Roberto Bachi, "HaYeludah be Yisra'el uvaYishuv vehaDerakhim le'Idudah," apparently 1944, CZA J1/3717/3.
161. Katz, Moran Hajo, and Engelman 1997. See also Bachi's report, 1944 (no specific date), CZA J1/3737/3.
162. Minutes of a meeting of the Committee on Birthrate Problems, Apr. 6, 1944, CZA J1/3717/2.
163. Program for a radio talk for a week devoted to birthrate issues, July 1944, CZA J1/3717/2; Roberto Bachi, radio talk, 1943, CZA J1/3717/1.
164. Minutes of a meeting of the Committee on Birthrate Problems, Apr. 6, 1944, CZA J1/3717/2.
165. Invitation from Ben-Yishai, secretary of the Committee on Birthrate Problems, to Dr. Noak, Nov. 23, 1943, CZA J1/3717/2.
166. See, for example, the public mock trial conducted in Tel Aviv against the use of the German language, Helman 2007, 50.
167. Minutes of a meeting of the Committee on Birthrate Problems, Sept. 21, 1943, CZA J1/3717/2.
168. Tova Berman, script for the mock trial on birthrate problems, 1943, CZA J1/3717/1.
169. Minutes of a meeting of the Committee on Birthrate Problems Executive, June 1943 (no specific date), CZA J1/3717/1.
170. Tova Berman, script for the mock trial on birthrate problems, 1943, CZA J1/3717/1.
171. Minutes of a meeting of the Committee on Birthrate Problems Executive, June 2, 1943, CZA J1/3717/1.

172. Minutes of a meeting of the Committee on Birthrate Problems, Dec. 14, 1943, CZA J1/3717/2.

173. Minutes of a meeting of the Committee on Birthrate Problems, Feb. 15, 1944, CZA J1/3717/2.

174. "Ktav Ha'ashamah Hamur neged haMosdot she'einam Me'odedim et haYeludah" (no byline), *Hamashkif*, Feb. 3, 1944, 4.

175. Minutes of a meeting of the Committee on Birthrate Problems Executive, June 1943 (no specific date), CZA J1/3717/1; report on the activities of the Committee on Birthrate Problems, during its two years of existence (May 1943–Apr. 1945), Apr. 29, 1945, CZA J1/1974. See also Minutes of a meeting of the Committee on Birthrate Problems Executive, Aug. 10, 1943, CZA J1/3717/2.

176. Minutes of a meeting of the Committee on Birthrate Problems, Feb. 15, 1944, CZA J1/3717/2; "HaYiten ha Yishuv leMi'ut haYeludah Livloa' et Hesegeinu be'Aliyah?" (no byline), *Davar*, Jan. 26, 1944, 4.

177. Minutes of a meeting of the Committee on Birthrate Problems, Sept. 21, 1943, CZA J1/3717/2.

178. Tova Berman, script for the mock trial on birthrate problems, 1943, CZA J1/3717/1.

179. For example, "Ktav Ha'ashamah Hamur neged haMosdot She'einam Me'odedim et haYeludah" (no byline) *Hamashkif*, Feb. 3, 1944, 4.

180. Minutes of a meeting of the Committee on Birthrate Problems, Feb. 15, 1944, CZA J1/3717/2.

181. Minutes of meetings of the Committee on Birthrate Problems, Dec. 14, 1943, Feb. 15, 1944, CZA J1/3717/2.

182. Roberto Bachi, "Maskanot Politiyot metokh Hakirotay 'al haHitpathut haDemografit shel haYehudim veha'Aravim beE"Y," Oct. 1944, CZA J1/3717/2, 5.

183. Kanievsky 1944, 20.

184. Tova Berman, "Ha'Emtza'im haDerushim le'Idud haYeludah baYishuv," Feb. 1945, CZA J1/3717/3.

185. Committee on Birthrate Problems, "Tokhnit lePolitikah Demografit," Apr. 22, 1945, CZA J1/2383.

186. Minutes of a meeting of the Committee on Birthrate Problems, June 22, 1943, CZA J1/3717/1.

187. Kanievsky 1944, 90.

188. Roberto Bachi, Offers for family wage, for workers in National institutions (1944 or 1945) (no specific date), CZA J1/3717/3.

189. Committee on Birthrate Problems, "Tokhnit lePolitikah Demografit," Apr. 22, 1945, CZA J1/2383.

190. Ibid.

191. Memorandum of a meeting of the Committee on Birthrate Problems, June 1, 1944, CZA J1/3717/3; Bachi, "Hakamat Kupat Hashva'ah Lemaskorot Ha'ovdim leshem 'Idud haYeludah," May 15, 1944, CZA J1/3717/3.

192. Roberto Bachi, Offers for family wage, for workers in National institutions (1944 or 1945) (no specific date), CZA J1/3717/3.

193. Bachi, "Hakamat Kupat Hashva'ah Lemaskorot Ha'ovdim leshem 'Idud haYeludah," May 15, 1944, CZA J1/3717/3.

194. Ibid.

195. Ibid.

196. Ibid.

197. Memorandum from a meeting with Tova Berman, Roberto Bachi, and Mr. Cohen, June 22, 1943, CZA J1/3717/2; Sh. Ze'evi, a suggestion to the national council, May 21, 1944, CZA J1/34358.

198. Committee on Birthrate Problems, "Tokhnit lePolitikah Demografit," Apr. 22, 1945, CZA J1/2383; Tova Berman, "Ha'Emtza'im haDerushim le'Idud haYeludah baYishuv," Feb. 1945, CZA J1/3717/3.

199. Leo Kaufmann, Questionnaire, 1944, CZA J1/3717/3.

200. Minutes of a meeting of the Committee on Birthrate Problems, June 22, 1943, CZA J1/3717/1.

201. Tova Berman, "Ha'Emtza'im haDerushim le'Idud haYeludah baYishuv," Feb. 1945, CZA J1/3717/3; minutes of a meeting of the Committee on Birthrate Problems Executive, May 27, 1943, CZA J1/3717/1.

202. Yocheved Bat-Rachel, "De'agat HaImahut," Merkaz Kupat Holim, Jan. 1945, YTA, 15-36/4/4, 11.

203. Tova Berman, "Ha'Emtza'im haDerushim le'Idud haYeludah baYishuv," Feb. 1945, CZA J1/3717/3.

204. Letter from Dr. Noak to the Committee on Birthrate Problems and Hadassah management, Feb. 15, 1944, CZA J1/3717/2.

205. Correspondence, 1941–1944, TAA 4-1427.

206. Letter, Sarah Herzog and H. Teitelbaum to the social welfare in the national council, Nov. 27, 1940, CZA J113/2312; letter from Dr. Haim Yassky to Rabbi Yitzhak Herzog, July 25, 1937, CZA J113/8087; correspondence between Y. Brumberg from Hadassah and HaEzra in Jerusalem, June 3, 1938, June 23, 1938, CZA J113/8087.

207. Letter from Mayor Israel Rokach of Tel Aviv to whom it may concern, May 22, 1940, TAA 4-1426; letter from Mayor Israel Rokach to Mrs. Rose Slutzkin, Aug. 9, 1939, TAA 4-1426.

208. Tova Berman, "Ha'Emtza'im haDerushim le'Idud haYeludah baYishuv," Feb. 1945, CZA J1/3717/3.

209. Ibid.

210. Yocheved Bat-Rachel, "De'agat HaImahut," Merkaz Kupat Holim, Jan. 1945, YTA, 15-36/4/4, 13.

211. Ibid., 16.

212. "Yukam Beit Holim Gadol" (no byline), *Davar*, Jan. 1, 1945, 5.

213. Tova Berman, "Ha'Emtza'im haDerushim le'Idud haYeludah baYishuv," Feb. 1945, CZA J1/3717/3.

214. Letter from Bachi to the committee's members, Feb. 16, 1945, CZA J1/3717/3; report on the activities of the Committee on Birthrate Problems, during its two years of existence (May 1943–Apr. 1945), Apr. 29, 1945, CZA J1/1974.

215. Report of the Committee on Birthrate Problems, Sept. 5, 1943, CZA J1/3717/2; minutes of a meeting of the Committee on Birthrate Problems, Sept. 21, 1943, CZA J1/3717/2.

216. "Litsumet Lev Va'adat haIdud laYeludah" (no byline), *Hatzofeh*, June 13, 1943, 4.

217. Letter from Ya'akov Yisraelov to the National Council, Feb. 22, 1945, CZA J1/1974.

218. Letter from Y. Hyman to the National Council, Mar. 25, 1945, CZA J1/1974.

219. Letter from the general secretary of the National Council, to Ya'akov Yisraelov, Mar. 5, 1945, CZA J1/1974.

220. Memorandum of a meeting of the Committee on Birthrate Problems, June 1, 1944, CZA J1/3717/3.

221. Letter from David Ben-Gurion to Tova Berman, May 22, 1944, CZA J1/3717/3.

222. Report on the activities of the Committee on Birthrate Problems, during its two years of existence (May 1943–Apr. 1945), Apr. 29, 1945, CZA J1/1974.

223. Roberto Bachi, "Be'ayat haYeludah BeYisra'el veHatza'ot leMediniyut haUkhlusiyah," undated, ISA 5588/2c; Committee on Birthrate Problems, "Tokhnit Shel Politikah le'Idud haImahut," 1945 (Copy was submitted by Bachi, Nov. 25, 1946), CZA A516/201.

224. L. Bein, "HaRibui haTiv'i veHishuvei he'Atid haKarov," *Hatzofeh*, June 8, 1945, 5.

225. A. Ben, "Teguvot," *Hamashkif,* July 16, 1944, 2.

226. Minutes of a meeting of the Committee on Birthrate Problems, Apr. 6, 1944, CZA J1/3717/2.

227. Tova Berman, "Ha'Emtza'im haDerushim le'Idud haYeludah baYishuv," Feb. 1945, CZA J1/3717/3.

228. Bachi 1943a, 19.

229. Minutes of meeting with Tova Berman, Roberto Bachi, and David Ben-Gurion, May 2, 1944, BGA/diaries/225700.

230. Ibid.

231. Ibid.

232. Kanievsky 1944, 97.

233. H. Myuzam, "Sekirah 'al haMegamot haDemografiyot haNokhehiyot ba'Olam, be'Am Yisra'el, uveYisra'el, 1964," CZA A516/276.

234. Dr. Grushka, minutes of a meeting of the Committee on Birthrate Problems, Feb. 15, 1944, CZA J1/3717/2

235. Bachi 1943a, 19.

236. Roberto Bachi, "Maskanot Politiyot metokh Hakirotay 'al haHitpathut haDemografit shel haYehudim veha'Aravim beE"Y," Oct. 1944, CZA J1/3717/2, 5.

237. Yehudit, "LeShalosh He'arot shel Ben-Gurion," *Hapo'el Hatza'ir* 47, Aug. 12, 1943, 25.

238. Ibid.

239. Rubinstein 1975, 11.

240. Letter from Dr. Grushka to Moshe Shilo, Oct. 24, 1949, CZA A516/73.

CONCLUSION
The Birthrate Issue as a Portrait of the Yishuv

"YOU THINK THAT YOU 'DECIDED' FOR yourself whether to have two children or five," an Israeli journalist wrote in June 2014. Not at all, he told Israeli Jewish mothers. "Sister, take a look at a tree. Did that leaf 'decide' to flutter in the breeze?"[1] Such autonomy is an illusion, he declared. Every person's ostensibly personal decisions are influenced by the zeitgeist. This insight, offered in a contemporary Israel in which average family size is large compared to other Western countries, is no less valid with regard to the Jewish community in Palestine under the British Mandate and its deliberately low birthrate.

The spirit of the times pervades my account of the Yishuv's attitudes toward childbearing and child rearing. It comprises attitudes deriving from the political, social, economic, and cultural aspirations of the new society the Jews in Palestine sought to fashion, their complex values and perceptions, and historical events of earthshaking proportions. No understanding of the Yishuv's birthrate is possible without a profound acquaintance with the human climate created by all these factors.

Demography was a more critical issue for the Yishuv than for other national communities, Roberto Bachi argued in 1943. A low birthrate threatened the Jewish people as a whole, and the Jewish community in Palestine in particular, more than it did other nations in other places, he maintained. Writing just as the full dimensions of the annihilation of Europe's Jews were becoming apparent, Bachi said that "the decline in the birthrate comes on top of physical annihilation and assimilation, leaving our nation without ground under its feet and without a governing body that can defend it and see to its future."[2] The Holocaust, the lack of a Jewish state, and the refusal of the British authorities to allow more than a trickle of Jewish immigrants to enter Palestine, amplified the demographic crisis from all angles.

The low birthrate, and the efforts to boost it, were inseparable from all other aspects of Yishuv life—education, health, economics, law, religion and tradition, women's rights, gender relations, and the concept of childhood, to name just a few. As such, the birthrate provides a lens through which the Yishuv can be viewed.

The discussion of the many reasons to avoid having more than one or two children casts light on how the people of the Yishuv lived. It highlights their difficult economic situation, and it illuminates in a new way their sense of physical insecurity in the face of attack from hostile Arabs. While this fear is well known from other research, the discussion here shows that this anxiety affected the most intimate decisions made by a man and a woman regarding the family they sought to have and to raise. On top of all this, the low birthrate reflected the Yishuv's aspiration to adopt Western social and cultural norms and to make them part of the new Jewish society in formation in Palestine.

A chronological examination of the factors repressing the Yishuv's birthrate shows just how much historical events played a role. The shaky economic and security situation at the time of the large waves of immigration that built the Yishuv intensified the decline in its birthrate.

All sectors and classes in the Yishuv, no matter where they lived, resorted to abortion as a means of family planning. Abortion was practiced in cities and rural settlements, by the nonreligious and religious Zionists. As in other Western societies, middle-class professionals tended to have small families. But in other countries, farmers served as the demographic reserve—rural families were large. In the Yishuv, the opposite was the case. The Jews who settled in far-flung kibbutzim and farming villages faced economic and security hardship that discouraged childbearing. But these people, men and women, also put off having children so that they could devote themselves totally to the national effort. Having children was an important contribution to the nation, but not having them allowed Zionist pioneers to devote their full efforts to farming, construction, and other fundamental tasks, rather than to child rearing.

The widespread use of abortion as a means of controlling family size was not unique to the Yishuv. It was typical of the West in general and of Jews in the West in particular. As in other Western countries, legal prohibitions did little to reduce the abortion rate. The Yishuv differed from Western Europe and the United States (but resembled Jewish immigrant society in the United States) in that most Yishuv couples resorted to abortion only after having one or two children.[3]

Having children was a very important imperative in Jewish tradition, and throughout Jewish history the family had been the fundamental unit of Jewish society. The Jewish national revival highlighted these values. As such, few in the Yishuv wished to avoid having children at all. It was a given that every couple would have one or two. What was new was stopping there. Theoreticians of modernization have noted how cultural heritage can leave an impression on society even as it modernizes.[4] This can be seen clearly in the Yishuv, which sought to carry out a social revolution and create a new society. While it was typified by modernization in many areas, Jewish values and tradition remained strong.

The immigrants who made up the Yishuv remained closely tied to their countries of origin in their worldviews, values, and practices, and having children was no exception. Most of them came from Europe and brought with them Western conceptions of ideal family size and family planning, as well as advanced means of performing abortions. But despite the prevalence of abortions in the Yishuv, it did not produce, as other Western societies did, a public movement that battled for the legitimacy and legality of family planning and abortions.[5] Members of the Yishuv practiced contraception and abortion without reference to the Mandate law prohibiting abortion and with disregard for the pronatalist position of the Zionist leadership. They did so privately and quietly, without demonstrations or formal protests. The individual stated her position through her behavior, not with slogans. The opposite was true of the leadership, which declared its position but did little in practical terms.

European countries viewed the birthrate as an issue of national importance, and thus instituted policies aimed at raising it, including the prohibition of abortion. The Yishuv also ascribed great importance to the issue, which it saw as key to national survival. "This is the only country," Bachi said in the 1940s, "in which our nation's future depends, at least in part, on our own volition."[6] Just as some European countries viewed the decline in their birthrates and the rise in abortions as evidence of national decline,[7] so the Yishuv's members, and in particular its doctors, were charged with disregarding their national duty.[8] Women in particular were expected to recognize that bringing a child into the world was not just a privilege they were granted by biology, but also a national imperative.[9]

The campaign to raise the Yishuv's birthrate was no less a mirror of its complex character. Larger families were a central Zionist goal, and were seen by many as a national rather than a personal matter. At the same time, the Yishuv sought to create a new and modern society. These two goals stood in conflict—on the one hand, this modern national community needed to grow so as to create the Jewish majority that was the necessary basis for a nation-state, while on the other modern European culture idealized small families in which each child received the full attention and care he or she deserved and in which parents were free to pursue careers and participate in political, cultural, and social life. Furthermore, the Yishuv wanted to be modern but also tied to Jewish tradition. This made it all the more difficult to achieve its diametrically opposed goals, and exacerbated existing ethnic and gender disparities.

The advocates of a higher birthrate placed the task of having and raising more children squarely on the shoulders of mothers. Women, according to the traditional view of gender roles shared by much of the Yishuv, were first and foremost responsible for their homes and families. That view was amplified by the belief that a high birthrate was vital for the nation's strength and survival. Yet, at the same time, the nation-building enterprise required the mobilization of all available forces, both men and women. Furthermore, the Yishuv's women were shaping a new female identity and demanded to be full partners in the national effort. Modernization and enlightenment shaped women's new conception of themselves, one in which motherhood was not their only, or even their central, destiny. Society's expectation that women devote themselves to motherhood collided with women's desire to play an integral role in public affairs. Yet the conflict was not between men in public leadership positions and women who sought to break out of the private sphere. It was a structural contradiction within the new society, which on the one hand adhered to traditional gender roles while at the same time advocating egalitarian socialism, of which gender equality was an inseparable part. The dissonance of welcoming women into public life and the national endeavor while still assigning them their traditional role in the family was a salient fact of Yishuv life—and remains so in today's Israel.

With abortions today still regulated by the state and private organizations encouraging a higher Jewish birthrate, Israeli society remains national and patriarchal in character. Abortions are seen as a public issue, not as a private matter for women to decide on. In contemporary Israel as well, wombs are enlisted to resolve demographic issues with political implications.[10] Such views persist today in Israel, a country in which women's rights are guaranteed by law and in which many women seek to fulfill their full personal potentials in their careers and in public life.

The conflict between these two conceptions of womanhood was all the more potent during the Yishuv period, when the establishment of new gender relations was still in its earliest stage. The Jews of this new society found it difficult to abandon the model of gender relations that had prevailed for generations untold, and, in the absence of social benefits such as maternity leave and laws establishing the rights of pregnant women and working mothers, and with a dearth of infant and childcare, upping the birthrate inevitably meant confining women to their homes. The Yishuv, constructing a modern, egalitarian state on traditional foundations, demanded, in practical terms, that women carry the torch of tradition. But that expectation was not consistent with the aspirations of many women and the way the Yishuv modernists wanted their society to look. The contradiction inevitably pushed the birthrate down.

The contradiction between creating a Jewish majority and building a modern Western society produced ethnic as well as gender gaps. Larger families were essential to realizing the goal of establishing a Jewish state. Yet the Zionists wanted that state to be an advanced one, and some kinds of large families could detract from that goal. These fell into two main groups. There were the Haredim, who kept themselves separate from the New Yishuv. They did not participate in elections to the Assembly of Representatives, did not accept the authority of Jewish national self-governing institutions, and had no allegiance to modern Western culture. The second group was made up of Jews of Asian and North African origin. Like the Haredim, they were a minority, but given their very high birthrate and the very low birthrate of the Ashkenazim, they were seen as a threat. While their birthrate was high, they lived for the most part in poverty, and the modernists looked down on their oriental culture. Subscribing to eugenic principles, the Yishuv leadership thus sought to boost the birthrate among the Ashkenazim while restricting it among these two groups.

It is important to stress that the Yishuv leadership sought to imbue all parts of society, both Ashkenazim and Misrahim, with common norms regarding the birthrate, the ideal being three or four children per family. Larger families were considered nonnormative and demographically threatening, while smaller ones were also undesirable.

But the ethnic factor subsumed in this attitude cannot be ignored. While the goal was a single norm for the entire nation, the rhetoric was not always in keeping with the principles. The rhetoric expressed demographic anxiety regarding a growing Mizrahi birthrate that could produce a population incompatible with the Zionist vision. It sought to encourage a higher birthrate among Jews of European origin, who were considered more desirable for the new society in creation. This rhetoric reflected and probably exacerbated ethnic divisions.

The selective encouragement of larger families in "appropriate" sectors, while the large families in other "inferior" sectors, such as the lower socioeconomic strata and ethnic minorities, was not unique to the Yishuv. It had been a feature of the Western discourse since the nineteenth century, focusing on the "quality" of the children born. In the Yishuv, nevertheless, the Mizrahi birthrate and the quality of the children being born was not the center of the public discourse in the period examined here. During the Mandate, most of the Jewish population was Ashkenazi, and most of the birthrate activity was directed at that community. After the establishment of the state of Israel and the arrival of huge waves of immigrants from the Islamic lands, pronouncements about the Mizrahi birthrate, including criticisms of both its quantity and quality, seen as a threat to the nation, became much more prominent.[11]

The contradictory messages aimed at different sectors did not make it easier for the campaign for a higher birthrate to carry out an effective policy to that end. It is not surprising, then, that the campaign was largely a declarative one, based on public education.

The focus on a public information campaign also highlighted other unique features of the Yishuv. It was an ideological society, motivated by an idea and mobilizing all its powers to achieve its goal of establishing a Jewish state. Zionist ideology had indeed succeeded in achieving a great deal in a very short time. Unsurprisingly, then, many advocates of a higher birthrate thought that they could advance toward their goal through ideological persuasion. Beyond this, the Yishuv suffered from a lack of funds, and had to devote the limited resources at its disposal to a range of other needs essential to the establishment of a Jewish state.

The birthrate issue sheds light on the Yishuv leadership. The power of the Yishuv leadership and its national institutions depended on the voluntary willingness of Palestine's Jews to accept their authority. The collective struggle to boost the birthrate was meant to empower the Jewish collective and strengthen the mutual responsibility needed to achieve Zionism's political and social goals. But it was the British who ruled, and the Yishuv was subject to their laws, with only limited legislative and enforcement powers of its own. Its leadership often had their hands tied, on the birthrate issue as on many others.

At the same time, the leadership's desire to take action to increase the birthrate shows that the Yishuv saw itself as the government of a state-to-be. As part of the struggle to found a Jewish state, the leadership sought to instill the Jewish public with a "sense of state" and to accustom it to living in an independent polity, no matter the uncertainty of the present. In taking up the birthrate issue, and the attempt to fashion a policy program just as other countries had, the Yishuv leadership acted as the government of a properly run state. The birthrate campaign can thus be seen as one more step toward an independent state, as a rehearsal for independence. At the same time, the difficulty of actually pursuing such a policy in practice clearly demonstrated that the Yishuv was not yet a state.

The concept of the family and its place in national society is not static. It changes in response to historical circumstances. Sometimes the family and the nation or state are perceived as two entities that reinforce each other, while at other times the family is seen as an expression of individualism that stands in the way of achieving national goals.[12] The period covered by this book, a seminal one in which the Yishuv was shaped, was a time of social and cultural conflict. The birthrate campaign can be seen seeking to mold the character of the future state and the relationship between the private individual and society that would prevail when it was founded. Historical circumstances led to a paradox. On the one hand, they prompted the Yishuv leadership to oppose families' individual and private decisions, which were based on their ideas of what a family should look like and what kind of upbringing children should enjoy. On the other hand, those same circumstances encouraged individuals and families to establish boundaries against social and national intrusion into their private affairs. The public acted as it saw fit and not as the nation wished—not because the public was devoid of national values, as the leadership argued, but because it had national values of its own, nourished in part by the cultural repertoire immigrants had brought from their countries of origin, regarding the national-modern character of the future society. Since, in the Yishuv, it was a matter of choice for the individual to affiliate with the national society, the birthrate issue can be seen as a conflict within a national-modern society and an attempt by the individuals of that society to lay out their private boundaries without crossing the borders of the nation.

Many studies of national societies, including those devoted to the Yishuv, have argued that nationalist indoctrination was a hugely powerful force that crushed the will of the individual and subordinated it to the communal imperative. The birthrate issue in the Yishuv shows what a limited impact indoctrination in fact had. The Yishuv, for all its national aspirations and for all the ideological commitment of many of its members, was fundamentally a collection of individuals of many different kinds who doggedly guarded their autonomy.

Seen through the prism of the birthrate issue, the project of turning the production of children into a tool in the national struggle should have further cemented the ostensibly monolithic nature of the Yishuv collective. Yet the opposite happened—the monolith cracked. In this light, the Yishuv is not the cohesive collective portrayed by many historians; it was rather a heterogeneous jumble of varying and often contradictory values that led in different directions. The period covered by this book was the acme of the national struggle. Even so, the Yishuv's complexity and the wide variety of views of its members overshadowed its national nature. The national discourse certainly dominated, but it was not decisive. The Yishuv's nationalism had clear limits. This was a society in the midst of a national revival that raised the banners of equality and social justice at the same time that it was riven by social, ethnic, and gender divides; it adhered to traditional values even as it sought to adopt modern ones; its perceptions and practices were Western but its place and time made it very different from the Western societies it sought to emulate.

In other words, while the birthrate issue and the campaign to encourage larger families may seem very specific, they in fact serve as a canvas on which a portrait of the Yishuv can be painted. It is a picture that displays the intricacies of day-to-day life, illuminates the nature of Jewish society in Palestine, and shows the give-and-take between the Zionist leadership and the multifaceted society it sought to shape. While the issue ostensibly at stake was the ideal size of families and whether, to what extent, and how the birth of babies should be regulated, the debate was really about the character of the society the Yishuv was building. It raised questions of the relations between different sectors of Jewish society, what the relations between genders should be, to what extent Jewish religious tradition should be a part of the new society, how its leaders should lead and whether its citizens would follow, where the boundaries between the individual and society should be drawn, and what the role of the individual was in modern society. These and other fundamental questions were the backdrop to the Yishuv's birthrate debate, and some of them would be addressed directly after the state was founded.[13] The birthrate issue was thus central to the formation of the state of Israel and its society.

NOTES

1. Dror Feuer, "Tenu'at Metutelet," *Globes*, June 26, 2014, 70.
2. Roberto Bachi, radio talk, 1943, CZA J1/3717/1.
3. Exler 2000, 89
4. Inglehart and Baker 2000, 19–51.
5. Grossmann 1995, v; Gordon 1997, 153; Usborne 2007, 3.
6. Bachi 1943a, 8.
7. For example in Ireland, see Brewer 2000, 93–100.
8. Dr. Noak, minutes of a meeting of the Committee on Birthrate Problems, June 22, 1943, CZA J1/3717/1.
9. Letter from Dr. Tova Berman to David Ben-Gurion, May 10, 1944, CZA J1/3717/3; report by Dr. Tova Berman, Feb. 16, 1945, CZA J1/3717/3.
10. Triger 2014, 99–100.
11. Melamed 2004; Rozin 2002.
12. For example in Japan, see Wilson 2006.
13. For example, Katvan 2012.

EPILOGUE

THE STATE OF ISRAEL WAS BORN on May 14, 1948. It was not an easy birth, involving as it did a bloody war with many victims. As the war was still in progress, the infant state labored intensively to bring in Jews from around the world. The first were Holocaust refugees from displaced persons camps in Europe, as well as Jews from Yemen and Iraq who were perceived to be in mortal danger. In the years that followed masses of immigrants arrived from all continents. The mosaic of immigrants redrew the country's social and economic profile. The influx was accompanied by an economic crisis involving severe shortages of food, clothing, furniture, housing, and other basic goods.

David Ben-Gurion, the country's founding father and its first prime minister, was optimistic at first. Not long before the birth he had proposed to double the population in four years by means of immigration and births.[1] In fact, it took one year less—but only thanks to immigration. The birthrate was far from satisfactory.

It had gone up in the mid-1940s, but that turned out to be short lived. In 1947 and 1948, the number of births dropped sharply.[2] Encouragingly, the Jewish birthrate rose during Israel's first four years, but that was mostly a result of the fact that the proportion of Jews from Asia and Africa, who characteristically had large families, was growing.[3] Beginning in 1951 the birthrate, and with it the rate of natural increase, again began to drop. It was especially notable given the steady rise in the birthrate and natural increase of Israel's Arab population. The huge influx of Jewish immigrants, a large number of whom had large families, could not hide the decline. In fact, in the 1950s it reached its nadir.[4] "The Israel birthrate has hit bottom. Ever more families are making do with two children or even one," a newspaper reported in 1960.[5] Ben-Gurion was not pleased. Fifteen years after the state was founded he declared that despite "the great increase by means of immigration, the rate of natural increase is declining inexorably."[6]

As had been the case in the Yishuv period, the abortion rate remained high despite the being outlawed.[7] The widespread practice of this means of avoiding children was a major factor in the decline in births.[8] Member of the Knesset Tova Sanhedrai presented that body with data showing that the number of abortions performed in Israel between 1951 and 1964 almost equaled the number of births. No attempt was made to prevent them, she said.[9] Women of all classes terminated their pregnancies, and for all reasons, from conception outside of marriage to the prospect of having two children less than twelve months apart. Mothers of three children had abortions because they wanted no more than that.[10] Ben-Gurion told the Knesset in 1963 that he was concerned that the abortion rate was reaching shocking heights.[11]

After the state was founded, the main reason for seeking out an abortion remained economic. The huge immigration rate and the scarcity that characterized the country's early years made their impact on the birthrate. "The numbers are frightening," said Moshe Sneh, a member of the Knesset for the Marxist-socialist Mapam party in May 1950. He attributed the decreasing birthrate to "a decline in the standard of living among the masses of the people."[12] Large families crumpled under the burden of providing for so many, declared Kalman Kahana, representative of the Haredi Poaelei Agudat Yisrael party in 1953. The decline was "an attack on internal immigration, so critical for the future of our country and its security."[13]

In the new state, as in the Yishuv, "educated white-collar people" continued to have a single child, or "one and a half," as Joseph Mayer put it, "while the poorer classes have many children."[14] In Israel's early years, some claimed—as they had in the Yishuv period—that the birthrate would have been even lower if it were not for Orthodox and Mizrahi Jews "who had not yet been spoiled by Western culture."[15] As in the past, in the 1950s fears were voiced, on the Knesset floor, that "the practice of restricting the number of births has already penetrated the Mizrahim."[16] These Jews, the press reported, "are beginning to calculate whether they can afford" a large family.[17]

Soon after independence, Dr. Betha Avramov, a German-born gynecologist who had immigrated to Palestine in 1939, began working in a clinic in Acre that cared for a heterogeneous population. It did not take her long to realize that the main problem women had was family planning, in two different and opposing aspects. Avramov divided her patients into two principal groups. One was composed of new immigrants from Islamic countries. They had many children who were born at short intervals, and they were barely able to bear the burden of caring for them. The second group was made up of immigrant women from Eastern Europe. They had few children and had learned, before their arrival in Israel, to plan their families by means of terminating pregnancies. A large proportion of them had undergone multiple abortions in their countries of origin, performed by experienced doctors in well-run hospitals, at no cost to them. Both groups, Dr. Avramov thought, needed to plan their families in a way different from what they had become accustomed to. But her advocacy of family planning was rejected by the Israeli authorities.[18]

The national concern about the low birthrate did not subside after the state was founded. This was remarked on as early as 1949: "Supervision of the birthrate is one of the urgent problems that our young country must address," one physician asserted.[19] Protests against the failure to enforce the abortion law were submitted on a nearly daily basis, and most of these noted that nonenforcement was endangering the country by keeping the birthrate down.[20] Concerned citizens continued to write to Ben-Gurion. "A horribly peculiar situation has emerged," a citizen wrote to him in 1954. "During our long years of exile, the Jewish people were fruitful and multiplied to supply people to the swords and furnaces of their enemies, and now that we have returned to our homeland and there is a chance that we need no longer give birth in fear, we have stopped having children."[21]

In short, the establishment of the state did not quell Ben-Gurion's worries about the birthrate. On the contrary, the demographic threat frequently preoccupied him during the 1950s. "Who can promise us that ten years from now the Arabs will not be in the majority. . . . Our urgent problem is a shortage of Jews, not a shortage of territory," he said at a meeting of the Knesset's Foreign Affairs and Defense Committee in 1958.[22] "The critical issue is from where we will bring Jews to Israel."[23] The most important contribution women could make to the Zionist effort was to be mothers, Ben-Gurion maintained, just as he had during the Yishuv period.[24] Yet at the same time he advocated an egalitarian society, symbolized in part by the fact that both women and men were required to perform military service. Ben-Gurion dismissed those who argued that mandatory military service for women would depress the birthrate. "If there is no settlement and no families are established and no children are born, what good is security?" he acknowledged, but also stressed that the conscription law took into account the vital importance of motherhood. For this very reason, while single women were expected to do their part for the defense of the state, married women, he noted, were exempted. "A woman who has married should not be kept from being a mother," he declared.[25]

But despite demographic concerns, nothing practical was done during the country's first decade to encourage a higher birthrate. The only measure taken was a symbolic one—Ben-Gurion declared in 1949 that a prize would be awarded to Jewish women who had given birth to and raised ten or more children. Similar prizes were awarded in other countries.[26] This highly publicized practice, which continued for a decade, was the epitome of Ben-Gurion's campaign to raise the birthrate.[27]

The transition from Yishuv to state presented Ben-Gurion with a dilemma. Was he prime minister of the Jewish state's Jews, or of all the new country's citizens? Could a state committed to social and political equality for all promote the birth of more Jewish babies over other babies?[28] When the prize for mothers of large families was announced, Arab mothers of ten children also demanded to receive it.[29] Ben-Gurion agreed.[30] He took a clear stand—he headed a government that represented and served all Israel's citizens regardless of nationality and religion.[31] Every mother, Jewish or Arab, who had given birth to and raised ten children who continued to live in Israel deserved a prize.[32] In doing this, he obviated the prize's demographic purpose and blurred the national focus of the birthrate issue. Mothers were awarded the prize as individuals who had devoted themselves to large families, rather than as servants of the national enterprise.

Two decades after the founding of Israel, at the end of the 1960s, Israel's birthrate turned around. Surprisingly, this came just as the advent of the birth control pill made family planning easier and empowered women to control their own fertility in the intimacy of their own homes and families. As the birthrate declined throughout the West, Israelis began to have more children; the typical Israeli family today has three. That change requires a book of its own.

NOTES

1. Rachel Kagan, Knesset session, July 4, 1949, Knesset protocols; Bar-Zohar 1977, 284.

2. From 1947 to 1948, the number of births dropped from 31 to 26 per 1,000 inhabitants. Moshe Sneh, Knesset session, May 16, 1950, Knesset protocols; according to Bachi, the figure dropped from 29 to 23. Roberto Bachi, "Be'ayat haYeludah BeYisra'el veHatza'ot leMediniyut haUkhlusiyah," undated, ISA 5588/2c.

3. Bachi and Matras 1962, 207–208.

4. Ben-Gurion's diary, May 8, 1961, BGA/Diaries/224363.

5. Arie Avneri, "Yesh Le'oded haNo'ar leHithaten beGil Tsa'ir uleHolid Yeladim," *Yediot Aharonot*, May 9, 1960, 8.

6. Letter from Ben-Gurion to Roberto Bachi, Sept. 5, 1964, BGA/Shabtai Tevet Collection/concepts/12–100.

7. The State of Israel adopted the British Mandate law that prohibited abortions. Since 1952, the law has been modified. Rimalt 2010, 138.

8. Dr Y. Asherman, "Dr. Asherman Mazhir Mipnei Hapalot Mela'akhutiyot," *Maariv*, Aug. 13, 1952, 3; Dr Y. Asherman, "Hapalah Mela'akhutit Mehabelet BePirion HaIsha," *Eitanim*, Nov. 11, 1952, 266.

9. Tova Sanhedrai, Knesset session, July 11, 1966, Knesset protocols. See also MK Shlomo Lorincz, Knesset session, Feb. 1963, Knesset protocols.

10. A report from a subcommittee on abortions issue, Feb. 18, 1965, CZA A516/73.

11. B–G Agrees, "Jewish birthrate too low; abortion rate is shocking," *Jerusalem Post*, Feb. 28, 1963, 3.
12. Moshe Sneh, Knesset session, May 16, 1950, Knesset protocols.
13. Knesset session, Mar. 16, 1953, Knesset protocols.
14. Dr. Joseph Mayer, "Hagbarat haYeludah o Ribui haYeladim," *Eitanim* 5:3–4 (Spring 1952), 76.
15. B–G Agrees, "Jewish birthrate too low; abortion rate is shocking," *Jerusalem Post*, Feb. 28, 1963, 3.
16. Arie Avneri, "Yesh Le'oded haNo'ar leHithaten beGil Tsa'ir uleHolid Yeladim," *Yediot Aharonot*, May 9, 1960, 8.
17. Dr. [Abraham] Spruch–Pevsner, in M. Meisels, "Mitargenim le'Idud haYeludah," *Maariv*, Apr. 4, 1955, 2.
18. Liberman House—Museum of the history of Nahariya, http://museum.rutkin.info/node/335.
19. Dr. M. Gelman, "HaPikuakh 'Al haYeludah biMdinat Yisrael," *Eitanim* 1:6 (Feb. 1949), 20.
20. Kalman Kahana, Knesset session, Mar. 23, 1954, Knesset protocols; Arie Avneri, "Yesh Le'oded haNo'ar leHithaten beGil Tsa'ir uleHolid Yeladim," *Yediot Aharonot*, May 9, 1960, 8.
21. A letter to Ben-Gurion, unclear signature, Jan. 1, 1954, BGA/correspondence/143315.
22. Sept. 19, 1958, BGA/diaries/220462.
23. Ben-Gurion's diary, Aug. 19, 1958, BGA/diaries/220462.
24. Knesset session, Sept. 5, 1949, Knesset protocols.
25. Knesset session, Jan. 16, 1950, Knesset protocols.
26. Dr. M. Gelman, "HaPikuakh 'Al haYeludah biMdinat Yisrael," *Eitanim* 1:6 (Feb. 1949), 21; Zerach Warhaftig, Knesset session, Sept. 5, 1949, Knesset protocols.
27. BGA/correspondence/128200. For information, lists, receipts, and correspondence on the birth award, see ISA 5587/C4.
28. For example, M. A., "Pras haYeludah," *Davar*, Nov. 22, 1949 (n.p.).
29. Letters from Arab women: ISA 5587/C4; B. Sela, "Bana'yikh Keshtilei Zeitim," *Maariv*, Jan. 14, 1951, 2.
30. His decision from Dec. 1949, ISA 5587/C4.
31. Knesset session, June 30, 1953, Knesset protocols.
32. ISA 340/C50; report containing data on the prizes distribution to Arab and Jewish mothers: June 30, 1952, ISA 5588/C20.

GLOSSARY

Ashkenazi
Jews of European origin.

Assembly of Representatives
The Yishuv's elected representative body, founded in 1920. The Assembly of Representatives was elected democratically, with voters voting for parties that were awarded seats on a proportional basis.

Committee on Birthrate Problems
The Committee on Birthrate Problems was established in 1943 to draw up a plan to encourage a higher Yishuv birthrate. It operated for two years.

Council of Women Workers
A feminist Zionist labor organization founded in 1921 to represent women of the labor movement. It operated under the auspices of the Histadrut.

Hadassah (The Women's Zionist Organization of America)
Founded in 1912 in New York by a group of Jewish women led by Henrietta Szold, Hadassah had two goals. The first was to advance health and medical services in Palestine, and the second to further the Zionist cause within the American Jewish community. Nurses sent to Palestine by Hadassah before World War I set up a clinic in Jerusalem, and these were followed by a mission of physicians and nurses in 1918 who founded clinics and hospitals in different parts of the country.

Hadassah hospital in Jerusalem
Founded by Hadassah in 1918 on the basis of the Rothschild Hospital, which had served the city since the nineteenth century.

Hadassah hospital in Tel Aviv (from 1931: Tel Aviv Municipal Hospital)
Founded by Hadassah in 1918 in Jaffa, it moved to Tel Aviv in 1920. In 1931, after years of expansion and facing budgetary problems, Hadassah handed it over to the Tel Aviv municipality.

Jewish Agency
Founded in 1930 to seek to incorporate the Zionist movement along with non-Zionists in Palestine and outside it, the Jewish Agency constituted the Jewish autonomous administration in Palestine.

Jewish immigration (*aliyah*)
Jewish immigration was central to the Zionist goal of establishing a Jewish state in Palestine in which the Jews would be the majority population. While the Mandate Administration initially allowed the influx of tens of thousands of Jews, it required that immigrants receive permits ("certificates"), which were restricted according to what number of newcomers the British thought the Palestinian economy could absorb economically.

Zionist pressure for more massive immigration increased in the 1930s with the rise of Nazism and antisemitism in Germany and other European countries. But Arab resistance to Jewish immigration, which broke out into violence periodically and into a full-fledged Arab Revolt in 1936, impelled the British to establish strict immigration quotas, as did internal British and international political considerations. These restrictions led to friction with the Zionist movement, which wanted larger numbers allowed in. One result was illegal immigration, with Jews entering the country by stealth, with the support of the Yishuv and Zionist institutions.

Jewish National Council (Va'ad Le'umi)
The presidium of the Assembly of Representatives, responsible for internal affairs such as health, education, religion, and immigrant absorption. The National Council and the Jewish Agency Executive overlapped in their membership and together constituted the Yishuv's leadership.

Kupat Holim
The general term for medical service and insurance organizations in the Yishuv and Israel. The first of these was founded in 1911. While there were a number of these during the Mandate period, the largest by far was Kupat Holim Clalit, which operated under the auspices of the Histadrut labor union. As such, the unmodified term "Kupat Holim" is often used to refer specifically to Kupat Holim Clalit.

labor movement
A general term for the labor and socialist parties and institutions that together made up the dominant force in the Yishuv. Its central institution was the Histadrut labor federation and its dominant political force was the Mapai party.

Mandate administration
The British government in Palestine under the Mandate.

Mandate Palestine
The British ruled Palestine from 1920 to 1948 on the basis of a mandate from the League of Nations (formally given in 1922), following the British conquest of the country from Turkey in 1917 and a brief period of military rule. The country's boundaries were established in the 1920s as part of the post–World War I settlement between the powers.

Mapai
An acronym for the Workers Party of the Land of Israel, Mapai was founded in 1930 and was the dominant political force in the Yishuv and during the first three decades of the Israeli state. It was led by David Ben-Gurion.

Mizrahim/Mizrahi Jews
Jews from the Islamic world, in particular from North Africa and Asia. Also referred to as Oriental or Sephardi Jews. *Mizrahi* is the term generally used in scholarly literature today, although technically it refers specifically to the ethnic subculture and consciousness that emerged among these Jews after the founding of the state. Confusingly, the word *Mizrahi* is a homonym—it also the name of the bourgeois religious Zionist party of the Mandate and early state period, and an element of the labor-religious Zionist party, Hapo'el HaMizrahi.

Old Yishuv/Haredim
The traditional religious Jewish population of Palestine, now termed the "ultra-Orthodox" or "Haredim." This population lived primarily in the four holy cities of Jerusalem, Safed, Hebron, and Tiberias and opposed the Zionist political project of establishing a Jewish state. Living largely off charity provided by Diaspora Jews, most of its men devoted themselves to Torah study.

Revisionist Zionists

A faction of the Zionist movement in opposition to the labor Zionists that dominated the Yishuv. Founded by Ze'ev Jabotinsky, the Revisionists advocated a more activist and confrontational policy toward the British, based on massive Jewish immigration rather than the more gradual approach taken by the labor Zionists and the mainstream Zionist leadership. The Revisionists demanded that the Jewish state also include Transjordan, originally intended to be part of the British Mandate territory but severed from it in 1922 to create the Arab kingdom of Transjordan. The Revisionists also opposed the socialism of the labor movement and advocated a liberal society based on free enterprise and individual initiative.

Union of Hebrew Women for Equal Rights

A Zionist feminist organization founded in 1919 to advance the political and legal status of women in Palestine. It led the fight for women's suffrage in the Yishuv in the 1920s, gaining women the right to vote for and to be elected to Yishuv representative bodies beginning in 1926.

Yishuv/New Yishuv

The modern Zionist Jewish population in Palestine that aspired to establish a Jewish state and participated in the new Hebrew-speaking society and culture that Zionist immigrants created there. This group is also known as the "New Yishuv." Scholarly work commonly uses the unmodified term *Yishuv* to refer to the entire Jewish population of Palestine.

Zionist Executive/Jewish Agency Executive

The "cabinet" or executive authority of the Yishuv's autonomous government under and recognized by the British Mandate as the representative of the Jewish population in Palestine. The Zionist Executive, an arm of the Zionist Organization, fulfilled this function until 1930, when it was superseded by the Jewish Agency Executive.

Zionist Organization

The institutional manifestation of the Zionist movement, founded in 1897 by Theodor Herzl to seek the establishment of a Jewish state in Palestine.

BIBLIOGRAPHY

ARCHIVES

BGA   Ben-Gurion Archive
CZA   Central Zionist Archive
ISA   Israel State Archive
LI   Lavon Institute for Labor Movement Research
RKMA   Religious Kibbutz Movement Archive
RZA   Archive of the Institute for the Research on Religious Zionism
TAA   Tel Aviv-Jaffa Municipal Historical Archives
YTA   Yad Tabenkin Archive

HEBREW NEWSPAPERS AND PERIODICALS

'Al Hamishmar
'Alonim
Bamishor
Batirah (Tirat Zvi)
Davar
Devar Hapo'elet
Do'ar Hayom
Eitanim
Globes
Ha'aretz
Ha'em Vehayeled
Hamashkif
Hapo'el Hatza'ir
Hatzofeh
'Iton Meyuhad
Jerusalem Post
Maariv
Mibifnim
Tesha' Ba'erev
Yediot Aharonot

Abrams, Lynn. 2002. *The Making of Modern Woman: Europe 1789–1918*. London: Pearson Education.

Ajzenstadt, Mimi. 2010. "Hitahdut Nashim 'Ivriyot LeShivui Zechuyot Be'Eretz Yisra'el veMa'avakan LeKhinun Tafkid Em haMishpakhah be'Eretz Yisra'el, 1919–1948." In Eyal Katvan, Margalit Shilo, and Ruth Halperin-Kadari, eds., *Nashim, Zekhuyot, veMishpat beTekufat haMandat*. Ramat Gan: Bar-Ilan University, 57–85.

Alpern Engel, Barbara. 2004. *Women in Russia, 1700–2000*. Cambridge: Cambridge University Press.

Alroey, Gur. 2004. *Immigrantim: HaHagirah haYehudit leEretz Yisra'el beReshit haMe'ah ha'Esrim*. Jerusalem: Yad Ben-Zvi.

———. 2010. "Nashim beEretz Yisra'el beTekufat haMandat: Hebetim Demografi'im." In Eyal Katvan, Margalit Shilo, and Ruth Halperin-Kadari, eds., *Nashim, Zekhuyot, veMishpat beTekufat haMandat*. Ramat Gan: Bar-Ilan University, 97–101.

Altshuler, Mordechai, and Ezra Mendelson. 1984. "Yahadut Brit HaMo'atzot uPolin bein Milhemot ha'Olam: Nituah Hashva'ati." In Jeffrey Wigoder, ed., *'Iyunim beYahadut Zmanenu*. Jerusalem: Institute of Contemporary Jewry, Hebrew University.

Amir, Delila, and Niva Shoshi. 2007. "The Israeli Abortion Law: A Gender and Feminist Aspect." In Shlomit Yanisky-Ravid, Yifat Biton, and Dana Pugach, eds., *Studies in Law, Gender and Feminism*. Kiryat Ono: Nevo, 777–808.

Andorka, Rudolf. 1978. *Determinants of Fertility in Advanced Societies*. London: Methuen.

Anson, Yonatan, and Avinoam Meir. 1996. "Datiyut, Le'umanut, uFiryon beYisra'el." *Bitahon Sotziali* 46 (September): 43–63.

Auerbach, Elias. 1997. *MeEretz haAv el Eretz haAvot: Parshat Hayav shel Tzioni she'Alah laAretz miGermaniyah, haRofeh haYehudi haRishon beHaifa beReshit haMe'ah*. Translated from the German by Daniel Or. Jerusalem: Yad Yitzhak Ben-Zvi, Leo Baeck Institute.

Avdeev, Alexander, Alain Bloom, and Irina Troitskaya. 1995. "The History of Abortion's Statistics in Russia and the USSR from 1900–1991." *Population: An English Selection* 7: 39–66.

Bachi, Roberto. 1941. *HaRibui haTiv'i haAmiti bekerev Yehudei Yerushalayim*. Jerusalem: Statistics Department of the Jewish Agency.

———. 1943a. *HaRibui haTiv'i beE"Y ve'Atido shel haYishuv*. Jerusalem: National Council.

———. 1943b. *Lema'an haYeludah—Lema'an haYeled*, Jerusalem: Mosad Lema'an haYeled vehaNa'ar.

———. 1944. "HaNohag baNisu'in uvaYeludah bekerev haShekhavot haShonot shel haYishuv veHashpa'ato 'al 'Atidenu." In David Gurevich, Aaron Gertz, and Roberto Bachi, *Ha'Aliyah, haYishuv, vehaTenua'h haTiv'it shel haUkhlusiyah beEretz Yisra'el*. Jerusalem: Statistics Department of the Jewish Agency, 242–243.

———. 1977. *The Population of Israel* (CICRED 1974 World Population Year Series). Jerusalem: Institute of Contemporary Jewry, Hebrew University.

Bachi, Roberto, and Judah Matras. 1962. "Contraception and Induced Abortions among the Jewish Maternity Cases in Israel." *Milbank Memorial Fund Quarterly* 40:2 (April), 207–229.

Baird, Robert M., and Stuart E. Rosenbaum, eds. 2001. *The Ethics of Abortion: Pro-Life vs. Pro-Choice [Contemporary Issues]*. Amherst, NY: Prometheus.

Bareli, Meir. 1986. *Lehavin et Ben-Gurion.* Tel Aviv: Yediot Aharonot and Edanim.

Barell, Ari. 2012. "Epistemologiyah Tzionit: Politikat haMisparim shel David Ben-Gurion." *'Iyyunim BeTekumat Yisra'el* 22: 92.

Bar-Zohar, Michael. 1975. *Ben-Gurion.* Vol. 1. Tel Aviv: Am Oved.

———. 1977. *Ben-Gurion.* Vol. 2. Tel Aviv: Am Oved.

Ben-Ami, Ilan. 2010. *HaIshah she'ito: Hayeihen haPrati'im vehaTziburi'im shel Neshot Rashei haMemshalah beYisra'el.* Tel Aviv: Matar.

Ben-Gurion, David. 1968. *Mikhtavim el Paula ve'el haYeladim.* Tel Aviv: Am Oved.

———. 1997. *Nilahem keUmah: Zikhronot min ha'Izavon (Sept. 1939–April 1940).* Tel Aviv: Am Oved.

Berkovitz, Nitza. 1999. "Eshet Hayil Mi Yimtza: Nashim veEzrahut beYisra'el." *Sotziologiyah Yisra'elit* 2:1, 277–317.

Bernstein, Deborah S. 1993. "Bein haIshah haAdam uvein Eshet haBayit: Ishah uMishpahah beTzibur haPo'alim haYehudi ha'Ironi beTekufat haYishuv." In Uri Ram, ed., *HaHevrah haYisra'elit: Hebetim Bikorti'im.* Tel Aviv: Bereirot, 83–103.

———. 1998. "Daughters of the Nation: Between the Public and Private Spheres in Pre-State Israel." In Judith R. Baskin, ed., *Jewish Women in Historical Perspective.* Detroit: Wayne State University Press, 287–311.

———. 2003. "Ka'asher 'Avodah 'Ivrit Enena 'Omedet 'al haPerek: Histadrut ha'Ovdim leNokhah haMigzar haMemshalti haMandatori." In Avi Bareli and Nahum Karlinski, eds., *Kalkalah veHevrah beYemei haMandat.* Sde Boker: Ben-Gurion University Press, 79–106.

———. 2013. "BeShuk ha'Avodah ubaHanut, baBayit uvaHutz: Hayei 'Avodah shel Nashim Meagrot beShuk ha'Avodah haFormali vehalo Formali." In Pnina Morag-Talmon and Yael Atzmon, eds., *Nashim Mehagrot beYisra'el.* Jerusalem: Mossad Bialik, 87–111.

Bernstein, Frances L. 2007. *The Dictatorship of Sex: Lifestyle Advice for the Soviet Masses,* DeKalb: Northern Illinois University Press.

Biale, David. 1992. *Eros vehaYehudim.* Tel Aviv: Am Oved.

Blom, Ida. 2008. "How to Have Healthy Children? Responses to the Falling Birth Rate in Norway, c. 1900–1940." *Dynamis* 28: 151–174.

Brewer, Michelle. 2000. "Eugenics Policies in the Republic of Ireland and the Impact of Nationalism." *Canadian Review of Studies in Nationalism* 27:1–2, 93–100.

Brezniak, Moshe. 2004. *Atzey haLivneh haZkufim: Lohem Yehudi baTzava haPolani, be-Geto Mezerich uvaMahanot.* Jerusalem: Sidrat 'Edut, 21.

Bridenthal, Renate, Atina Grossmann, and Marion Kaplan. 1984. "Introduction." In Renate Bridenthal, Atina Grossmann, and Marion Kaplan, eds., *When Biology Became Destiny: Women in Weimar and Nazi Germany.* New York: Monthly Review Press, 1–28.

Burton, Chris. 2000. "Minzdrav, Soviet Doctors, and the Policing of Reproduction in the Late Stalinist Years." *Russian History* 27:2, 197–221.

Chatterjee, Nilanjana, and Nancy E. Riley. 2001. "Planning an Indian Modernity: The Gendered Politics of Fertility Control." *Signs: Journal of Women in Culture & Society* 26:3 (Spring), 811–846.

Clark, Christopher, and Wolfram Kaiser, eds. 2003. *Culture Wars: Secular-Catholic Conflict in Nineteenth-Century Europe.* Cambridge: Cambridge University Press.

Coale, Ansley J. 1986. "The Decline of Fertility in Europe since the Eighteenth Century as a Chapter in Demographic History." In Ansley J. Coale and Susan Cotts Watkins, eds., *The Decline of Fertility in Europe.* Princeton, NJ: Princeton University Press, 1–30.

Coale, Ansley J., Barbara Anderson, and Erna Harm. 1979. *Human Fertility in Russia since the Nineteenth Century.* Princeton, NJ: Princeton University Press.

Coale, Ansley J., and Roy Treadway. 1986. "A Summary of the Changing Distribution of Overall Fertility, Marital Fertility, and the Proportion Married in the Provinces of Europe." In Ansley J. Coale and Susan Cotts Watkins, eds., *The Decline of Fertility in Europe.* Princeton, NJ: Princeton University Press, 31–79.

Coale, Ansley J., and Susan Cotts Watkins, eds. 1986. *The Decline of Fertility in Europe.* Princeton, NJ: Princeton University Press.

Cohen, Gerda. 2001. *Lihyot 'im Agam.* Tel Aviv: Sifriyat Poalim.

Coser, Rose L., Laura S. Anker, and Andrew J. Perrin. 1999. *Women of Courage: Jewish and Italian Immigrant Women in New York.* Westport, CT: Greenwood.

Cotts Watkins, Susan. 1991. *From Provinces into Nations: Demographic Integration in Western Europe, 1870–1960.* Princeton, NJ: Princeton University Press.

Cotts Watkins, Susan, and Angela D. Danzi. 1995. "Women's Gossip and Social Change: Childbirth and Fertility in the United States, 1920–1940." *Gender and Society* 9:4 (August), 469–490.

Dayan, Shmuel. 1959. *'Al Gedot Yarden veKineret.* Tel Aviv: Masada.

DellaPergola, Sergio. 2002. "Elef Shanim shel Demografiyah Yehudit." *Tahapukhot Vetemurot,* 7–29.

———. 2009. "Tzmihah, Shever, veHemshekhiyut: Ha'Am haYehudi lifney ve'ahrey haShoah: Mabat Demografi." *Bishvil Hazikaron* 3: 2–11.

Drezgic, Rada. 2010. "Religion, Politics and Gender in the Context of Nation-State Formation: The Case of Serbia." *Third World Quarterly* 31:6 (September), 955–970.

Eitan, Rafael (Raful). 1985. *Sipur shel Hayal.* Tel Aviv: Sifriyat Ma'ariv.

Engel, David. 2012. "Ketivat Toldot Yisra'el 'al pi Dubnow: Bein haMekomi laUniversali." *Zion* 77: 307–315.

Eshkoli-Wagman, Hava. 2012. *'Arvut Yehudit beMivhan: HaTziyonut haDatit beEretz Yisra'el lenokhah haShoah (1939–1945).* Ramat Gan: Bar Ilan University.

Even Hen, Aviva, ed. 2006. *Hod-haZikaron: Sefer Ti'ud veHantzahah shel Nitzolei Shoah Toshvei Hod haSharon.* Hod HaSharon: Hod HaSharon Municipality.

Exler, Lisa Fran. 2000. *Birth Control Practices of Eastern European Jewish Women Immigrants to America.* Senior honors thesis, Brandeis University, YIVO Archives, New York.

Falk, Walter. 1994. *Letters of a Doctor From the Cyprus Camps,* Translated and edited by Raphael Falk. Tel-Aviv: Yaron Golan.

Falk, Rafael. 2006. *Tziyonut vehaBiyologiyah shel haYehudim.* Tel Aviv: Resling.

Feldman, David. 1998. *Birth Control in Jewish Law.* Northvale, NJ: Jason Aronson.

Fogiel-Bijaoui, Sylvia. 1991. "Imahot veMahapekhah: HaMikreh shel haNashim baKibbutz, 1910–1948." *Shorashim* 6: 143–162.

———. 1999. "Mishpahot beYisra'el: Bein Mishpahtiyut lePost-Moderniyut." In Dafna Yizraeli, Ariella Friedman, Henriette Dahan Kalev, Hanna Herzog, Manar Hasan, Hannah Naveh, and Sylvia Fogiel-Bijaoui, eds., *Min, Migdar, Politikah*. Tel Aviv: HaKibbutz HaMe'uhad, 107–166.

Fraenkel, Abraham Halevy. 1944. *HaYeludah baYishuv uVa'ayotehah*. Jerusalem: Dov Ber Aharonson.

———. 1967. *Lebenskreise: Aus den Erinnerungen eines jüdischen Mathematikers*. Stuttgart: Deutsche Verlags-Anstalt.

Frankel, Alona. 2004. *Yaldah*. Tel Aviv: Mapah.

Frevert, Ute. 1997. *Women in German History: From Bourgeois Emancipation to Sexual Liberation*. New York: St. Martin's Press.

Gantz, Michal. 2003. *Yeludah veKoakh Nashi baHevrah haHaredit beYisrael*. M.A. thesis, Bar-Ilan University, Ramat Gan.

Goldman, Emma. 1931. *Living My Life: An Autobiography*. New York: Knopf.

Golz, Avishay. 2013. *Batey Holim Prati'im beEretz Yisra'el*. Zikhron Ya'akov: Itay Bahur.

Gordon, Linda. 1976. *Woman's Body, Woman's Right: A Social History of Birth Control in America*. New York: Grossman/Viking.

———. 1997. "The Struggle for Reproductive Freedom." In Andrea Tone, ed., *Controlling Reproduction: An American History*. Wilmington, DE: SR Books, 147–155.

Greenbaum, Masha. 1999. *Hayyim 'al pi haTehom*. Jerusalem: Yad Vashem.

Grossmann, Atina. 1984. "Abortion and Economic Crisis: The 1931 Campaign against Paragraph 218." In Renate Bridenthal, Atina Grossmann, and Marion Kaplan, eds., *When Biology Became Destiny: Women in Weimar and Nazi Germany*. New York: Monthly Review Press, 66–80.

———. 1995. *Reforming Sex: The German Movement for Birth Control and Abortion Reform, 1920–1950*. New York: Oxford University Press.

Grushka, [Theodore]. 1958. "Hafsakat Herayon keBe'ayah Tziburit." *Harefuah* 55:8 (October), 193.

Halamish, Aviva. 2001. "Aflayat Nashim ba'Aliyah beTekupat haMandat: Ha'Uvdot, ha-Sibot, haHashlahot." *Proceedings of the Twelfth World Congress of Jewish Studies* 5, 49–57.

———. 2004. *MiBayit Le'umi leMedinah baDerekh: HaYishuv haYehudi beEretz-Yisra'el bein Milhamot ha'Olam*. Vol. 1. Tel Aviv: Open University.

———. 2006. *BeMerutz Kaful neged HaZman: Mediniyut Ha'Aliyah HaTzionit beShenot haSheloshim*. Jerusalem: Yad Yitzhak Ben-Zvi.

———. 2012. *MiBayit Le'umi leMedinah baDerekh: HaYishuv haYehudi beEretz-Yisra'el bein Milhamot ha'Olam*. Vol. 3. Tel Aviv: Open University.

Halevy, Nadav. 2008. "HaHitptkhut haKalkalit Shel haYishuv haYehudi beE"Y, 1917–1947." In Moshe Lisak, ed. *Toldot haYishuv haYehudi beEretz Yisra'el me'az ha'Aliyah haRishonah: Tekufat haMandat haBriti*. Part 3. Jerusalem: Israel Academy of Sciences and Humanities and Bialik Institute, 545–583.

Hashiloni-Dolev, Yael. 2013. *Mahapekhat haPiryon*. Ben Shemen: HaUniversita haMeshuderet, Modan.

Hazelton, Lesley. 1978. *Tzela' Adam: HaIshah baHevrah haYisra'elit*. Jerusalem: Eidanim.

Helman, Anat. 2007. *Or vaYam Hikifuha: Tarbut Tel Avivit biTekufat haMandat.* Jerusalem: Haifa University Press.

———. 2012, *Bigdei ha'Aretz haHadashah: Medinat Yisra'el haTze'irah bire'i haLevush vehaOfnah.* Jerusalem: Zalman Shazar Center.

Hirsch, Dafna. 2014. *"Banu Hena Lehavi et hama'arav": Hanhalat Higyena ubeniyat Tarbut baHevrah haYehudit biTekufat haMandat.* Sde Boker: Ben-Gurion Research Institute for the Study of Israel and Zionism, Ben-Gurion University of the Negev.

Hoffer, Peter Charles, and N. E. H. Hull. 2010. *Roe v. Wade: The Abortion Rights Controversy in American History.* Lawrence: University Press of Kansas.

Hoffmann, David L. 2000. "Mothers in the Motherland: Stalinist Pronatalism in its Pan-European Context." *Journal of Social History* 34:1 (Fall), 35–55.

Hunter, John C. 1962. "The Problem of the French Birth Rate on the Eve of World War I." *French Historical Studies* 2:4 (Fall), 490–504.

Hyman, Paula. 1997. *HaIshah haYehudit biSvakh haKidmah.* Jerusalem: Zalman Shazar Center.

———. 1998a. "Me'ever laYam: Hemshekhiut veTemurah baMishpahah haYehudit haMehageret beARH"B." In Israel Bartal and Yeshayahu Gafni, eds., *Eros, Irusim, veIsurim: Miniyut veMishpahah baHistoriyah.* Jerusalem: Zalman Shazar Center, 335–344.

———. 1998b. "East European Jewish Women in an Age of Transition, 1880–1930." In Judith R. Baskin, ed. *Jewish Women in Historical Perspective.* Detroit: Wayne State University Press, 270–286.

Inglehart, Ronald, and Wayne E. Baker. 2000. "Modernization, Cultural Change, and the Persistence of Traditional Values." *American Sociological Review* 65 (February): 19–51.

Ir-Shai, Ronit (Naamat). 2006. *Piriyon, Migdar, veHalakhah: Hebetim Migdari'ium biFsikat haHalakhah Bat Yameinu beShe'elot shel Piriyon.* PhD dissertation, Bar-Ilan University, Ramat Gan.

———. 2008. "Tefisot Migdariyot biFsikat Halakhah: Sugiyat haHapalot keMikreh Mivhan." In Aviezer Ravitzky and Avinoam Rozenak, eds., *'Iyyunim Hadashim beFilosifiyah shel haHalakhah.* Jerusalem: Van Leer and Magnes, 417–451.

Jacobs, Aletta. 1996. *Memories: My Life as an International Leader in Health, Suffrage and Peace.* New York: Feminist Press.

Jungho, Kim. 2010. "Women's Education and Fertility: An Analysis of the Relationship between Education and Birth Spacing in Indonesia." *Economic Development and Cultural Change* 58:4 (July), 739–774.

Kaminski, Tamar. 2012. *Neshot 'Ein Harod keMe'atzvot Hevrah Mehadeshet uMishtanah.* PhD dissertation, Bar-Ilan University.

Kanievsky, Yitzhak. 1944. *Be'ayat haUkhlusin vehaBitahon haSotziyali.* Tel Aviv: HaSifriyah haDemografit shel Knesset Yisra'el.

Kaplan, Marion A. 1998. *Between Dignity and Despair: Jewish Life in Nazi Germany.* New York: Oxford University Press.

Katvan, Eyal. 2012. "Refu'ah Mona'at (Nisu'in veGerushin): Bedikot Trom-Nisu'in veha-Medikalizatziyah shel Alimut baMishpahah." *Alei Mishpat* 10: 73–124.

Katvan, Eyal, and Ruth Halperin-Kedari. 2011. "Kesheha'Ishah Na'aset 'Orekh Din: 'Al Hitpathutah shel Zehut Femenistit." In Eyal Katvan, Margalit Shilo, and Ruth

Halperin-Kedari, eds., *Nashim, Zekhuyot, veMishpat beTekufat haMandat*. Ramat Gan: Bar-Ilan University, 253–292.

Katz, Esther, Cathy Moran Hajo, and Peter C. Engelman, eds. 1997. *The Margaret Sanger Papers Microfilm Edition, Collected Document Series*. Bethesda, MD: University Publication of America.

Katzburg-Yungman, Mira. 2008. *Nashim Tziyoniot beAmerikah: Hadassah veTekumat Yisra'el*. Sde Boker: Ben-Gurion Research Institute for the Study of Israel and Zionism, Ben-Gurion University of the Negev.

Katzenelson, Avraham. 1929. *HaTenu'ah haTiv'it shel Ukhlusei E"Y: Sekirah Demografit*. Jerusalem: n.p.

Kimelman, Miryam. 2003. *Soreget ba'Or haGanuz*. Edited by Leah Tzivoni. Jerusalem: Tzivoni.

Klapper, Melissa R. 2013. *Ballots, Babies and Banners of Peace: American Jewish Women's Activism, 1890–1940*. New York: New York University Press.

Knei-Paz, Mira, ed. 2012. *Rak haYaldut Einah Mizdakenet: BaShoah Hayinu Yeladim*. Jerusalem: Carmel.

Kozma, Liat. 2010. "Oto haSex Bidiyuk." *Te'oriah Uvikoret* 37, 96–124.

Kuklien, Fridolf. 1990. "The German Response to the Birth-Rate Problem during the Third Reich." *Continuity & Change* 5:2 (August), 225–247.

Lamdan, Arela. 2004. *MiShtikah leZe'akah leDibur: Shloshah Dorot shel Imahut veKibbutz*. Ramat Efal: Yad Tabenkin.

Lapid, Shulamit. 2011. *Ve'Ulai Lo Hayu*. Jerusalem: Keter.

Lavsky, Hagit. 2006. "Mishaphot veYeladim beTahalikh haHishtakmut shel Nitzolei haShoah beBergen-Belsen." *Yalkut Moreshet* 81 (April), 9–23.

Leibler, Anat E. 2008. *Nationalizing Statistics: A Comparative Study of the Development of Official Statistics during the Twentieth Century in Israel-Palestine and Canada*. PhD dissertation, University of California, San Diego.

Lesthaeghe, Ron. 2010. "The Unfolding Story of the Second Demographic Transition." *Population and Development Review* 36:2 (June), 211–251.

Levy, Nissim. 1998. *Perakim beToldot haRefuah beEretz Yisra'el, 1799–1948*. Tel Aviv: HaKibbutz HaMe'uhad.

Levy, Nissim, and Yael Levy. 2008. *Rofeiha shel Eretz Yisra'el, 1799–1948*. Zikhron Ya'akov: Itai Bahur.

Linders, Annulla. 1998. "Abortion as a Social Problem: The Construction of 'Opposite' Solutions in Sweden and the United States." *Social Problems* 45:4 (November), 488–509.

Lustig, Andrew, Baruch Brody, Tristram Engelhardt, Laurence McCullough, and Thomas Bole, eds. 1993. *Theological Developments in Bioethics: 1988–1990 [Bioethics Yearbook 3]*. Dordrecht: Kluwer Academic Publishers.

Maloy, Kate, and Maggie J. Patterson. 1992. *Birth or Abortion? Private Struggle in a Political World*. New York: Plenum.

Margalit-Stern, Bat-Sheva. 2011. "Bein 'Hok haTeva' leDin haTenua'": Imahut ve'al-Imahut baHevrah haTzionit beEretz Yisra'el (1920–1945)." In Margalit Shilo and Gideon Katz, eds. *Migdar beYisra'el*. Jerusalem: Ben-Gurion Research Institute for the Study of Israel and Zionism, Ben-Gurion University of the Negev, 170–197.

————. 2013. "Mi Ya'azor la'Ezer keNeged? Hevdelei Migdar beMishpahot Mehagrim Ye-
hudiot baEretz Yisra'el." In Penina Morag-Talmon and Yael Atzmon, eds. *Nashim
Mehagrot beYisra'el*. Jerusalem: Bialik Institute, 112–142.

Maynes, Mary Jo, and Ann Waltner. 2012. *The Family: A World History*. New York: Oxford University Press.

McRae, Susan. 1991. "Occupational Change over Childbirth: Evidence from a National
Survey." *Sociology* 25:4 (November), 589–605.

Melamed, Shoham. 2004. "'Ka'Avor 'Asarot Shanim Mu'atot Nehiyeh Kulanu Bnei 'Edot
haMizrah': Imahut, Piryon, veHavnayato shel 'HaIyum haDemografi' be Hok Gil
haNisu'in." *Teoriah Uvikoret* 25 (Autumn): 69–96.

Mendelson, Ezra. 1976. "Polin." In Ya'akov Tzur, ed. *HaTfutzah: Mizrah Eiropah*. Jerusalem: Keter, 169–211.

Morag-Talmon, Penina, and Yael Atzmon, eds. 2013. *Nashim Mehagrot beYisra'el*. Jerusalem: Bialik Institute.

Moran Hajo, Cathy. 2012. *Birth Control on Main Street: Organizing Clinics in the United
States, 1916–1939*. Urbana: University of Illinois Press.

Mosse, George. 2008. *Le'umiyut veMiniyut be Eropah haModernit*. Jerusalem: Zalman
Shazar Center.

Mouton, Michelle. 2007. *From Nurturing the Nation to Purifying the Volk: Weimar and
Nazi Family Policy, 1918–1945*. New York: Cambridge University Press.

Nash, Mary. 1991. "Pronatalism and Motherhood in Franco's Spain." In *Maternity and
Gender Policies: Women and the Rise of the European Welfare States, 1880s–1950s*.
London: Routledge, 160–177.

Netzer, Ruth. 2012. *HaHathalah: Numah 'Emek*. Jerusalem: Carmel.

Nir, Henry. 2008. *Rak Shvil Kavshu Raglai: Toldot haTenu'ah haKibbutzit*. Jerusalem:
Mossad Bialik, HaKibbutz HaMe'uhad, and Ben-Gurion Institute for the Study of
Israel and Zionism, Ben-Gurion University.

Noonan, John T., Jr., ed. 1970. *The Morality of Abortion: Legal and Historical Perspectives*.
Cambridge, MA: Harvard University Press.

Ofer, Dalia, and Lenore Weitzman. 1999. "Tafkid haMigdar beHeker haShoah." *Yalkut
Moreshet* 67 (April): 9–24.

Offen, Karen. 1991. "Body Politics: Women, Work and the Politics of Motherhood in
France, 1920–1950." In Giesela Bock and Pat Thane, eds., *Maternity and Gender
Policies: Women and the Rise of the European Welfare States, 1880s–1950s*. London:
Routledge, 138–156.

Pass Freidenreich, Harriet. 1996. "Aletta Jacobs in Historical Perspective." In Aletta Jacobs. *Memories: My Life as an International Leader in Health, Suffrage, and Peace*.
New York: Feminist Press, 179–196.

Pedersen, Jean E. 1996. "Regulating Abortion and Birth Control: Gender, Medicine and
Republican Politics in France." *French Historical Studies* 19:3 (Spring), 673–699.

Pekelman, Henia. 1935. *Hayei Po'elet baAretz*. Tel Aviv: Lakol.

Porat, Dina, and Yehiam Weitz, eds. 2002. *Bein Magen David leTlai Tzahov: HaYishuv
haYehudi beEretz Yisra'el veSho'at Yehudei Eropah, 1939–1945*. Jerusalem: Yad
Vashem and Yad Yitzhak Ben-Zvi.

Portugese, Jacqueline. 1998. *Fertility Policy in Israel: The Politics of Religion, Gender and
Nation*. Westport, CT: Praeger.

Proskauer, Erna. 1989. *Wege und Umwege: Erinnerungen einer Rechtsanwältin*. Berlin: Dirk Nishen.

Razi, Tammy. 2009. *Yaldei haHefker: HaHatzer ha'Ahorit shel Tel Aviv haMandatorit*. Tel Aviv: Am Oved.

———. 2010. "'Re'uyah haMishpahah sheYivnuhah meHadash': Tefisot shel haMishpahah haYehudit ha'Ironit beTekufat haMandat." In Eyal Katvan, Margalit Shilo, and Ruth Halperin-Kadari, eds., *Nashim, Zekhuyot, veMishpat beTekufat haMandat*. Ramat Gan: Bar-Ilan University, 21–56.

Reagan, Leslie J. 1997. "'About to Meet Her Maker': The State's Investigation of Abortion in Chicago, 1867–1940." In Andrea Tone, ed., *Controlling Reproduction: An American History*. Wilmington, DE: SR Books, 109–138.

Reggiani, Andres H. 1996. "French Procreating France: The Politics of Demography, 1919–1945." *French Historical Studies* 19:3 (Spring), 725–755.

Remennick, Larissa I. 1996. *Fertility Regulation Problem: The Israeli Scene in the International Context, A Background Paper*. Jerusalem: Israel Women's Network.

Rimalt, Noya. 2010. *HaFeminism haMishpati miTe'oriah leMa'aseh: HaMa'avak leShivyon bein haMinim beYisra'el uva'Artzot haBrit*. Haifa: Pardes and University of Haifa.

Rose, June. 1992. *Marie Stopes and the Sexual Revolution*. Boston: Faber & Faber.

Rosenbaum, Judith. 2011. "'The Call to Action': Margaret Sanger, the Brownsville Jewish Women and Political Activism." In Marion A. Kaplan and Deborah Dash Moore, eds., *Gender and Jewish History*. Bloomington: Indiana University Press, 250–265.

Rosenberg-Friedman, Lilach. 2005. *Mahapchaniot be'al Korhan: Nashim veMigdar bi-Tekufat HaYishuv*. Jerusalem: Yad Ben Zvi.

———. 2008. "Nationalization of Motherhood and Stretching of its Boundaries: *Shlihot Aliyah* and Evacuees in Eretz Israel in the 1940s." *Women's History Review* 17:5 (November), 767–785.

———. 2012. "The Marriage Debate in the Shertok (Sharett) Family: A Case Study of Religious-Cultural Perceptions in the Yishuv during the 1920s." *Israel Studies Review* 27:1 (Summer), 98–124.

———. 2013. "'Itzuv Zehut Nashit-Datit Hadashah: HaMikreh shel haIshah baKibbutz haDati beReishito." In Sylvie Fogiel-Bijaoui and Rachel Sharabi, eds. *Bein haPrati laTziburi: Nashim baKibbutz uvaMoshav*. Ramat Efal: Yad Tabenkin, 53–83.

———. 2015. "Godfather of Fertility: David Ben-Gurion and His Dualistic Approach to Natalism, 1936–1963." *Middle Eastern Studies* 51:5 (September), 742–766.

Rozin, Orit. 2002. "Tena'im shel Slidah: Higyenah veHorut shel 'Olim meAratzot haIslam be'einei Vatikim beShenot haHaimishim." *'Iyunim beTekumat Yisra'el* 12: 195–238.

Rubinstein, Amnon. 1975. *Akhifat Musar beHevrah Matirantit*. Tel Aviv: Schocken.

Ruppin, Arthur. 1934. *HaSotzioligiyah shel haYehudim*. Vol. 1. Berlin: Shteibel.

Sabar, Shalom, Ella Arazi, Avriel Bar-Levav, and Roni Weinstein, eds. 2006. *Ma'agal haHayyim*. Part of the series: *Kehilot Yisra'el baMizrah beMe'ot ha-19 veha-20*. Jerusalem: Ministry of Education.

Sanger, Margaret. 1931. *My Fight for Birth Control*. New York: Farrar & Rinehart.

Saraceno, Chiara. 1991. "Redefining Maternity and Paternity: Gender, Pronatalism and Social Politics in Fascist Italy." In Giesela Bock and Pat Thane, eds., *Maternity and*

Gender Policies: Women and the Rise of the European Welfare States, 1880s–1950s. London: Routledge, 196–212.

Schenkolewski, Zehavit. 2009. *Hazon uMetzi'ut beTahalikh Binui Umah: Yeladot vaYaldei 'Ir beShenot haBayit haLe'umi (1918–1948).* PhD dissertation, Bar-Ilan University, Ramat Gan.

Schweid, Sabina. 2003. *Milhamah, Milhamah, Gevirah Nehedarah: Yaldut veNe'urim biTekufat haShoah bezborow.* Jerusalem: Yad Vashem.

Shapira, Anita. 2009. "HaHistoriografiyah shel haTzionut uMedinat Yisra'el beShishim Shenot Medinah." *Lizkor veGam Lishkoah, Tzion* 64: 287–309.

———. 2012. *Israel: A History* (Schusterman Series in Israel Studies). Waltham, MA: Brandeis University Press.

———. 2014. *Kechol 'Am Va'am: Yisrael 1881–2000.* Jerusalem: Zalman Shazar Center.

Shatil, Yosef. 1995. *Meshek haKibbutz beYisra'el: Toldot ve'Ekronot.* Tel Aviv: Sifriyat Poalim.

Shaul, Michal. 2009. *Pe'er tahat Efer: Nitzolei haShoah, Zikhronah, vehaHitmodedut 'im Hashlakhoteiha, Perek Merkazi beShikum haHevrah haHaredit haAshkenazit baYishuv uveMedinat Yisra'el, 1945–1961.* PhD dissertation, Bar-Ilan University, Ramat Gan.

Shechter, Tamar. 2011. *Likhbosh et haLev: Sipurah shel Rachel Katznelson Shazar.* Jerusalem: Yad Yitzhak Ben-Zvi.

Sheffer, Gabi. 1997. "David Ben-Gurion keManhig Me'atzev." *Iyyunim beTekumat Yisra'el* 7: 583–600.

Sheffer, Yosef, and Sylvia Fogel-Bijawi. 1993. *HaMishpahah baKibbutz (HaHevrah haKibbutzit: Shinui veHemshekhiyut 6).* Tel Aviv: Open University.

Shehori-Rubin, Zipora. 2013. *Dr. Tova Berman-Yeshurun: HaGiveret haRishonah beMamlekhet Kupat Holim (1898–1997).* Tel Aviv: Dekel.

Sheshar, Michael. 1991. "Hayu Zemanim: Re'ayon 'im Aharon Nahlon, miRishonei Sde Eliyahu." In Moshe Krone. *Gevilin leMahshavah Datit Le'umit* III (January), 107.

Shilo, Margalit. 1998. *HaZehut haMishtaneh shel haIshah ha'Ivrit haHadasha beE"Y.* Jerusalem: Research Institute for the Study of the History of KKL-JNF.

———. 2007. "Zehut Nashit Umahut Nashit Besi'ah Po'alot ve'Ezrahiyot." In *Etgar Hamigdar: Nashim Ba'Aliyot Harishonot.* Tel Aviv: Hakibbutz Hameuchad.

———. 2013. *HaMa'avak 'al haKol: Neshot haYishuv veZekhut haBehirah 1917–1926.* Jerusalem: Yad Yitzhak Ben-Zvi and Ben-Gurion University.

Shilo, Margalit, Ruth Kark, and Galit Hazan-Rokem, eds. 2001. *Ha'Ivriyot HaHadashot: Nashim ba Yishuv uvaTzionut beRe'i haMigdar.* Jerusalem: Yad Yitzhak Ben-Zvi.

Shoham, Hizky. 2013. *Mordekhai Rokhev 'al Sus: Hagigot Purim betel Aviv (1908–1936) uVeniyatah shel Umah Hadashah.* Ramat Gan: Bar-Ilan Press.

Shvarts, Shifra. 2002. *The Workers' Health Fund in Eretz Israel.* Rochester, NY: University of Rochester Press.

———. 2008. *Health and Zionism: The Israeli Health Care System, 1948–1960.* Rochester, NY: University of Rochester Press.

Shvarts, Shifra, and Sachlav Stoler-Liss. 2011. "'HaHeigeinah shel Hayei haIshah léTekufoteiha': Migdar, Le'umiyut, ve'Avodah beKhetaveiha shel Rof'at haNashim D"R Miriam Aharonova (1889–1967)." In Margalit Shilo and Gideon Katz, eds. *Migdar beYisra'el*. Jerusalem: Ben-Gurion Research Institute for the Study of Israel and Zionism, Ben-Gurion University of the Negev, 85–105.

Sicron, Moshe. 2004. *Demografiyah: Ukhlusiyat Yisra'el: Meafyenim uMegamot*. Jerusalem: Carmel.

Sinai, Smadar. 2003. *Miriam Baratz: Diyukanah shel Halutzah*. Ramat Efal: Yad Tabenkin.

———. 2013. *HaShomrot shelo Shamru: Nashim uMigdar be-"Hashomer" uveKibbutzo Kfar Gil'adi, 1907–1939*. Tel Aviv: Yad Tabenkin and HaKibbutz HaMe'uhad.

Spargo, John. 1914. *Socialism and Motherhood*. New York: B. W. Huebsch.

Stopler, Gila. 2008. "HaMediniyutah haDemografit shel Yisra'el beTehum haYeludah vezekhuyot Nashim uMi'utim." *Mishpat Umimshal* 11:2, 473–516.

Taylor Allen, Ann. 2008. *Women in Twentieth-Century Europe*. New York: Palgrave Macmillan.

Therborn, Göran. 2004. *Between Sex and Power: Family in the World, 1900–2000*. London: Routledge.

Tomlinson, Richard. 1985. "The Disappearance of France, 1896–1940: French Politics and the Birth Rate." *Historical Journal* 28:2 (June), 405–415.

Tone, Andrea. 1997. "Contraceptive Consumers: Gender and the Political Economy of Birth Control in the 1930s." In Andrea Tone, ed., *Controlling Reproduction: An American History*. Wilmington, DE: SR Books, 211–232.

Triger, Tzvi. 2014. *Pesha'aim neged haPatriarkhiyah: Ni'uf, Hapalot, veHomosexualiyut beMishpat uveTarbut*. Moshav Ben Shemen: Modan and Misrad HaBitahon.

Tsur, Muki. 2002. "HaKevutzah: Mabat miVereshit baPerspektivah." *Cathedra* 104 (Tamuz), 149–156.

———. 2014. *Fania Bergstein: Sipurah shel Meshoreret veHalutzah*. Tel Aviv: HaKibbutz HaMe'uhad.

Tsur, Muki, and Aharon Yisra'eli, eds. 1985. *'Al Sfat Agam Soen: Bentzion veHaya Yisra'eli*. Tel Aviv: Am Oved.

Tsur, Muki, Tair Zevulun, and Hanina Porat, eds. 1981. *Kan 'al Pnei haAdamah*. Tel Aviv: HaKibbutz HaMe'uhad and Sifriyat Poalim.

Tydor Baumel, Judith. 1997. "DPs, Mothers and Pioneers: Women in the She'erit Hapletah." *Jewish History* 11:2 (Fall), 99–110.

Tzhor, Zeev. 1986. "HaSotzializm veMashma'uto etzel Ben-Gurion." *Kivunim* 29: 103–114.

———. 1996. "Ben-Gurion keMe'atzev Mitos." In David Ohana and Robert S. Wistrich, eds., *Mitos veZikaron: Gilguleha shel haToda'ah haYisra'elit*. Jerusalem: Van Leer and HaKibbutz HaMe'uhad, 136–155.

Una, Yitzhak. 1975. *LeMa'an haAhdut vehaYihud: Mishnato veHayav shel MOHR"R Yitzhak ben Moshe Una ZTz"L*. Jerusalem: Kiryat Sefer.

Usborne, Cornelie. 2007. *Cultures of Abortion in Weimar Germany*. New York: Berghahn.

———. 2011. "Social Body, Racial Body, Woman's Body: Discourses, Policies, Practices from Wilhelmine to Nazi Germany, 1912–1945." *Historical Social Research* 36:2, 140–161.

Van de Kaa, Dirk. 1999. "Europe and Its Population: The Long View." In Dirk Van de Kaa, Henri Leridon, Giuseppe Gesano, and Marek Okolski, eds., *European Populations:*

Unity and Diversity [European Studies of Population, 6]. Dordrecht: Kluwer Academic Publishers, 1–49.

Van der Tak, Jean. 1975. *Abortion, Fertility, and Changing Legislation: An International Review*. Toronto: Lexington Books.

Warhaftig, Zerach. 1984. *Palit veSarid beYemei haShoah*. Jerusalem: Yad Vashem.

Weeks, John R. 1999. *Population: An Introduction to Concepts and Issues*. 7th ed. Belmont, CA: Wadsworth.

Weinberg, Sydney S. 1988. *The World of Our Mothers: The Lives of Jewish Immigrant Women*. Chapel Hill: University of North Carolina Press.

Wilson, Sandra. 2006. "Family or State? Nation, War, and Gender in Japan, 1937–45." *Critical Asian Studies* 38:2 (June), 209–238.

Winckler, Onn. 2007. "Yisra'el vehaPetzatzah haDemografit: Sipuro shel Mitos Shagui," *Iyyunim Betekumat Yisra'el* 17: 197–237.

Woycke, James. 1988. *Birth Control in Germany, 1871–1933*. London: Routledge.

Yuval-Davis, Nira. 1987. "Woman/Nation/State: The Demographic Race and National Reproduction in Israel." *Radical America* 21:6, 37–59.

———. 1997. *Gender and Nation*. London: Sage.

Zahra, Tara. 2009. "Lost Children: Displacement, Family and Nation in Postwar Europe." *Journal of Modern History* 81:1 (March), 45–86.

Zalashik, Rakefet. 2008. *'Ad Nefesh: Mehagrim,'Olim, Plitim vehaMimsad haPsikhiatri beYisra'el*. Tel Aviv: HaKibbutz haMe'uhad.

Zameret, Zvi. 1987. "Teddy Kollek: MeVina le'Ein-Gev." In Mordechai Naor, ed., *Yemei Khoma uMigdal, 1936–1939* [Idan 9]. Jerusalem: Yad Ben-Zvi, 107–116.

INDEX

raising of, 87–88; costs of, 62, 84; deaths of in kibbutzim, 56; disincentives for bearing, 71–72, 74, 77–78; versus job, 74; objections to support for unborn, 148; "parents' rebellion" against, 70–79; role of under modernity, 84; taking labor from kibbutzim, 59, 75–76; time required to care for, 75–77; women's desire for, 1, 74

Childhood Psycho-Hygienic Station, 133

Cohen, Gerda (Kibbutz Hulata), 79

Cohen, Leo, 155

coitus interruptus/"withdrawal method," 103–104

collectives' rights over individuals, 115–116

"collective suicide," declining births as, 23

Committee on Birthrate Problems: April 1945 report by, 93; birthrate research by, 148–149; on birthrates among Holocaust survivors, 90; economic incentives proposals, 164–168; education or economics dispute, 149–153; effectiveness of, 168–171; establishment of, 145, 146–148; on family size and modernity, 83; lack of enforcement resources, 159; mock trial, 160–164; monitoring yearly birthrates, 25; objections to, 148; public education program, 153–154, 159–160, 168; public meeting deferred, 154

communism and abortion, 83

conception as beginning of life, 5

contraception: among European Jews, 11; celibacy, 104; contraceptive devices, 6; premodern methods of, 17n31, 103–104; for spacing of births, 130–131

cost of private abortions, 61–63

Council of Women Workers, 104, 155–156, 163–164, 197. *See also* Bassewitz, Lilia; Bat-Rachel, Yocheved; Katznelson-Shazar, Rachel

criminalization of abortion, 5, 7

Dayan, Devorah, 77

Degania kibbutz, 75–76, 115

"deliberate barrenness," 31

demographers, 10–11, 33, 117–119, 132, 139, 146. *See also* Bachi, Roberto

Devar Hapo'elet, 89, 104

diaphragm, 6

displaced person (DP) camps, 90–92

documentation of births, abortions, 3–4

economics and abortion decisions, 47–59; Committee on Birthrate Problems and, 164–168; cost of private abortions, 61–63, 106, 142; poverty in kibbutzim, 53–59, 88; wives' need for outside work, 77–78; in Yishuv generally, 47–53

education and abortion decisions: Committee on Birthrate Problems proposals, 153–155; in Europe, 139–140; propaganda not helpful, 150–153

Egypt, 11, 129, 144

Ein Gev kibbutz, 4

Ein HaHoresh, 57

Ein Harod, 76

Eitan, Rafael (Raful), 53, 106

Essay on the Principle of Population, An (Malthus), 116

eugenics, 46, 130–132, 139, 172, 188

Europe: concerns about birthrates in, 138, 186; criminal laws against abortion, 7; family planning in, 7; fertility policies in, 138–142; fertility rate trends in, 6–8; Jewish birthrate patterns, 9–10 (10t)

Falk, Walter, 91

family-planning clinics, 6

family planning in Europe, 7

family size preferences, 114, 150, 154, 159, 186–187

farm cooperatives/kibbutzim: abortions in, 53, 74, 83; asking for help during wartime, 123; under British Mandate, 12–13; children taking labor from, 59, 75–76; differences among, 29; family size among, 28–29, 173, 185; lacking basic needs, 56

father's role in abortion decision, 49–50

fertility rate: in Europe, 6–8; in Yishuv versus contemporary Israel, 1

Fischler (Dr.), 46

Fraenkel, Abraham Halevi: abortion and halakhah, 58–59, 79–80; abortion as murder, 126; active in Mizrahi party, 117, 126; commencement speech on abortion, 117–118, 124; concerned with family size, 82; Holocaust necessitating high birthrate, 129; on lack of anti-abortion enforcement, 107; meeting with Herzog, 157; member of Committee on Birthrate Problems, 146, 148, 158, 169–170; and mock trial, 161–163; on pressures for abortions, 50; on Yishuv abortion rates, 32

France, 6; abortion laws and customs in, 140–141; economics and abortion in, 47

Franco, Francisco, 7

Frankel, Alona, 46, 80, 82, 83

Gellner, Hedwig, 26, 49, 52, 74, 79

gender ratio: after Holocaust, 119; of Yishuv under Mandate, 15

genetic diseases, preventing, 131–132

Germany, 6; abortions in, 7–8, 45, 139–140; birthrate falling under all governments, 7, 139; birthrate policy before Nazism, 141; birthrate policy under Nazism, 7, 8, 140; economics and abortion in, 47. *See also* Holocaust; Nazism

Gertz, Aharon, 119

Goldman, Emma, 43

Great Depression, abortions during, 8

Gruenfelder, Benno, 53

Grushka, Theodor, 158–159

Gurevich, David, 20, 118–119

Hadassah (Women's Zionist Organization of America), 16n8, 197; and Committee on Birthrate Problems, 155; manual on infant nutrition by, 16; positions on abortion, 157; pressured to address declining birthrate, 142–143; prize committee, 145

Hadassah Central Bureau of Medical Statistics, 118

Hadassah Hospital (Jerusalem), 46, 53, 130, 147

Hadassah Hospital (Tel Aviv)/Tel Aviv municipal hospital: abortions at, 32–34, 59–60, 105, 107–108, 130; board actions to support new mothers, 143; overcrowding in, 23, 166–167; recordkeeping by, 3–4, 32. *See also* Grushka, Theodor

Hadassah Medical Organization, 11, 60–61, 102, 143, 145

HaEzra Association, 166–167

Haifa, 15, 27t, 28, 60, 102

Halamish, Aviva, 12, 107

Hamashkif newspaper, 110

hapalah (abortion, miscarriage), 4

Haredim/Old Yishuv, 19n82, 23, 26, 28, 132, 188, 199

Harkabi, Tzidkiyahu, 162

HaShomer HaTza'ir movement, 45, 57–58, 133

Hatzofeh newspaper, 25, 84, 91, 129, 150, 168–169

Hauser, Emil, 147

Hebrew Medical Association, 158

Herzog, Sarah, 127

Herzog, Yitzhak HaLevi, 79, 127–129

Himmler, Heinrich, 140

Histadrut labor organization, 9

Hitler, low birthrate as aiding, 120

Holocaust: abortions in concentration camps, 12, 92; Bachi on birthrates following, 25, 90, 92, 184; birthrate patterns among survivors, 12, 90; deaths of children in, 125; desire for smaller families after, 93; gender imbalance after, 12, 92, 119; as God's punishment for abortion, 127–128; high birthrate needed to counter, 129; and loss of extended family, elders, 45, 71, 93, 167; mar-

riages in DP camps after, 90–91; public discussions on birthrate following, 115, 120, 125, 127–128, 144–145. *See also* Germany; Nazism

hospitals: cost of pregnancy care, 60–61; overcrowding in, 23, 44, 60–61, 166–167; private, 60–62, 85, 107

housing shortages, 51–54, 166

hygiene and infant mortality rates, 9–10

Hygiene of Women's Lives Stage by Stage, The (Aharonova), 131

Idelson, David, 29

immigrants/immigration to Palestine/Israel: birthrate patterns among immigrants, 42–46, 52–53; under British Mandate, 2, 14–15, 21–22; effects on existing population, 94; illegal immigration, 21; wartime drop in, 121

Immigration, the Yishuv, and the Natural Movement of the Population of Palestine (Bachi, Gurevich, Gertz), 119

individual freedom, 89

infant mortality rates, 6

intermarriage, 119

internal descent *(yeridah penimit)*, 121–122

"internal immigration," 126

Islamic societies, countries, world, abortion laws and customs in, 11, 15, 23, 134, 189

Israel, State of, 1, 2, 15, 42, 92, 93, 134, 165, 168, 174, 187–189, 191–195

Israel, State of, current birthrates, 1

Israel, war of independence, 25, 126

Italy, 7, 141

Jabotinsky, Ze'ev, 120

Jacobs, Aletta, 6

Jewish abortion policies historically, 9

Jewish Agency, 14, 16, 118, 121, 125–126, 128, 155, 162, 171

"Jewish question," low fertility as answer for, 11

Jewish tradition regarding family, 126

journalism, role of, 158

Kagan, Helena, 35, 72, 146–147, 159

Kahana, Kalman, 193

Kanievsky (Kanev), Yitzhak, 151; birthrate by subgroups, 25; call for public discussion, 116; effects of immigration, 15; effects of war, 85; Jews saved from extinction by fertility, 9; member of Committee on Birthrate Problems, 146, 148, 164; objections to pronatalist propaganda, 152; poverty, housing and family size, 48, 52, 54, 57, 151, 164

Therborn, Göran, 84

Tirat Zvi kibbutz, 29–30, 59, 77, 86

Torah's "Be fruitful and multiply" commandment, 117

traditional versus progressive versus revolutionary views, 155–156

Tsur, Muki, 56

two-children norm, 82–83

Tzadok, Yonah, 34, 50, 80

Tzila (Tirat Zvi), 77

ultra-Orthodox Jews (Haredim/Old Yishuv), 23

Una, Yitzhak, 107

Union of Hebrew Women for Equal Rights, 156

unmarried women and abortion, 49, 79–80, 127, 171

UNRRA (UN Relief and Rehabilitation Association), 92

Von Weisl, Ze'ev Binyamin (Wolfgang), 1, 33, 71, 120, 126

war, insecurity during, 85–86

Weimar Republic: abortion laws and customs in, 7–8; eugenic approach, 139

What Every Girl Should Know (Sanger), 43

withdrawal method, 103–104

WIZO (Women's Zionist Organization), 147

women: blamed for low birthrate, 123; calls for stay-at-home mothers, 124; desire for children, 1, 74; gender imbalance after Holocaust, 12, 92, 119; military service for, 194; modernity and role of, 187; mother role versus women's rights, 154, 172–173; national versus personal needs, 173–174; "new Hebrew women," 16; pregnant women's fears, 71; protections for working women (1954), 168; public demands for support for, 143–144; role as mother of nation, 138; shortage of in kibbutzim, 57; traditional versus progressive versus revolutionary views of, 155–156; views of city women, 77; women's organizations, 155–156; working women's birth statistics, 73–74, 78–79. *See also* Council of Women Workers; Hadassah (Women's Zionist Organization of America)

Women's Zionist Organization (WIZO), 147

World War I birth rates, 6

World War II, 47, 52; abortions up, birthrate down during, 9, 12, 47, 86; and birth issues within religious kibbutzim, 59; death penalty for abor-

tionists during, 8, 140; economic crisis during, 52; halting immigration from Europe, 15; lack of census data during, 20; and Palestinian economy, 63; public discussion of birthrate during, 117, 121. *See also* Holocaust

Wronsky, Sidi, 35, 146

Yahalomi family (mock trial), 161, 163

Yarbeh Ha'Am (The People Will Multiply), 145

Yassky, Haim, 46

Yehudit (Kfar Yehoshua), 78–79, 86–87, 150, 173

Yemenites in Israel, 26, 27t, 53, 105, 133–134

yeridah penimit (internal descent), 121–122

Yishuv: age distribution within, 21; Bachi on declining birthrates, 23–24, 30, 31–32, 184, 186; Bat-Rachel's concern over future of, 24; birthrate patterns in contemporary Israel versus, 1; under British rule, 7; Committee on Birthrate Problems, 145, 146–149; declining birthrate of, 1, 20–21, 22t, 26; defined, 12; emphasis on autonomy, 12; European influences on, 5; Fraenkel on abortion rates in, 32; gender ratio under Mandate, 15; growth during Mandatory Palestine, 14–15, 172, 184; Haredim/Old Yishuv, 19n82, 23, 26, 28, 132, 188, 199; limited enforcement power within, 170; mortality rate, Berman-Yeshurun on, 30; mortality rates in, 30, 53, 56, 82; natural increase in, 15, 24, 46, 57; as society of immigrants, 5, 15; a voluntary public association, 141; war for independence, 9. *See also* Ben-Gurion, David

Yisraeli, Chaya, 45, 55, 76, 87

Zaslevsky, H., 146

Zionism/Zionists: abortion/birth control among, 26, 28, 35, 45, 53, 185; anti-abortionism among, 89, 110; babies unwelcome among pioneers, 54, 56, 58, 75, 82, 86–87; "be fruitful and multiply" command, 23; Ben-Gurion on motherhood and, 194; concern about Arab birthrate, 31; favoring modern (small) families, 133, 172–173, 186, 188; Haredim/Old Yishuv, 19n82, 23, 26, 28, 132, 188, 199; historiography of, 5; religious position on abortion, 126–129, 155; views on birthrate issue, 1–2, 10, 115–123, 133; WIZO (Women's Zionist Organization), 147. *See also* Bachi, Roberto; Hadassah; *Hatzofeh* newspaper; Jewish Agency

Zionist Executive, 14–16, 20, 130. *See also* Jewish Agency

Zondek, Samuel, 130

LILACH ROSENBERG-FRIEDMAN is a historian and Associate Professor of the Martin (Szusz) Department of Land of Israel Studies and Archaeology at Bar-Ilan University, Israel. She is the author of *Revolutionaries despite themselves: Women and Gender in Religious Zionism during the Yishuv Period* [Hebrew].

CPSIA information can be obtained
at www.ICGtesting.com
Printed in the USA
LVOW12s2055141117
556263LV00004B/418/P